D1512095

Sails Full
and By

Sails Full
and By

DOM DEGNON

SHERIDAN HOUSE

First published 1995 by
Sheridan House Inc.
145 Palisade Street
Dobbs Ferry, NY 10522

Library of Congress Cataloging-in-Publication Data

Degnon, Dom.
    Sails full and by / Dom Degnon.
        p.   cm.
    ISBN 0-924486-75-9
    1. Taku (Boat)   2. Voyages around the world.   I. Title.
    G440.T14D44   1995
    910.4'1—dc20   94-44861
                                                         CIP

Design by Jeremiah B. Lighter

Printed in the United States of America

ISBN   0-924486-75-9

For my wife, Catherine,
and my children, Carol, Mandy, Peter, and Martha

An aspect of the cruising lifestyle that fascinates me is the time and space networking . . . I imagine hundreds of giant cat's cradles lacing up the world's oceans, the anchoring fingers the ports of call, the strings the routes of friends and acquaintances.

CATHERINE BAKER DEGNON

There was so much visibility one day that they bottled some in flasks and stored the flasks tightly capped in one of the forward holds. On the first day of no visibility, a day of blinding fog, they made their experiment. The mate walked forward into the bows, uncorked the first flask, held it at arm's length, and released its contents into the thick air.

At once blue sky streaked and leaked from the flask and ripped across the fog. It was a banner of clarity; it floated. In it, the mate could see a petrel dashing along the top of the water; he could see calm seas clear to the horizon. He climbed the rail and looked down through the banner of clarity; he could see several feet into the water, which was green and full of jellyfish.

The banner-shaped patch of visibility was ten feet long and as narrow as the flask's neck. As their schooner drew slowly along—for there is rarely a wind in fog—all aboard realized that they would soon lose the visibility over the stern. The captain gave an order, and a man on the afterdeck reached out with a belaying pin and snagged it. He moved it in carefully, moving the pin until the center of the clear patch wrapped around it. He lowered it from the air, gingerly pinched it at a corner, and, trailing it from his fingers, carried it to the captain.

It was all the officers could do to keep the men from feeling of it— for the officers suspected, and rightly, that touching it would smear the visibility with fingerprints, or worse, tear it. Accordingly, the captain held it by the same corner and waved the men away. Slowly he brought a shred of it before his eyes; he looked through it thoughtfully to the horizon. He passed the flowing thing, as if it were an angel, to the sailmaker, who sat and brought his curved needles to bear on its corners. He fashioned delicate grommets there, and whipped their edges with cord. Then the mate lashed the visibility on the lee side of the bows between the forestay and shroud. There it cut a crack of clear and colored vision in the fog. It revealed the sea and sky, far and near in their own colors. The dumb, pale fog lay all around the crack, like a wall.

The mate sent a man forward for another flask. The ship had altogether two dozen flasks of visibility. The captain would decide how many to use now and where to hang them. They hoped to sight the Azores after dawn.

ANNIE DILLARD
"Notes on a Voyage"

Contents

PART ONE: OUTWARD BOUND

PART TWO: HOMEWARD BOUND

P A R T
ONE

OUTWARD BOUND

Prologue

Pack Your Bag and Go

Listen! If you are reading this to find out the secret of successfully sailing around the world, here it is: Pack your bag and go. Really, it's as simple as that. If you choose to read further, do so because you are into redundancy, for everything else that follows will lead you to the same conclusion. Start now and avoid the rush. Those of you with a compelling need for order in your lives, believe me when I tell you that everything that follows, the pages and chapters that all lead to the conclusion "pack your bag and go," is inextricably related. Events may seem disparate and the connections between them obtuse, but it all relates in the end. Be on the lookout for the subtle connections, those cosmic flashes of insight that give underlying meaning and substance to the mundane happenings of life.

On the other hand, those of you with no compelling need to have things relate, you free spirits for whom each moment is separate and distinct, an essence in and of itself, need not worry. Believe me when I tell you that what follows is a mere random sampling, a book of words dipped from the trough of experience. Sipping them, one enjoys the rejuvenation while recognizing the impetuousness and disconnectedness of life, the grab bag nature of existence.

There may be some of you who are not sure where you fit, neither suffering from a need to have things relate nor feeling overwhelmed by the apparent randomness of existence. Pack *your* bag and go. Read on, reassured that what follows is neither a random passage of one life nor a subtle revelation of the intricacies of existence.

I am an English major. What that means really is that I am one of those people who was told all through college and into my adult years that I wasn't able to do anything. English majors read poetry (and are reported even to understand it at times); they read books, plays, articles, magazines, graffiti . . . whatever comes their way. But, and this is a But with a capital "B", they aren't able to *do* anything. What follows is an account of seven years of not doing anything, or so those who so categorize English majors would have you believe.

I have found being an English major a helpful career umbrella. You never know when it might come in handy. Dealing with bureaucratic employees such as you might find at the Department of Motor Vehicles who stare you down and give you incomprehensible directions as to why you cannot renew your car registration or driver's license causes me always to interject, "I'm sorry; you see I'm an English major. I can't possibly understand you." Once on a beach in North Yemen (more on that later), I engaged in a heavy conversation with an animated group who were shouting at me in Arabic by nodding, smiling, and telling them over and over: "Right; you see I'm an English major." You can see how it might be useful in all sorts of difficult situations. I would encourage any of you to use this stratagem whenever you wish, English major or no. There are, of course, some situations where it might be inappropriate; Northern Ireland, for example, jumps to mind. But, I leave it to you.

Before you get too far into this account I'd like to offer you some poetry to help set the theme for what follows. Alfred Lord Tennyson wrote a poem called "Ulysses" in which he described Ulysses back home some years after the Trojan War. I had always wondered why it took Ulysses nine years to find his way back across the wine-dark seas to home. I'm sure it wasn't poor navigation, which is the excuse I offer when asked why it took me seven years to sail around the world. Whatever it was, Ulysses eventually arrived home and reunited himself with his patient wife, Penelope, who had spent all those years weaving and unweaving her tapestry and fighting off the suitors. Ulysses settled down to the day-to-day routine of running his kingdom, and Tennyson describes, in part, that existence.

"For always roaming with a hungry heart
Much have I seen and known; cities of men
And manners, climates, councils, governments,
Myself not least, but honour'd of them all; . . .
I am a part of all that I have met;
Yet all experience is an arch wherethro'
Gleams that untravell'd world, whose margin fades
For ever and for ever when I move."

Hold those thoughts as you pack your bag to go.

1

"Whee-Whew"

One of the peculiar things that happens to me from time to time is what I fondly refer to as a mystical experience. Although these do not occur frequently in my life, when they do happen I am so struck by their congruity, that I am thrown, however briefly, into the camp of those who see everything as being connected. Mystical experiences can make you a believer fast. A case in point:

Midnight . . . I am lying in my bed in my apartment in Cambridge, Massachusetts, unable to sleep. For months I have poured my energy into getting TAKU, my Cuttyhunk 41-foot ketch, ready for departure on what will turn out to be a circumnavigation of the world. I am apprehensive about what lies ahead. I have read all the books. Well, not actually all, but enough of them to recognize how much I don't know, how much I need to learn. This foreknowledge keeps me asking questions, seeking answers. More than anything, the growing anxiety makes it difficult for me to sleep at night. I idle away my insomniac hours by listening to the radio beside my bed. At this particular moment I am listening to Larry Glick, a late-night talk show host on Boston's WBZ radio. I fear that I am becoming a 'glicknick,' a regular who tunes in every night and endures the darkness through the shared experience of a radio call-in show. Larry's programs center on various topics to which the listening audience responds by calling in and participating in a sort of round-table discussion. They frequently deal with bizarre events like UFO sightings or other uncertainties in our otherwise ordinary world. I like Larry's sense of the absurd, and I like his sense of humor.

Callers will call in and Larry, invariably, will gently "pull their legs" to get them to talk. The routine goes something like this:

"Hi. This is Larry Glick; you're on the air."

"Hello," [this from the caller] "Larry?"

"Hi. This is Larry Glick; you're on the air."

"Larry?"

"This is Larry Glick; you're on the air."

At this point I always find myself smiling in the dark. Larry can be the master of noncommunication. The rest of us know how dumb the caller is being. We would, if we called, speak right up. The conversation usually continues like this:

"Larry!" Now a statement, not a question. "How ya doin?"

Larry must get asked this question by almost every caller every night. His answer is always the same. "Let me check," followed by a two-pitch whistle. "*Whee-whew.* I am fine, thanks. What's on your mind?" The caller will offer his views on the day's topic and be challenged by Larry. Not very heady stuff, I admit. Certainly not Alfred, Lord quality by any means, but in the early morning hours with the light off and insomnia hanging around, it isn't bad.

Sometimes Larry invites special guests, and this particular midnight is one of those occasions. He has a woman on the air who claims to be a psychic. Probably is a psychic. Kurt Vonnegut wrote somewhere that you "have to be careful what you pretend to be when you grow up" because at some point people start taking you seriously. I accept the woman as a psychic even though as she speaks I don't believe that she can intuit anything. She is taking callers, and based on their saying hello and sometimes their answers to one or two questions, she reveals something about them over the air. She receives, according to her, this information psychically. Larry isn't convinced, and neither am I, but as she's the guest he goes along.

The calls go something like this:

"Hi. This is Larry Glick; you're on the air. Tell us your name and what town you live in."

"My name is Mary, and I live in Chelmsford."

Then the psychic takes over. "I sense, Mary," she says beginning slowly, "that you are troubled. I sense that you have something going on in your life that may produce a change. I feel something about a hospital or medical work. I think it is this that concerns you."

Larry takes over. "Are you there, Mary? How does that sound? Is she reading you?"

"Yes, Larry, I'm here. I just recently got out of the hospital and my doctors are advising me to move to a milder climate."

The psychic: "Mary, I sense that things will be all right for you. I see a move coming up, and I sense that that scares you. I see your health improving and a lot of new and exciting opportunities for you. Please don't worry."

"Thanks for calling, Mary. Hi! This is Larry Glick; you're on the air." The calls go on and on. The psychic seems to have everybody pegged. I try to figure out how she does it. I listen for telltale signs in the voices of the callers. I wonder if I could be a psychic. How much is there to know about human nature? How many general questions can there be about life situations? Health, relationships, jobs. I figure with a little practice anybody can do it.

I decide I should call in and be vague and see if she can guess that in a few short days I am heading off on an ocean voyage that may take me around the world. I know she'll never guess that. I go through the conversation in my head. "Hi. This is Larry Glick; you're on the air." I, being supremely cool and confident will get right to the point with no "how are you's." "Larry, my name is Dom (I say to myself). I live in Cambridge and am changing my lifestyle. I wonder whether that's a good idea at this time?" The words rattle around in my head. I look at the clock and see that it is a quarter to one in the morning, and I picture myself getting out of bed and going into the other room and calling on the phone and catching the psychic out. But I stay in bed and play the conversation over and over in my head.

"Hi. This is Larry Glick; you're on the air." The next caller is Bill from Brockton who wants to know whether the direction he is taking with his life is the right one. I smile as I think of my own change of direction. Suddenly I am caught by the voice of the psychic.

"I see a sea voyage for you, Bill," she says. "You are leaving your old life behind and heading out. You are apprehensive, but I see success. You have the confidence it will take to deal with the elements. You should feel good about this direction of your life." I am overwhelmed. I can't believe what I am hearing; she's talking about me. Is Bill taking a voyage as well?

"So Bill, how are we doing? Did she get close to your problem?" Larry asks.

"Larry," says Bill, "I own a small trucking company, and I am not going anywhere. I'm trying to decide whether to expand my business a bit. You know, buy another truck or two."

"It's me!" I scream in my head. I've jammed the psychic. She was picking me up. How about that? I want to go and call Larry, to say that it is me, that after long years of thinking and planning I'm about to head off around the world on my own boat. I can imagine his incredulity; I can hear the conversation, the questions. I decide to keep it to myself as my own mystical experience, an omen of things to come. I click off the radio and soon fall asleep. From that night on my insomnia is gone. The orderly part of me wishes I had called and followed through on the experience. The side of me that prefers spontaneity finds comfort in having left it uncertain. "Whee-whew; let me check," I say when people ask me how I am.

2

Climbing the Ladder

November, St. Thomas

Dear Mom,

Thanks for all the mail. I realize now that it wouldn't all fit in one envelope as I requested. I have received four, but as they aren't numbered I'm not sure if that's all. One note mentioned a bill and a credit card, but I haven't found that envelope. Enjoyed the "Pirates: New Sea Menace" clipping.

Love,

If you are to make sense of life on the high seas, that sense comes in sharp contrast to what has been left behind. Feelings for home are not nostalgic. Rather, the recollections serve to highlight the differences of a cruising life—as if they needed highlighting. Nonetheless, the joy found upon receipt of some frail jotting from the folks at home remains hard to describe. Traveling from port to port, from country to country, each time the question is the same, "Any mail for me?"

In Post Office Bay, Floreana Island, Galápagos, sits a barrel that gives the bay its name. This barrel acts as a repository for mail from out- and homeward-bound ships of the whaling trade. It, or its predecessor, has been there since the early 1850s. Outbound ships would drop off letters, and ships coming the other way would pick them up and deliver them to their first port of call. The departing sailor was assured of one last communication with home before heading into the vast Pacific for an indeterminate time. This process would often take many months, but ran on a sort of honor system that still works today for yachts much as it did in Herman Melville's day for the whalers. Surprisingly, the Post

Office barrel is often more reliable than the sophisticated mail systems of the modern world. The average time today for a letter deposited there to reach home still remains at about two months.

To cope with the need for mail and the problems connected with receiving it, most yachts devise strategies. These are varied and include giving mail addresses well ahead of time (often six months to a year) to the folks back home, having a "reliable" relative or friend send mail to each address in time and act as a clearing-house, and having all mail sent in one large envelope to each address so that you needn't search for more than one package of mail at each port of call. The people who devise and advise these strategies never had to deal with my mother.

I left the air-conditioned post office, a building the size of a large supermarket, and went out into the warm, tropical, December morning. The sun burned strongly overhead, and although the palm trees rustled with the spill off the tradewinds that made it across the island, the heat reflecting from the pavement and the paved roads surrounded me and made me realize that winter in the tropics was as unlike winter in New England as it could be. Ten months before I hadn't even completed the purchase of TAKU, and yet here I was. I moved along the sidewalks of St. Thomas in my short-sleeved shirt, khaki shorts, and boat shoes *sans* socks, and looked at all the Christmas decorations in the windows. A fake winter scene in a jewelry store window caused my mind to drift.

The weather was cold. Bundled to the ears, I was driving to Marblehead, Massachusetts, in the dark of an early February morning to be on hand for the survey of what I hoped would be the new TAKU, the boat of my dreams. The dreams included not only a boat, but a long sojourn in the South Seas.

I was a bit late, having stopped to get a cup of coffee to ward off the cold. Nevertheless, the chill seeped into my bones as I got out of the car and heard the sound of a hammer tapping inside the hull, which was looming large above me. In the early winter light the boat looked gigantic. Beside her, I felt dwarfed. Looking up at the full-keeled, 41-foot-plus ocean sailing ketch swathed in winter covers, I felt my stomach constrict. *What was I doing here?* This thing was much larger than the old TAKU, a Bristol 32, which I'd sold two months before. During four years of owning that boat, I had come to feel attached to her, having sailed her from Canada to Florida and back. Thirty-two feet was a manageable size, but *this*! Suddenly I was having difficulty envisioning being the owner of this large boat, let alone sailing it anywhere.

"I must be out of my mind," I muttered aloud.

When I'd first glimpsed the boat back in November, I'd imagined sailing her, suntanned, sunglassed and swimsuited, perhaps with a hat on and definitely with a cold drink in my hand. Fueled by this romantic vision, I'd made an offer on FANTASY, written out a check for deposit and signed an agreement to buy subject to survey. Buying a boat called FAN-TASY—there has to be a message there!

Now, I found myself climbing the boat's ladder, but instead of wearing shorts, I was outfitted against the numbing winter cold in long johns, heavy wool pants, two pairs of socks and a pair of boots, turtleneck, wool shirt, sweater, down vest, hat, gloves, and large parka with fur-lined ruff on the hood. Even decked-out like an Arctic trapper, I shivered from the cold and could only move stiffly, like a small child bundled up to go out in the snow. The weatherman on the car radio had reported that it was four degrees below. I believed him.

Reaching the top of the ladder, I pushed my head under the canvas cover and out of the biting wind that blew in off the dark water of Marblehead Harbor and the North Atlantic beyond. I took a deep breath to calm my nerves and only succeeded in making myself colder. Instead of being cool and calm for the surveyor I was yet to meet, I would be cold and frozen. I wiggled farther under the canvas and discovered, suddenly, that I was stuck. With all the clothes I was wearing I couldn't fit through the tiny space available for access to the deck. My coat was caught on the framework for the cover; I tried to back down the ladder and in the process managed to kick it out from under my feet. This left me hanging balanced at my waist over the rail of the boat, my top half under the cover and my lower half suspended in space.

I contemplated shouting for help, but on reflection decided it wouldn't do to have the surveyor find the prospective buyer of this enormous yacht, for that is how it now seemed as I looked right and left along the seemingly endless teak decks, trapped in this unseamanlike position. Resolving to save myself, I grabbed a stanchion. Wiggling like a stranded fish trying to get back to water, I inched my way under the cover and flopped onto the deck, panting clouds of vapor into the freezing air. So much for the captain coming masterfully aboard his ship.

I found the surveyor below. He was wearing a set of coveralls and, despite the cold, no hat and no gloves. He carried a large yellow pad on which he was writing as fast as he could. We exchanged introductions, and since he was a taciturn New Englander, he went on with his job as though I, bulging dramatically in my layers of clothes, were invisible. From time to time he would grunt and write something down, and occasionally he would hand me his work light to hold. I was dying to ask him what he thought.

Finally he turned to me. "Are you getting cold?" he asked. Cold! I could hardly move. My lips felt so frozen I was sure that if I tried to answer him my skin would rip. The cabin temperature must have been below 10 degrees; it was still around zero outside. I nodded my head in agreement, and he said, "Me too. Let's go in and look at the sails." Then I remembered the ladder. But before I could say anything he was up on deck untying the canvas. "Good thing you tied this back down after you came aboard," he said. "The wind sometimes comes up suddenly and tears it." Tied it back down? Of course! No wonder I had gotten stuck. "Looks like the wind blew the ladder down," he said, nimbly climbing over the side and down the cradle to the ground. Before I could follow, he had put the ladder up; I descended, retying the cover behind me.

Off we went to the sail loft, he walking quickly in the cold and me waddling along behind. Inside the loft it was warm and cozy and the hum and whir of the sewing machines and the sound of scissors were a pleasant accompaniment as we shed our footwear—protocol requires that you never walk on a sail loft floor in street shoes to prevent dirt from being tracked in and damaging the sails that are constantly being stretched out and worked on. I removed my gloves, coat, hat, and down vest. Someone gave us each a cup of steaming coffee, and we proceeded to check over the 14 bags of sails that comprised FANTASY's wardrobe. The surveyor made notes as he went through each sail seam by seam with the sailmaker. I stood around and tried to look knowledgeable, like I did this all the time, but my mind was racing.

Fourteen bags of sails ! The four bags on the old TAKU had seemed like a lot. Well, FANTASY was a ketch but still, fourteen bags of sails; *what was I getting into?* Bags with the words *running staysail, mizzen staysail, storm staysail, drifter* were emptied, checked over and repacked. Before I knew it we were finished. Bundling back up, we proceeded in turn to the spar shed to examine the spars and then to battery storage to check the batteries. It was now well after noon. The surveyor turned to me and announced that it was time for lunch. We walked back to FAN-TASY, which sparkled brightly in the cold winter sunlight. The surveyor took a turn around the boat, came back to me, nodded sagely, and got into his car. I was left standing there. He opened his window.

"If you want to eat, you'd better stop staring and get in."

He took me to his house, where his wife had a hearty New England lunch awaiting us. He was as businesslike about food as he was about the survey, and we went quickly about the chore of eating.

Lunch finished, we drove back to the boat. For the next few hours he proceeded to tap and prod, inside and out, always noting his findings on the yellow pad. Eventually I looked at my watch and realized that it was four o'clock. When we finally emerged from the boat an hour later, daylight had already faded into winter darkness. One more trip down the ladder, and the job was finished.

"You understand," the surveyor told me, "that I haven't done a machinery survey so I can't really comment on the engine or the electronics or the windlass or any of the lights or battery-dependent gear. They all look okay, but looks can be deceptive. If you want, I'll come back when the boat is launched, and we can check out whatever we haven't seen. I'll be delighted to go on some sea trials if you wish."

"But what about all those pages of notes?"

"Don't look so worried; it isn't all bad. When we do a survey we comment on all aspects of the vessel in question. So what you'll get when I send this to you is an overall assessment of the vessel. My notes just help me to remember what I've seen when I prepare my report. All in all she looks pretty good. With a few minor modifications you should have yourself a vessel you can be proud of. She has the look and feel of a good sailing boat. She'll be up to anything you want to put her to."

Up to anything I want to put her to—but what about me?

I considered my performance all day, from getting stuck under the cover to feeling overawed in the sail loft. Suddenly I realized that I would have to stretch and grow to fit the boat rather than the other way around. The surveyor was telling me that she was a good boat to grow into. I smiled in the dark; we shook hands. In a moment he had driven off into the night.

I stood for a few more minutes under the hull of FANTASY. What a name! It looked like she would be TAKU soon enough. A few more negotiations and adjustments on the price and once again I'd own a boat.

Only this time it would be a boat capable of crossing oceans and taking me to the ends of the world. As I looked up at her in the dark, she seemed to be a bit smaller than she had that morning. The new TAKU seemed at that moment, and since, just right. I opened the car door, shed my hat, gloves, and coat, and threw them inside. After all, it would only be a matter of months before I'd be sailing, shirtless and sun-tanned, upon the oceans of the world. Wondering where I would be in a year, I climbed behind the wheel and headed for home. It seemed warmer already.

3

My Mother's Trophy

January, St. Thomas

Dear Mom,

I went, as you suggested, to the Postmaster. He says you'll have to trace the letter from your end and that perhaps it went to some other St. Thomas. I asked him if he knew of another St. Thomas, and he said he didn't. To trace it you'll have to know when it was sent. We can't wait here and have to get on our way "down island," as they say. I'm glad you got the postcard from North Carolina. I mailed it in October.

Love,

People always ask me how I came to sail around the world. "Gosh," they tell me, "I really envy you. That's the kind of thing I have always wanted to do." Reflection tells me that I always wanted to go sailing and that circumnavigating was just a natural extension of that desire. On my mother's side I come from a long line of adventurers and, as they used to call them, "boaters". Not the straw hat type, but the ones that went out on the sea in boats.

For me my earliest recollection of anything to do with boats is tied in with a silver trophy that until my mother's death sat proudly on the mantle of her house. The trophy isn't exactly silver; it is plated and much of the plate has worn off, though you can still read the engraving. My mother kept it polished and the frequent polishing has, in part, hastened the plating's demise. She displayed the trophy in a prominent position wherever she has lived. The trophy is almost as old as I am and has the date April 25, 1942, engraved upon it. The silver, a loving cup with big ears for handles, is little more than four inches tall; even so my mother kept it for all those years. She always referred to it as "the trophy my son won."

I was never sure whether my mother's preoccupation with this silver cup reflected genuine parental pride or provided a perverse opportunity, often repeated, to make me squirm. Were the trophy for an extraordinary achievement or an athletic skill I wouldn't have been bothered. I would have been especially proud if it had been awarded to me for sailing. But, alas, I never went to camp, and much as I would have loved to have been part of a yacht club junior sailing program, our family didn't belong to a yacht club, and probably, for that matter, didn't know anyone who did.

The funny thing about my mother's trophy—and you will notice that I refer to it as I always have, as "my mother's trophy," just as she always referred to it as "the trophy my son won"—the funny thing about the trophy is that the rest of the engraving following the date reads:

FIRST PLACE
S.P.C.A. DOG SHOW
MR. MUGGINS

Now, if you are to really understand this, you must also see the somewhat faded photograph that was always kept prominently displayed in a polished silver (real not plated) frame near her (my) trophy. The photo shows a small child of about four (me) standing on a chair looking grimly at the camera and holding in each hand the paws of a white raggedy dog who is smiling brilliantly at the photographer, all canines, bicuspids, and incisors revealed. The dog, who has just won first place, sits upright on a small stool.

The facts are always slightly different, as they always are, from the remembered history of an event. We need to always keep that in mind when we hear or tell stories. I am immortalized in a photo, which, as my mother always pointed out, "was featured in *The Philadelphia Inquirer*." Having little news other than World War II, *The Inquirer* had run the photo of the first-place Mr. Muggins and me. I was dressed for the occasion in white shoes, pressed white duck trousers, a white shirt and black tie, all topped with a blue blazer decorated with gold stripes on the sleeves. My hair, which was curly and blond, was slicked down and par-

tially hidden under a white captain's hat with a dark bill set rakishly to one side of my head. How could the judges in the patriotic fervor of World War II not award the prize to the kid in the sailor suit, no matter what kind of dog towed him around. Mr. Muggins got his name on the trophy, we both got our pictures taken and "featured" in *The Philadelphia Inquirer*, and my mother gained in perpetuity the phrase "the trophy my son won." Had I not gone on to grow up and to be involved with sailing in my later years I suspect I would be less troubled by this early appearance in a sailor suit.

My mother treasured her trophy and the silver-framed photo. Though she was behind the scenes herself, for her the fame of that moment endured unforgotten. Families, though, have a way of sensing or knowing the truth behind the facts of the histories we create. My uncle John, younger than my mother and used to her promotions as he was often a victim himself, suggested that we had won the trophy because my ears stuck out exactly like the handles on the silver cup.

My admiral's suit was not my only exposure as a kid to boats. My uncle Harry had a go-fast Chris-Craft speedboat. She was all varnished and gleaming and threw up the most beautiful rooster tail as he ran her up and down the Delaware River. He managed eventually to shipwreck her on the Jersey coast after attempting to navigate from Philadelphia to Atlantic City, New Jersey, one steamy Fourth of July. Impressing my Uncle John (he of the ears that stick out comment) as crew, Harry set out bright and early. Now, ordinarily, the trip down the Delaware, across Delaware Bay, around Cape May, and then up the Atlantic Ocean to Atlantic City is a challenge at the best of times. One faces strong currents, long distances, and some important navigational decisions.

The trip had taken far longer than they expected. I should have learned from their experience. The two brothers started out into the Atlantic Ocean at dark to run up the coast to the inlet between Ocean City and Atlantic City. The ground swell of the Atlantic was a different story from the tide in Delaware Bay, and they were forced to reduce speed so as not to swamp the boat.

By this time John was definitely ready to mutiny but had no place to go. They forged ahead in the darkness, staying well offshore to keep clear of the surf. As the story was later told, they started to run low on fuel, and Harry, seeing what he believed was the bridge between Wildwood and Sea Isle, decided to put into port. Before they knew it, they were caught in the surf and cast up on the Wildwood Beach right in front of the boardwalk and roller coaster, which Harry in his fatigued state had mistaken for a bridge. They waded ashore, found a phone, called home, and called the Coast Guard. During the night the surf pushed the boat up the beach, and when we all arrived in the morning, it was high and dry, surrounded by stakes with a rope slung between them to keep sightseers away. A fully uniformed and armed Coast Guardsman kept watch.

The sight of the "ship wreck" had attracted all manner of visitors; we, being the next-of-kin, were permitted under the rope and up close to the vessel itself. It rested on its side like a stranded whale. I, myself, was less interested in the boat now that it was high and dry and more interested in the Coast Guardsman and his uniform. Here was a real *salt*, not a kid in an admiral's costume. Years later my own decision to join the Coast Guard and the four years I spent on active duty as a Coast Guard officer had as much to do with that moment on the beach as it did with my desire to learn navigation and seamanship so that I would be able to voyage successfully around the world.

My uncles always inspired me, but they also showed me how it shouldn't be done. We remained for a while at the beach staring at the wreck, and then eventually we all dispersed. The mood, even though John and Harry were alive and safe, was gloomy. Something, some sense of ebullience, had disappeared. I think the sight of the boat on the beach with the man in uniform reminded everyone of the war their generation was being called upon to fight. Harry's boat, in need of repairs, was taken over and salvaged by the Coast Guard, which painted her military gray and used her as a mini-patrol boat and launch for the duration. The boat, like the more carefree time she represented, was not to be seen again.

4

Can Dead Men Vote Twice

April, Antigua

Dear Mom,

Took a one-hour bus ride from English Harbour to pick up a package and found out when they opened it that it was full of small lemonade packets from you. The customs man kept me the better part of the afternoon trying to determine what I was smuggling, and when he finally decided it was lemonade mix, he spent another hour trying to determine the duty. He couldn't find it anywhere in his books so he finally let me and the lemonade go. Appreciate the thought.

Love,

One doesn't get to Antigua, or to any of the islands in the Caribbean, without some effort. Cruising, like many things in life, is probably 25 percent planning and 75 percent execution. The lovely thing about cruising is that the planning usually turns out to be of little use. Murphy and his law take over. As someone once wrote: "A ten-cent fuse is designed to protect a $2,000 piece of electronic equipment. In the event of a malfunction, the $2,000 piece of equipment will burn out and save the fuse almost every time."

My mother and I lived with my grandmother in Philadelphia from the time I was thirteen until I went away to college and eventually on to the Coast Guard. I spent a lot of time by myself and my greatest passions were books, movies, and boats. My grandmother was in what I referred to as her Madame Defarge period. She had, as a quasi-concierge, accumulated a large collection of keys which she kept in a cigar box. I would come upon her sitting in a chair in front of a door where she would daily attempt to match up the keys in the box on her lap. Her eyes fixed in concentration on her task. Her black hair streaked with grey framed her solid face as she peered for hours into the box of keys. Those that seemed to match would be set aside to try in one of the many doors she was responsible for overseeing. Over the years she had had so many locks changed that the collection of keys represented mere memories of times past rather than actual useful elements. Still she would sit busily clicking her keys, attempting to match them.

One day she interrupted her sorting to tell me that my third uncle, Charlie, had finally called to invite me to go for a three-week cruise with him and his family aboard their power boat. I remember my grandmother sitting there sorting keys and off-handedly saying that I was to go off on a cruise despite my generally lackadaisical, or as she put it, "ungentlemanly-like" behavior. It seemed that all I did was read books or go to the movies. I am struck now as to how clearly I picture this. Her phrasing and intonation echo in my mind like a bell. I am also struck by how little else I remember of what, to that point in my life, was to be my greatest adventure

I do recall that in anticipation of the invitation from my uncle I had spent the winter taking a United States Power Squadron safe-boating course. Under age and ineligible to participate officially, I had persuaded my mother to enroll in the course and take me along. She would be the straw figure; I would do the work. My mother's attendance at the weekly meetings was physical rather than cerebral. Her little admiral was growing up. My enthusiasm and diligence more than made up for her disinterest. I hung on every word.

I had read books about voyaging, of course. I devoured the Hornblower books and Kenneth Roberts' *Captain Caution* and *Lydia Bailey*, this latter giving me my first real feel for the Caribbean. I had dogeared to pieces my copy of Howard Pease's *The Jinx Ship* as I read and reread it. How I longed to be Tod Moran, the mate, traveling the world on a tramp steamer and finding excitement and adventure. Handsome, clean-cut, and self-assured was how I imagined him. The books, though, never seemed to unlock any navigation secrets. And each year at school we would get to see the Charles Laughton, Clark Gable version of *Mutiny on the Bounty*. How they found their way I couldn't fathom, but each time I saw the movie I hung on every detail.

I hold a memory of a dignified, blue-serge-suited, grey-haired man in steel-rimmed glasses asking "Can Dead Men Vote Twice?", the mnemonic for unlocking the secrets of the ship's compass and thus navigation itself. Compass, deviation, magnetic, variation, true—the words are engraved permanently on my mind, and I need no mnemonic to recall them. Perhaps out of deference to my mother, or to me, he refrained from offering the more popular reciprocal mnemonic, which I was to learn years later, "True Virgins Make Dull Company." I suspect that had he suggested anything about virgins and the company they make, I, in my youth and innocence, would have been forced to confront yet another then unfaced area of my education and been too embarrassed ever to have found out the difference between magnetic and true compass courses at all! Piloting, seamanship, and small boat handling were tangible things that I could learn and someday use.

I recall that fortified with my certificate, or rather my mother's, as she was the one officially enrolled, I set out to teach my long-suffering Uncle Charlie and Aunt Kay all there was to know about piloting, seamanship, and dead men voting as we made our voyage from Philadelphia to the Chesapeake and back. Of the cruise itself, I recall little. That my uncle didn't throw me overboard is either to his everlasting credit or shame. While I tried to set things right for him, he, in turn, set out to teach me a little humility. His principal teaching tool for this monumental endeavor was the mop. When he wasn't employing this effective measure he taught me the principles of the sponge and Ajax in various combinations.

When I wasn't carrying out a cleaning task for 'Captain Hitler,' as I secretly referred to my uncle, I worked on my plotting (chart not mutiny), on knots, and on steering the boat by the compass even though the next buoy was always visible up ahead. I had found myself ecstatic with this part of the experience; the cleaning I could do without. Tod Moran never seemed to do any cleaning work on the Jinx Ship and Captain Caution was too busy fighting the Revolutionary War, outgunned as he was by the British men-at-war.

My last and most vivid recollection of this time is of my uncle offering to help me back aboard from the dock in Annapolis, Maryland, the turn-around point of our trip. Disdaining the outstretched arm, I made the attempt on my own, as Tod Moran would have, only to slip and scrape myself along the edge of the dock and collect a load of splinters in the back of my thighs and elsewhere too painful to mention. Aunt Kay said nothing; she merely fixed her baleful brown eyes upon me, got me face-down on the settee, and spent the afternoon working with a pair of tweezers, a needle, and a bottle of mercurochrome while attempting to keep my uncle and my younger cousin, Mimi, away.

Of our trip home I recall little except that I stood up a lot and slept face down when I could get comfortable. I do know that as we turned to head back toward home I had glimpsed further horizons that beckoned and that opened up the possibilities of future voyaging. If I was in pain, if I was humbled, no matter; my life had, indeed, opened up.

I have tried consciously over the years to recapture other moments of this experience from within my memory, but they remain, if there are any, elusive and ethereal. What decision in our minds says that *this* I will remember but *this* I won't be able to recall? Sometimes when things are calm, especially late at night in the middle of an ocean passage out under a canopy of stars with only the sounds of the sea and the wind, I am able to edge past the peaks of memories and slide into the unexplored valleys of forgotten experiences. What process, I wonder, what inexplicable connection, allows these hidden memories to surface?

I was to visit Annapolis many times before setting out around the world. It is a splendid place, but it never quite holds the excitement now that it did in 1952; humbled and splintered, I perceived it then as a place of wonder, as the key to the cruising lock. If one could make it to Annapolis, one could, with some planning and organization, make it anywhere around the world. Before commencing my circumnavigation I entertained my cousin Mimi and her husband, Les, aboard for a day of sailing in Annapolis where TAKU underwent her final fitting out and provisioning. Mimi and I reminisced about our earlier boating adventures, which included many more days afloat with Charlie after that first cruise. We remembered Annapolis, and she chided me about the splinters. We laughed about all the cleaning that she and I had been forced to do.

As the day ended she touched my arm and said, "I am so glad you are finally getting to sail around the world; that's all you talked about the whole time we were growing up." I was startled. All my years of secretly (or so I thought) wishing to go, to sail around the world, had been far more public than I thought. At first I was put off that Mimi knew, but remembering all our toiling together to scrub and polish Charlie's boat,

I decided I must have somehow revealed my deepest desires. Two days later, the day before TAKU's final departure, I climbed out of the cockpit to go on deck and managed to walk right into the end of the boom, laying open my scalp so that I required stitches to close it up. Annapolis, I thought, was still out to get me, even after all the years since I had taken a backside full of splinters away from my first visit.

5

A Man Dressed All in White

TAKU's first long offshore passage was nothing like the ones that I had read about in books. Accompanied by my cousin Tip, who had taken some time off from his job with the government and crew mate Celia Lowe, who had sailed with me before on my previous boat, we had set out confidently from the Morehead City, North Carolina, inlet bound for the Virgin Islands some 1,100 miles away.

We managed to cross the Gulf Stream without incident on the second day and even took turns jumping from the deck into its warm deep blue waters. But on day three the weather deteriorated; we were down to a single jib and crashing along in the most enormous seas I had ever seen. Celia was seasick and confined to her bunk, where she would remain for five days, unable to eat or move about. If this was ocean voyaging I hated it already. By calculations from the log we trailed and some imprecise sunsights that we shot when we were able to see the sun, we calculated we were making a little over 100 miles a day.

The fresh food that we had stockpiled was rolling around the floor uneaten, and it seemed that the most we could do was stagger out and stand watch and then crash on a bunk for the off-watch periods. The point of sail we were making was a wet one, and wave after wave would hit the boat and toss dollops and buckets of water into the cockpit and all over the weary watchstander.

I felt that we had to make as much easting as possible, and here we were in the teeth of a 25- to 30-knot northeast wind. Fatigued and discouraged after five days of this bashing, we hove-to for the night, slept, and then discussed whether we should give it up.

"We could turn and run off for Florida and regroup," I told Tip. "Celia is really pretty sick, and you have to be back within a week. I really don't know what to do. This isn't quite what I pictured life at sea to be all about."

"Look," Tip replied, "it's your decision; you have to make up your mind. I think you should fight it. This awful weather can't last forever, and besides, we're more than halfway there."

"I'm worried about our easting. If we run off now we can avoid the Bahamas, but I'm afraid the set from this storm is pushing us too far west. I wish we would get a good fix so that we could be sure where we were, and a good weather report to see what this is all about. The only one I can get on the radio is from Nova Scotia." Celia's only input was a groan and more dry heaves. "Let's sleep on it and see what tomorrow looks like."

"It's up to you," Tip told me again, and I realized that it was my responsibility, indeed. I wondered if I was really ready for it.

The morning brought a diminishing of the wind and a clear sky with bright warm sunshine. Our dead-reckoned position (DR), based on distance traveled and course and speed being made, put us some 400 miles out of the Virgin Islands. I decided we would push on. We were able to get more sail up, and TAKU's motion became more comfortable. Celia managed to keep down a small can of mandarin oranges and suddenly craved food. Her seasickness was over. The decks that had been continually wet started to dry out. The worst was over, or was it?

Suddenly I felt sick and drained. The long build-up of getting off to sea followed by the impact of the bad weather had caught up with me. I was, unaccountably, depressed and lethargic. I sat huddled in a corner of the cockpit and tried to make sense of what I was doing out here. Tip and Celia tried to cheer me up.

"C'mon cousin, cheer up. Look, we're doing over six knots. Another 48 hours or so and we'll be there. Celia and I are going to make a Mexican dinner to celebrate our progress."

I closed my eyes and tried to doze in the warm afternoon tropical sunshine and to imagine myself anywhere else. There wasn't really anything else I wanted to do; I was just in post-departure depression, I told myself. I peeked through my half-closed eyelids and saw the cottony trade wind puffers in the bright blue sky. We had obviously hit the trades. The weather was perfect, the boat was sailing well, and the anxieties of the past few days, weeks, and months were draining out of me.

I gave myself over to the rhythm of the boat, and with a few lingering thoughts about needing to make more easting, fell into a deep sleep.

"Dinner is coming up, señor," Celia told me as she nudged me awake. "You were really out." I looked around; the blue sky was gone, as were the clouds. Instead it was a crystal clear starlit evening, and TAKU was still sailing smoothly.

"We let you sleep," said Tip, as he emerged from below with three plates of dinner. "Do you feel better?"

"Yeah. That's the best sleep I've had in months." I looked out at the horizon and at the star-studded heavens. "Boy, it's amazing how much clearer things are out here. Look at the milky way up there. What's on the plates?"

"Tacos," replied Celia. "I brought a can of them as a special treat; this seemed like a good time to try them."

I picked mine up and by the faint red of the compass light guided it to my mouth. I took a bite and started to chew. It was terrible. I didn't want to say anything as Tip and Celia were in such high spirits and had obviously gone to some effort to make a special dinner. I chewed slowly.

"This is awful," said Tip, as he chewed on a mouthful.

"I thought they would taste better," remarked Celia. "They taste like cardboard."

"Cardboard; oh, no!" exclaimed Tip, who had obviously done the cooking. "I forgot to take the cardboard layers out between the tacos."

Three Mexican dinners splashed over the side. When the laughter died down, Tip heated a can of stew, and we sat in the cockpit eating it as TAKU ate up the miles to the Virgin Islands.

"I figure we have about 90 miles to go, so by tomorrow night we should be in. We'll need to keep a good lookout during the morning watch since I'm afraid we are getting set west and may end up closer to Puerto Rico than St. Thomas. We're getting there, you guys."

With the arrival of morning twilight we were overwhelmed by the sight that greeted us. Stretched out as far as we could see on the horizon ahead were islands. They were gigantic. I had never seen pictures of the Virgin Islands and had in my mind low sandy atolls with white beaches. These were high, almost mountainous, islands. We looked at the chart and then at the islands that stretched across the horizon on either side of the bow.

"Let's face it. We have no idea where we are. Looking at the chart I think that we are probably coming down just east of Puerto Rico. See all these islands here. That one could be Culebra." It could, but the chart didn't match what we were looking at. "I think we'd better pinch a little farther east," I said as I altered course. "If these are the islands off Puerto Rico, we will have to beat east once we get there." The islands were clearly still some 10 to 20 miles away. "Let's keep moving south-eastward until we can get a good fix, and then we can just alter course for St. Thomas and slide right in."

We all agreed on this plan, and I took the watch while Tip and Celia rustled up some breakfast. I stood behind the helm and peered ahead. And then I saw it. A fishing boat. It looked like a big trawler about four miles ahead in the early morning light.

"There's a fishing boat ahead," I cried out. "I'm going to head over to it, ask for a position, and find out which island is St. Thomas." I altered course and felt a sense of relief fill me. The navigation anxieties would soon be over. With a little help, we would be able to identify the mass of islands that we were seeing.

Tip and Celia appeared on deck. "It looks like a trawler," Tip said, as we began to close the distance.

"What's that?" Celia asked, pointing to starboard.

It was a small motorboat with a cuddy cabin. It was headed almost right for us and having tough going plowing into the trade wind seas. On deck, leaning against the side of the cabin was a man dressed all in white: white pants, white shirt, and white cap pulled down over his forehead. He was steering with one foot while hanging on to the cabintop to afford himself a better vantage point. He looked like he was headed for us, but if he saw us he gave no notice. We waved and hailed, but he kept his course, which was bringing him to pass us several hundred yards astern.

"Let's ask him where we are," I said, as I wheeled TAKU 90 degrees and set a course to intercept the mysterious man in white.

"Hey," Celia screamed toward the little boat. Suddenly the man changed course and ran his boat over alongside in the lee of TAKU. As he did so, I thought I caught a glimpse of something green off in the direction that we had been heading, but it was gone as quickly as I had seen it.

Tip took charge and leaning out over the side of TAKU, pointed to the largest island. "Puerto Rico?" he shouted.

"No," replied the man.

"Culebra?" Tip enquired.

"No."

Tip looked at the chart in his hand and then shouted again. "Vieques?"

"No," came the reply with an emphatic head shake. Tip looked at the chart again.

"Tip, there are thousands of islands in the world. You could be here forever. Why don't you just ask what islands those are?" I suggested.

Celia picked up on my thought. "What islands are those, please?" she shouted.

"British Virgin Islands," the man pointed off in the direction that we had been headed. "No, no, no!" he shouted. "Bad reef. Anegada. See shipwreck." We could now see the trawler canted to one side, obviously up on a reef. He gunned his engine and roared off out to sea.

I went below and pulled a chart from the chart drawer. It was the chart of the eastern British Virgin Islands, of which Anegada, a low, reef-encircled island that had claimed many, many vessels, was one. By climbing up the rigging a little we were able to make out part of the reef and to see the palms on the beach beyond. Obviously, the palms had been the patch of green I had seen as TAKU had risen to the top of a large swell. Between us and the now obviously wrecked fishing boat were masses of reefs just below the water's surface. We had been headed right for them and unable to see them because of the early morning sun. We had not been set west as I had thought, but had come some 15 to 20 miles farther east than we had needed. With the right chart in hand we were able to recognize the islands that spread across the seascape and soon had a safe course charted for the U.S. Virgins and St. Thomas, some 40 miles away.

By late afternoon we were safely anchored in Charlotte Amalie Harbor in St. Thomas. I was overwhelmed by the number of boats. There was no hero's welcome. As a matter of fact, no one even noticed that we had arrived. As we snugged down the boat, we reviewed the day.

"That guy on the little boat thought we didn't speak English," Tip commented. "I guess he didn't see our flag."

"We were lucky he came along," added Celia. "We were headed

right up toward the reef. We were lucky, too, that it wasn't dark. I wonder where he went or was going. I mean, he just disappeared out to sea."

"Maybe he's my guardian angel," I offered, feeling more truth to the statement than I wanted to believe. We had been very lucky. Luck had a way of running out if you trusted to it too long. If TAKU was going to make it safely around the world, I wasn't going to be able to count on mysterious men in white magically appearing at every trouble spot to take care of me. I would have to learn to be more prudent and to take care of myself, of TAKU, and of the people who helped sail her. It was an enormous responsibility. The man in white had given me an eleventh hour reprieve. It was now up to me to prove that I was worthy of it. As we went ashore to celebrate our arrival after eleven days at sea, I hoped that I would be.

6

My Aunt's Pen Is on the Table

One of the dreads that people have when setting out to travel anywhere is communication. Suppose you wake up in a foreign country and find that not only can no one understand you, but you, yourself, are unable to make even the remotest sense of what people are trying to tell you. Phrase books only go so far. Knowing how to say phonetically "Where can I get my trousers dry cleaned today?" is of little help when what you really want to know is where to buy diesel fuel. There are many phrases you need to know in foreign languages if you travel around the world. This is particularly true if you sail in a small boat.

One of the first things that you discover is that the complete French or Spanish vocabulary that was, you thought, implanted forever in your brain by the various Señorita Hoskins or Madame Simone of the school language departments has been programmed to vanish completely any time your boat enters foreign waters or you, yourself, meet anyone who is a native speaker of the language. The vanishing phenomenon was always there. Early manifestations seemed to occur when you were called on to recite in class; you just didn't recognize it as a cruising phenomenon.

Therefore, those of you contemplating world travel would do well to consider problems in making yourself understood in countries where the mother tongue is other than English. That English is the *lingua franca*—and already we aren't even using English to describe it!—of today's world may be true, but the fact remains that in many harbors of the world frequented by cruising yachts or long distance travelers the local folk may never have heard of *lingua franca*, let alone English, or if they do speak it, they speak a form that hardly resembles that spoken by the good old folks back home in the U. S. of A.

What are the poor travelers of today to do? In Panama and the Galápagos you speak Spanish. If you are bound across the Pacific as I was, you will discover that French Polynesia is exactly that, and that there, French and various forms of Polynesian dialect are the norm. Most of the inhabitants of the Polynesian and Melanesian islands speak their own *tok place*, or local language, as well as a bit of English and whatever language was brought to them by the colonial powers that ruled them.

I felt fortunate when I set out to sail the oceans of the world to think that I had some linguistic capabilities. I had studied both Spanish and French back when being able to say, "My aunt's pen is on the table," meant that you were practically fluent. Like many travelers, I felt my high school and college French and Spanish would tide me by. What local in the far-off Marquesas or Tuamotus, say on the exotic island of Fatu Hiva, wouldn't be impressed with *"La plume de ma tante est sur la table."* It was a sure opener and bound to win me fast and true friends wherever we went and wherever French was spoken.

Then I encountered the vanishing language phenomenon. My first experience with *vlp* occurred in the Caribbean at the French Iles des Saintes, off Guadeloupe. We had gone ashore to search out some dinner with fellow cruisers Roland and Lisa, who had been sailing in company with TAKU aboard their Valiant 40, KLEE. Unable to find anyone who spoke English or any place to cash traveler's checks or to change money, we were about to return to our boats. In a small side street we passed by a lovely, elegant restaurant. Candles flickered on the tables, and the glassware and the silverware seemed to sparkle in the early evening twilight. As it was early for the locals, though not for us, the place was still empty. "Maybe they take American Express cards," said Roland. "It's worth a shot; go ask them."

"You go ask them," I replied. "You grew up in Germany, and that's right next to France, so you ought to be able to talk with them easily."

"Baloney," (or something to that effect) said Roland, displaying his years in America and his familiarity with our idiomatic expressions. "When I grew up, the Germans hated the French and vice-versa. We *never* talked to each other." At this point the others with us withdrew from the Alsace-Lorraine territorial dispute fast developing in front of the empty restaurant.

"What about you?" gibed Roland. "Where's all that high school and college French you told us about? Surely you must be able to ask if they take American Express cards?" And suddenly I was being propelled in the door by Roland. My mind raced through all the French I knew, stumbled repeatedly over the *franglaised* "acceptez-vous" that kept trying to surface and secure itself upon my tongue, and just in time got the query together in correct French. Then it happened. The well-attired woman at the back of the restaurant glided forward through the candlelight and, raising one Gallic eyebrow quizzically, inquired: "*Oui, Monsieur?*"

I was dazzled—here I was speaking real French. Well, to be truthful, I hadn't actually said anything yet. I opened my mouth and out came: "Do you take American Express cards?" In English! The woman smiled and said, "*Oui, Monsieur!*" and escorted us to a table. Trying to regain my composure and save what I could of the situation, I turned to Roland and as nonchalantly as I could, said softly, "She says they take American Express cards!"

"Really," rejoined Roland sardonically, "I'm glad we had you along to interpret for us." The dinner was excellent—true French cuisine— and we had lots of laughs about my failed French. We decided that at that rate I was probably fluent in Spanish, German, Greek, Italian, and Russian, not to mention Chinese. Clearly, I was ready for the world; the question remained whether the world was ready for me.

7

I Am Cristina

May, Colón, Panama

Dear Mom,

Thanks for the packet of mail. I am writing the credit card company immediately. Thanks especially for the article "Collision at Sea." I know it can happen to me.

Love,

Mothers, I have decided, have a direct pipeline into a disaster clipping service. What you choose to pursue doesn't matter; your mother will send you clippings about disasters that have occurred. Mountaineering? Stand by for clippings on avalanches, frostbite, exposure, hostile sherpas. Suppose tropical fish are more your wont. In come clippings on *ciguatera* and other exotic fish-born diseases, shark attacks, aquarium heaters that have exploded or caught on fire, fingers bitten off by pet piranhas. You get the general idea. At almost every mail stop around the world fellow yachties would shake out large envelopes containing clippings of various sea disasters. It keeps you on your toes.

There are basically two ways to sail around the world: east or west. West takes you with the prevailing winds and keeps you, for the most part, in the warm tropical latitudes, permitting you to call at exotic locations around the world. East, on the other hand, is a more difficult route. It involves miles of beating to windward, fewer days in the tropics, and fewer exotic ports of call. East is like pedaling a bicycle uphill almost all day; west is downhill, a lovely slide in the trade winds around the world. If you think I chose east, you're wrong. West all the way for me.

But pushing westward out of the Caribbean through Panama and into the vast reaches of the Pacific and beyond is not something one does glibly. North Carolina to the Virgins had shown me that everything does not always go smoothly. Cruising from island to island in the Caribbean, with the next destination always in sight, was a far different story from making the 1,400 miles from Panama to the Galápagos across the doldrums and into the southern hemisphere. And certainly it was far different from the more than 3,300 miles that separate the Galápagos Islands from the Marquesas, the first Polynesian stop on the way west around the world.

My friend and colleague, Armen Dedekian, was planning to join TAKU in Panama for the passage to Tahiti, and although he wasn't a sailor, he was an avid traveler and adventurer. I looked forward to his company. But we still had to get from Antigua to Panama, and evening conversations in the cockpit while TAKU bobbed gently in the placid waters of English Harbour concerned the issue of crew. Should we or shouldn't we?

The problem with crew is that you can argue either side clearly and cogently, and in so doing you become more confused than ever on where you stand. "Well, what do you think about taking crew along? Friends and relatives are one thing, but someone unknown is a bit more of a risk. There seem to be a great many available people here in Antigua. Do you think you'd prefer a male or a female?" I had asked Celia one night after dinner .

"It's your idea," she replied, "but I guess I'd want a girl. I wouldn't want two guys trying to boss me around. Besides a girl takes up less space, and she might be a good cook and that would help." Remembering the cardboard Mexican dinner, I had to agree on that. "She'd have to know how to sail," Celia continued, "and she's got to have some offshore experience." Suddenly we found that we were both agreeing and that we had made the decision to take extra crew along. We left ourselves an out; we'd try the person as far as Panama and if she didn't work out, we could ask her to leave there.

Although I lacked first-hand experience, and knew no friends who had sailed with unknown crew, I felt it was a common enough practice to get involved. Next to the monkey, from whom some say we have descended, sailors seem to have the most imitative urge. Perhaps we are the missing link in the evolutionary chain. *Sailor see, sailor do* might well be a catch phrase today if monkeys hadn't adopted it first.

The lack of experience severely handicapped us in our search; as we were to learn later, a frustrated skipper trying to unload a bad crewmember may sound very much like a satisfied skipper heartbroken to see a favorite watchstander depart. So it was with Cristina.

A neatly typed card with a green-inked border stood out among myriad requests for crew positions pinned to the notice board at Nicholson's in Nelson's Dockyard, English Harbour, Antigua:

> Experienced sailor (female) desires
> onward passage to the Pacific. Can
> leave anytime. Excellent cook. Can
> navigate. References available. See
> Cristina. British yacht RELIABLE.

Of all the notices, this one jumped off the board and reached out to us. "Look," I said. "She even took the time to type it." I turned to Celia: "I'll go over to RELIABLE and meet her and check her out, and if she seems okay, I'll bring her back so you can meet her and talk with her as well."

"No way," Celia immediately replied. "Suppose she is some fabulous, gorgeous creature who doesn't get seasick, is a gourmet cook, and turns out to be personable as well?" Intent on helping out, I hadn't thought much along those lines at all. "If you bring her back," Celia continued, "I won't be able to say no to those qualifications; I'll spend the rest of my time aboard feeling envious and like a drip. Cristina . . . I'll bet! I'll go and see her, and if I think we can both put up with her, *I'll* bring her back for you to meet."

A bit later Celia returned alone. "Well?" was all I could muster.

"Well, everyone on RELIABLE thinks she is fantastic. Apparently she is Italian. They couldn't say enough about her. They seemed really sorry that she is going off to the Pacific."

When Celia said Italian, I immediately pictured either Sophia Loren or Gina Lollobrigida dressed in a neat little yachting costume or bikini, fully made up as in the movies, steering TAKU, while I sat idly by enjoying the view. For some reason, which I was to regret later, my mind didn't get past Loren and Lollobrigida to the M's, and I didn't get a flash of Anna Magnani in her basic peasant black, hair unwashed and unkempt, standing defiantly in a garden hoeing turnips while World War II went on all about her.

Trying to sound my most casual, I asked: "So, did she get on another boat? Or what's the story?"

"Well, that's a problem," came the reply. "See, she's ashore for a few days, and she won't be back until after I fly out to the States for my three weeks at home, and by the time I get back, we'll be leaving for Panama and it will be too late to get anyone else. She sounds really good. So I guess *you* will have to interview her and decide."

"Me? Yeah . . . sure . . . why not? I guess I can do that."

Celia flew out, and I went about the business of getting TAKU ready for the passage to Panama and the Pacific beyond. The oil in the engine needed to be changed, the rigging to be tuned and checked.

Two or three days later a dinghy bumped heavily alongside, barely under the control of an overweight woman in her mid-twenties. She had flaming red hair, obviously dyed, for the original brown was well on its way to growing back in. Her clothes, like her hair, went every which way and seemed merely to have happened by chance rather than by design. Anna M. could have played her and won an Academy Award even without the turnips or World War II for support.

"I am Cristina," she announced in heavily accented English. "I understand you will take me to the Pacific; I want very much to get there. May I come aboard? Thank you." Before I could even say Anna Magnani, she was in the cockpit.

I was stunned and could think of nothing to say. Finally, in a last ditch defense of Sophia and Gina, I blurted: "You're Bulgarian!" It was the only thing I could think of at the time.

"No. I am Italian," she replied, "but I speak French, English, Spanish, and a little German. But not Bulgarian. Where is the American girl who came to the yacht RELIABLE looking for me?"

"Ah . . . well . . . yes . . . she's in the States at the moment." I proceeded to conduct the interview fairly sure of the outcome even before we began. It turned out that Cristina had sailed extensively in small boats in Italy. She had even been a ski instructor. She had crewed on a yacht from the Canaries to Barbados, and she had been on two other yachts in the six months that she had been in the Caribbean. She liked to cook and wanted to learn more navigation.

She asked when we planned to depart for Panama, and suddenly I found myself explaining about the trial period and the necessity of her being financially independent and able to post the required bond in French Polynesia. To all of this she gave reassuring answers, and before I knew it we had agreed that she could crew at least as far as Panama. With Cristina, Celia needn't worry about being turned into a drip.

Before Celia returned I also signed on a personable Australian, Ron, whom I had met and who wanted only to get to Panama. He, like Cristina, came highly recommended. Thus it was that we set off from Antigua to Panama, a distance of some 1,100 miles, with two, rather than one, additional crewmembers aboard.

Our passage, unlike the 1,000 miles from the U.S. to the Virgin Islands, went swiftly. The weather was picturebook perfect. Puffy white fair-weather clouds hung against a brilliant blue sky as we fairly flew along before the trades with all sail crowded on. We double-poled our yankee and our big drifter wing-and-wing, and pushed out the main as far as we could and fixed it with a preventer; with the added canvas of the working staysail, mizzen staysail, and mizzen, TAKU kicked up her heels, took the bone in her teeth, and drove gaily for the Isthmus. I gave thanks for all those bags of sails that I had worried over at the survey.

With four watchstanders there was ample sleep, and since Ron and Cristina liked to cook and were vying with each other for the culinary prize, the food situation was great. They didn't even mind doing the washing up. The most difficult task of the passage, aside from taking the daily sights and perfecting my navigational skills, became the task of finding something to do until I could get back into the round-robin backgammon tournament that went on all day in the cockpit. Even the Aries windvane that controlled the helm cooperated, rarely needing to be adjusted. If having extra crew could produce such an idyll, "Why," I asked myself, "didn't everyone have them?"

We breezed into Panama on the good weather high that had carried us all the way from Antigua and on our own personal highs that had developed on the passage. No matter that space was a bit crowded and that Cristina never combed her hair, cruising had become, almost overnight, a snap. I was even learning a smattering of Italian and had added *un sógno dorato* (sleep well) to my previously limited *pizza, ciao, grazie, Fiat,* and *Lamborghini.* There was no question of signing

Signorina Cristina off in Panama. Sail across the Pacific shorthanded? Ridiculous.

Ron signed off in Colón, and Armen arrived from Boston. Did we really want to give up the fourth watchstander? And what about the potential cook? It was over 4,000 miles to Tahiti. Cristina wanted to go *Pacifico*. With visions of antipasto, lasagna, and the spaghetti that we had been introduced to in mind, I made the decision: Cristina would stay aboard. Even Armen, who was at that point neither much of a sailor nor much of a cook, welcomed the decision.

Mark Twain once remarked: "If a man wants to carry a cat home by the tail, I say let him. He will profit by the experience. If he chooses to carry a cat home by the tail a second time, perhaps he has gotten something from the experience that the rest of us can't perceive."

I had carried the cat home by the tail from Antigua to Panama. No crew horror stories aboard TAKU. Now the choice had been made to do it again. The Pacific was a big ocean to cross. The question was whether the crew experience would continue to be successful. Cat lovers, stay tuned!

8

You Won't Believe This

June, Colón, Panama

Dear Well-Known World-Wide
Credit Card Company,

You won't believe this, but I never received your bill as it was lost in the mail somewhere between the U.S. and one of the St. Thomases. If you will note please on the bill enclosed, your computer seems to be in error. I know you will find that hard to believe as well. I *did* charge an electric sander for my boat last August, for which I paid $79.23 in September. But as I have been away from Boston and the U.S. since then I don't see how I could have purchased identical sanders each month for $79.23 or why, for that matter, I or anyone would want to. Obviously something is wrong.

Thanks,

Colón, or Cristóbal as it is also known, the Caribbean port of entrance to the famed Panama Canal, keeps us busy. TAKU is hauled on the shaky marine railway of the tiny Cristóbal Yacht Club, and her bottom given a coat of antifouling paint. Provisions for the impending Pacific crossing are bought and stowed. Charts are dug out and made ready. The lists seem endless, but gradually they are whittled away. And Armen finally arrives.

He had gotten what he believed was a cheap ticket from his travel agent in Boston. With school over for the year, and his bags packed, he had set out to find his way to Panama City where we were to meet him at the airport. My last word from Armen was an arrival time at Panama

City and a promise to telex me if there were any changes. The telex arrived in the middle of the day.

Arriving Panama City 11:30 p.m. your time stop not 6 p.m. stop will explain on arrival stop sorry stop

Armen

With Armen safely in hand we proceeded back to TAKU while he explained the change in his flight arrival time. "There I was," he told us excitedly, "sitting in the Miami International Airport and feeling so happy to be out of school and finally on my way to catch up with TAKU. I got talking with a man sitting next to me and explained to him how I was about to sail across the Pacific, but that I had never been overnight on a boat. I told him that I had sailed some day trips with you, Dom, but that this was really the big adventure. We got to talking further, and I told him what a great deal I had gotten on my plane ticket—140 bucks to Miami and only another 37 to Panama City. He said that was hard to believe given how far Panama was from Miami, so I showed him my ticket. Wouldn't you know; it was for Panama City, Florida!" I got to thinking that if there were two Panama Citys, perhaps there really were two cities named St. Thomas as well. Was that where all the missing mail had gone?

After several days' delay and three attempts to schedule our transit of the canal, we finally succeed. We are told that we will lock through with a Russian ship, the MAXIM GORKY. This causes us a certain amount of amusement as Armen, though born in Boston, ended up living in the Soviet Union from age two until 18. In addition to English, he speaks fluent, unaccented Russian.

We have chosen to lock through with a center chamber moor, which requires, in addition to the helmsman, four line handlers and four 200-foot lines. We are also required to have a pilot aboard; in our case this turns out to be Gilbert Card, a soft-spoken man born in Honduras who has worked for the Canal Commission for over 20 years. Gilbert arrives on schedule, delivered to TAKU by a small tug, and with his walkie-talkie in hand, he informs the control that TAKU, now known as 14-ALPHA for the day, is underway for her transit.

True to the Canal Commission's word, as we stand into the first of the series of locks that will lift us from the level of the Caribbean to Gatun Lake we find ourselves positioned under the stern counter of a very large Russian ship. Our 41-foot ketch with its American flag seems dwarfed behind the representative of the hammer and sickle in front of us. We learn from Gilbert that uplocking to the lake, the smaller vessel will always enter the lock chamber after the larger vessel to prevent its being crushed against the forward gates in case of accident.

The Russians seem to be as fascinated with sharing the lock chamber with us as we are to be sharing it with them. The world has yet to arrive at *glasnost* and *perestroika*, so we each eye the other a bit warily. Once moored in the lock, Armen shouts to the crew visible on the stern of the GORKY. They are startled and look to see where the voice, speaking perfect Russian, is coming from. Soon there is a crowd of sailors, each attempting a conversation with Armen. At one point there is a pause, and then they are all laughing.

"What did you say, Armen?" I ask.

"Oh, the one in the green shirt—he's from the Republic of Georgia; I recognized his accent. I asked him what a good little Georgian boy was doing so far away from the farm. They all are teasing him."

More shouts, more exchanges. The water level in the chamber rises, and above the lock gates that had towered overhead I see the port of Cristóbal/Colón and catch what will be my last glimpse of the Caribbean for six years. The forward gates open, and we follow the GORKY into the next chamber. This will be our routine as we uplock to Gatun Lake. Each time we are moored, the conversations between Armen and the GORKY's crew continue. They are all shouting questions at Armen, trying to determine who he is and whether, indeed, he is truly a Russian.

As we are about to leave our last uplock, Armen shouts one last time to the Russians as they wave goodbye.

"What did you say?" I ask again.

"I told them they should come to America. I said, 'Look at me! I have only been in America for a few months, and already I own this magnificent sailboat and I'm off to sail around the world!'" I warn Armen that they are liable to send a small boat with some KGB agents or something to take him away.

The Canal Commission had informed us that yachts are only permitted to transit the canal during daylight hours, and as it is now getting late in the afternoon we ask Gilbert if we must anchor in Gatun Lake for the night and then proceed the remaining 40 miles to the Pacific the next day. He tells us that the rules are loosely interpreted; as long as a yacht enters the lock system in the daylight, no one seems concerned about when it finally emerges. Traffic continues 24 hours a day every day.

At the moment a backlog of merchant ships waits to transit and many are temporarily anchored in Gatun Lake awaiting an orderly and evenly spaced passage. Since we are only a small yacht and can be squeezed into a lock chamber with almost any ship, we are told to proceed. Even though we are headed toward the Pacific, we watch as the sun sets behind us over our stern. This oddity is explained by the west-to-east angle that the canal makes as it crosses the Isthmus of Panama. Doubters, check your maps.

We slide along through the twilight waters of Gatun Lake. The channel is abundantly marked, and getting lost would be impossible, particularly with Gilbert's ever-watchful eye. By midnight we are at the Miraflores locks at the Pacific end of Gatun Lake. We are ready to downlock. As instructed, we enter the chamber first and watch as a large merchant ship follows us in and is positioned just astern of us. With the forward lock gate a mere boatlength in front, we experience a few anxious moments as the mules—now powerful diesel engines on tracks—tow our chamber mate into the lock and moor her securely with stout wire pennants.

The water level is gradually lowered, and at last we pass through the final gate to the Pacific. The dark water swirls around our hull, and we shoot forward into the night, propelled in part by the emptying lock waters behind us. We've made it! To cross to a new ocean and all the wonders it holds has taken a brief 14 hours. The entire trip has cost us only $90, including all fees and the services of the pilot for the day. Gilbert has told me that the highest toll ever was $89,154.62, paid by the QE II in January 1980, while the lowest fee for the 50-mile canal passage was 36 cents, paid by Richard Halliburton for swimming the canal in 1928.

We prepare to spend our first night in the Pacific. I am almost too excited to sleep. The events of the day keep flashing through my head. The locks, the lake, the Pacific. The Pacific; here I am at last. I fall asleep wondering what stories will go back to the Soviet Union, what photographs might have been taken of TAKU from the GORKY. Will they ever find out who the Russian last seen headed into the Pacific was? I wonder.

9

Dos Días

Five days out of Panama and we are in the ITCZ, more familiarly known as the doldrums. Now, my sense of the doldrums was a place where not much happened, a sort of no man's land out in the ocean. How often have you heard someone say, "Oh, he's a little depressed; he's in the doldrums today?" Well, life in the intertropical convergence zone is more than a little depressing. The winds that are blowing one way in the northern hemisphere bump up against the winds blowing the opposite way in the southern hemisphere, and where they meet, meteorological life is confused and unsettled. It rains. And then it rains some more. And then it rains from a different direction. When the weather finally clears up a bit, it is only so it can rain again.

By this particular point of time three things had occurred:

1. We had been unable to get a sight for the full five days, so I was basically navigating by the seat (wet as it was) of my pants. The wind was on the nose, and we were tacking every six hours trying to beat our way southwestward to the Galápagos. I was trying desperately to keep an accurate idea of where I thought we were.

2. A 14-foot seam in the mainsail had blown out. We were forced to remove the sail from the boom and take all 375 square feet of soaking wet Dacron down below, where it took up most of the available space. Repairs to the seam took two people, as one had to help hold the sail steady while the other pushed and pulled the needle through the layers of wet Dacron. We needed to double-stitch the seam so that it wouldn't let go again. That meant 28 feet of hand sewing at the rate of about a foot an hour. It would take us two and a half days to get the sail repaired and reset. So much for waiting to play round-robin backgammon.

3. Cristina had become morose. For hours she would sit on the floor of the forward V-berth cabin humming to herself. "I am so depressed," was all she would say when she could be made to say anything. Greta Garbo had made "I vant to be alone" famous, but I had my doubts that "I am so depressed" in heavily Italian-accented English was worth anything but trouble. It rained, we sewed, and TAKU sailed ever onward.

"She says our systems are poisoned and that we need to eat more garlic and onions to purge them," came Celia's comment one day after she had attempted to interview Cristina.

"Do you mind if I move my sleeping bag out of the V-berth and back behind the chart table to the little quarterberth?" asked Armen a day later. "The smell of garlic and onions is killing me; I think I'll sleep better nearer the main hatch where I can get some air." Good friend that he was, Armen had kept his peace about Cristina and perhaps, as Twain had suggested, believed that *we* were getting something from this experience that *he*, Armen, couldn't perceive.

To be fair, Cristina did some sewing on the mainsail and stood her watches, although by this time I found myself watching her. "This is ridiculous," I said to Celia, as I shed my wet raingear after yet another two hours in the continual downpour. "Here we have a crew to help with the watchstanding, but she acts so *looney-tunes* half the time that now I not only stand my watch, but I feel I have to keep a weather eye on her as well."

"We have only another three days to the Galápagos if your calculations are correct. Maybe she'll cheer up when we get in."

"I hope so." Armen, having not had the benefit of our trial-by-ordeal passage to the Virgin Islands, was beginning to get a bit woeful looking himself. He hadn't counted on constant rain, miles of sewing, a half-crazy Italian woman, and a skipper who had only a vague idea of where we were.

We got the main back up and drawing, and morale improved. I was concerned that we would run into Costa Rica's Cocos Island. Lying some hundreds of miles from the Costa Rican mainland, Cocos is virtually the only obstacle in the vast expanse of water between the Gulf of Panama and the Archipelago de Colón, as the Galápagos Islands are officially known. The way my luck seemed to be running, and with no fix to show on the chart because of the continued overcast, I felt we were fast becoming prime candidates for the next disaster.

"Everyone must keep an especially sharp lookout tonight. My best guess puts us within about 50 miles of Cocos Island. We'll keep heading west until midnight, and if we haven't sighted it by then we'll tack off south until daylight so that we won't run into it. It's a big island, and we need to keep a sharp watch. We haven't had a fix for seven days so we need to use extra care."

I was concerned. I knew that there would be no boat with a fisherman in white to greet us this time. I could barely sleep. Every half hour or so I would poke my head out to make sure the individual on watch was keeping a good lookout. Things felt wrong. The sense of unease was one I was to experience other times in later passages. The rhythms of the boat and the sea felt wrong. I debated tacking south earlier than we had planned.

I pushed open the companionway to check on Armen. He stood behind the wheel peering into the darkness ahead. Looking over his shoulder I saw the reason for my unease. A jet-black squall line stretched across the sky and was bearing rapidly down on us. I threw a set of foul-weather gear out to Armen and, grabbing my own, hurried on deck.

"Quick, get that gear on," I exhorted Armen, as I took over the helm and disconnected the windvane.

"I should have looked back," said Armen. "I was keeping a great watch ahead like you said. I never thought to look back."

The squall line was on us. The wind speed indicator rocketed to 45 and then 50. TAKU leapt ahead, hard pressed by the increasing wind. The rigging screamed. Celia's head appeared in the hatch. "Are we okay?" she shouted.

"I think it's just a line." The wind had already dropped back to 40 as the line raced past. "Everything's under control." As the wind died back down I realized that the unease that I had felt was gone. TAKU was doing fine. We would make it. Armen looked rattled as he helped tack the boat over, and we started south for the last leg to the Galápagos.

The squall passed, and as I was to learn as the months went on, that very often brought clearing weather. Some stars appeared in the sky, the first we had been able to see in over a week. My watch passed quickly, and I was delighted to see an orange glow off to the east as the sky lightened and the sun made its first appearance as well. We would be able to get some sights and an accurate fix. Although he had only been asleep a short while, I went down and woke Armen and told him to come up on deck as I had something to show him.

He crawled out of his sleeping bag, rubbed his eyes to clear them, and followed me up into the cockpit. "That, my friend," I said, pointing off the port side toward the east, "is the sun." I was grinning. We could feel the warmth of the rays hitting our skin. I pointed off to the starboard where a low bank of clouds hung on the horizon. "And right over there should be Cocos Island."

We both peered at the bank of clouds to our right, and as the sun came up a little further, they warmed and lifted. About 20 miles to starboard, Cocos Island emerged as though painted on the backdrop of the sky. I was more astonished than Armen, but pretended that I knew it was there all the time. Armen turned to me and smiled and gave me a big hug. "I should never have been worried," he declared as he went below. "I won't worry again."

Celia appeared shortly thereafter for her watch. "The sun woke me up," she said. "Isn't it great."

"You bet."

"Armen told me you showed him Cocos Island."

"Yeah. Right over there." I pointed to starboard, but the clouds had lowered again and Cocos lay obscured. "We saw it a few minutes ago, but it's back in the clouds now." We weren't to see Cocos again, nor would we see land until two days later when we crossed the Equator while in sight of the first of the Galápagos Islands. No matter. The vision of Cocos Island appearing from the clouds had come at an opportune time to validate my dead-reckoned navigation. I felt truly, for the first time, that I, on whom everyone else was counting, could count on myself.

We were across the Equator, in the fabled South Pacific. Celia, who had been to South America by plane and was therefore the only one of us who had been across the Equator, dressed up as Queen Neptune and, welcoming us to her realm, inducted us into the ranks of the Equator-crossers with a bowl of freshly-popped popcorn. The chill mist produced by the north-flowing Humboldt Current drove us into sweaters, jackets and watch caps. Here we were, new shellbacks, on the Equator and dressed for winter! It was not what I had imagined at all.

Academy Bay opened before us. Sails slithered down, we rounded up, the anchor slid over the roller, the chain rattled out of the hawse, and suddenly there was silence as TAKU swung peacefully to her chain. The Galápagos—the enchanted islands—the province of Darwin and Melville and now of TAKU and her hearty crew. And also the Ecuadorian Navy, which administers the Galápagos Islands for Ecuador. Within minutes a launch was alongside bearing a starched and pressed, fully-attired naval officer and his retinue. In a flash he was on board and in the cockpit. In another flash he had given us a dazzling Latino smile and a fast-from-the-hip *"Buenos Días,"* and then a frown and in Spanish, "Why are you here?" Celia took a turn in the interpreter's hot seat.

"He wants to know why we are here," translated Celia. "What shall I tell him?"

"Tell him we've come to visit the beautiful Galápagos." With better luck than I had in the Caribbean with my French, Celia relayed this information to the capitano de porto.

"Dos días!" he replied.

"He says we can have two days," interpreted Celia. Like Roland in Iles des Saintes, I was discovering that at the current level of communication, fast-paced as it was, I could keep up and handle the translation myself.

"That's bullposterous," I sputtered. "Tell him we want more time; we didn't come all this way for only a two-day stay. Make something up. Get us some more time—I know, tell him we're exhausted and need to rest and that 48 hours isn't enough. C'mon—charm the hell out of him."

Celia turned to the port captain and started to translate into halting Spanish. She turned to me. "Dom, I don't know the word for exhausted in Spanish."

"Try *cansada*," came a voice speaking perfect English from the mouth of the port captain. Oops! And there we were. My mind clawed back over my remarks of the past minutes as I tried to remember what I had said that had been meant for Celia but that the port captain had obviously understood. Celia filled the gap of silence by attempting to continue the explanation. Finally the stalemate was broken by Cristina, who had been silent until this moment.

"You must be nicer to us," she said in Spanish. "Today is my birthday."

This simple statement seemed to let the port captain off the official hook. In honor of the birthday, he immediately gave us 72 hours and then later extended that by 48 and yet another 48 a few days later. He took us for drinks one evening to the "disco" *cantina*, a small watering hole with canned music and cold beer. Another afternoon we were invited to tea at his office. We reciprocated and invited him and his retinue for a party on board TAKU. Ironically, on his way to visit with us on our seventh day in port, he stopped and ordered to sea two yachts that had used up their requisite *dos días*. He stood by in his launch and waited until the boats weighed anchor and departed.

We, who had struck up a friendship, probably could have stayed forever. The inequities of the port administration were beyond understanding. If Cristina had not announced her birthday we would have been ordered out after 48 hours to face the 3,300–mile passage to the Marquesas. Instead, we used our time to rest, prepare the boat, and visit the Darwin Station to see the magnificent Galápagos tortoises and the fascinating marine iguanas who were as much at home in the water as they were on the land.

It was time to move on. July was already upon us; Armen needed to be in Tahiti, more than 4,000 miles away, by early September. We managed to purchase a 55-gallon drum of diesel from an Ecuadorian Navy vessel that put into port one day. We topped off our water tanks with water purchased by the gallon from one of the two small hotels doing business here on Isla Santa Cruz. Some last minute extra, and expensive, provisions, from a local store, and we were off on what was the longest mileage leg of the trip around the world: 3,300 miles from Academy Bay, Galápagos, to Hiva Oa, Marquesas, French Polynesia, a fair distance to sail nonstop under any circumstances.

10

Looney Tunes

We worked our way southwest from Academy Bay and were fortunate to pick up the trades within the first 12 hours. Twenty-one days later, having been given a boost of 15 to 20 miles per day by the current, TAKU nosed into the handkerchief-sized cove that served as the harbor at Hiva Oa and dropped her anchor for the first time in Polynesia.

For the most part the passage was uneventful. We slept, ate, navigated, cooked, cleaned, read, and watched the ever-changing marine landscape as TAKU scudded along under a pair of poled-out running staysails, the mizzen staysail, and the mizzen. We also raised and sheeted tight the storm trysail to cut the side-to-side motion as much as we could. This gentle rolling motion of the trades made me understand why sailors were always thought to walk with a rolling gait when they returned ashore.

As I watched our track extend along the chart and bring us nearer and nearer to the fabled South Pacific islands, I experienced the vastness of the world in a way that I never had before. Especially wonderful were the clear nights with the heavens blazing star formations that became more and more familiar with each nightwatch. Everything would have been perfect—except for Cristina. She became depressed again. The time ashore in Academy Bay had rejuvenated her, but once more out at sea she grew more withdrawn.

She took to roaming at night (difficult to do on a 41-foot boat with three other people aboard); sleep, when she got any, was at odd times. Once I found her asleep on night watch and the boat disengaged from the windvane and way off course. I took over her night watches for the rest of the trip. Armen and Celia kept an eye on her during the day as well as standing their own watches. I was glad to arrive at Hiva Oa. I had one item of business to do as soon as possible. I intended to get Cristina signed off the boat.

"But she must post a bond, *monsieur*, and as she is Italiano," said the gendarme, "she must pay enough francs to repatriate her to her home country if necessary."

"How many francs is that?" I asked, already dreading the answer.

"Oh, *monsieur*," he replied with a Gallic shrug that I remembered from Iles des Saintes, "a mere _____." He named a figure that I managed to calculate was, at the then-current rate of exchange, in excess of $1,800 U.S.

"*Sacrebleu!*" I muttered as I worked on my French. We held a council. "Cristina, you want to get off TAKU, right?

"Yes," she replied languorously. "I think it is very beautiful here. I think I am staying here for a while."

"Fine, Cristina. There's just a little practical matter of the $1,800 bond. You told me in Antigua that you had sufficient funds."

"I did; the bond in Antigua was only $500. That's what I have, $500." I worked on my French some more.

If we wanted her off the boat it would cost us $1,300, and she would be stuck ashore with no money whatsoever. I considered paying the $1,300 and giving her some extra money to get her ashore. Celia was annoyed and adamant.

"Now who is *looney-tunes* around here?" she would ask me. "That's a sizeable chunk out of your cruising budget. You'll never get it back."

"I am so depressed," I thought to myself in an Italian accent. I contemplated finding an unoccupied corner of the V-berth floor to hum on.

Finally Celia took matters in hand, figuratively and literally. Taking Cristina forcibly by the hand, she escorted her to the post office and had her book a call home to Italy. Some hours later they returned.

"What happened?" I asked anxiously.

"You'll never believe it," answered Celia. "She called home, and they asked her if she had gotten the money they sent to the Indo-Suez Bank here in the Marquesas for her. We went to the bank, and there was the $1,000 her family had cabled her. I guess they figured she'd need money when she got to French Polynesia in case she got depressed or something. So $1,800 minus $500 and then another $1,000 only leaves us short $300."

Off I went once again to the gendarmerie. "Look, Cristina has the money for the bond (I mentally included our $300); she wants to get off the boat. We *want* her to get off the boat. Can *you* please get her off the boat?" Ah, the French; ah, their bureaucracy.

"But, *monsieur*, I have not the permission to sign her off. I must call Tahiti. Come in two days; I will have your answer."

"But if you are calling, why can't I wait?"

"But, *monsieur* (palms up, shoulders raised), these things take time. Here in *Paradise* one should relax. You will hear, *monsieur*; you will hear!"

Two days later I heard. Papeete had refused permission for Cristina to disembark in the Marquesas. "She can leave the boat, *monsieur*," said the gendarme when I went back to see him, "but only in Tahiti where she will pay the bond." Case closed; Tahiti it was to be.

Time in paradise had been flying by. July somehow had turned into mid-August, and we were only as far as the Marquesas. Sailing around the world was taking longer than I had imagined. On top of that Armen was getting closer to his departure date from Tahiti, but we weren't getting closer to the Tahiti airport. We discussed the issue at length. If we went direct, we could be in Tahiti in a little over a week, but that would mean missing the Tuamotus altogether. It was Armen who found a solution to his problem.

While we had been waiting to hear about Cristina, Armen had looked into flying to Tahiti. The difficulty was that there was only one flight every other week on a six-passenger plane but all seats were booked for several flights to come. Armen had been commiserating with Susan and George on the Danish yacht JOHANNA BRUNE, whom we had met in Panama and had run into in the harbor of the Marquesan island of Fatu Hiva.

"George and Susan are pushing on to the Tuamotus and then Tahiti in just a few days. Susan's son, Christopher, has to fly out on September 8 to go back to school. He's actually on the same outbound flight that I'm on," Armen told us. "They said they would be happy to have me come along, and then I could keep Christopher company on the flight to the States." Christopher was eleven and going to live with his uncle while he went to school.

I had to admit that Armen's solution seemed logical. JOHANNA BRUNE was a wonderful boat. She had been a working Danish fishing trawler. Her main hold had been converted to a spacious and gracious living space with mahogany paneling and even an oil painting or two. Her high, bluff bow hid teak decks that led aft to a cozy pilothouse complete with chart table and bunk. "You don't need to wear foul-weather gear on night watch," Armen told me as he pointed out this cruising comfort. I was sure he would be safe and that he would have a wonderful time with Sue and George.

My biggest regret was losing him as a shipmate. We had shared a lot of experiences in the past few months, and Armen, though he had started out as a landlubber, had developed into a competent watchstander and an excellent crewman. More importantly he had always been a close friend.

"Why don't you just stay on, Armen?" I asked him. "They won't even notice you aren't back at school for a few months until the mail starts piling up in your box."

He laughed. "I'd love to, Dom, but I'm not ready for my circumnavigation yet. But I'll miss TAKU; it's been different from what I expected. And wonderful. I'm not sure I will be able to explain it to everyone back in Boston, but I'll try."

We had a farewell dinner, and the next morning I dinghied Armen over to JOHANNA BRUNE. George was already cranking in the massive anchor chain on the trawler's big windlass. Armen climbed over the rail, and I passed him his seabag. We waved good-bye. We shouted a few bantering phrases over the noise of the windlass. I sat in the dinghy and watched as Armen helped Sue and George raise JOHANNA BRUNE's tanbark sails. They quickly filled with wind, and with a toot of her whistle, the converted Danish trawler spun over on to the port tack and was soon a spot on the horizon as she rolled along for the Tuamotus and Tahiti. Armen was gone.

I had contemplated sending Cristina as well. George and Sue were willing to take her, but I had been given specific instructions that she was to arrive in Tahiti on TAKU and was not to be signed off until her bond was paid. I didn't want to get George and Sue in trouble with the authorities. If Cristina was TAKU's nemesis, TAKU's nemesis she would remain.

11

"Toto," Dorothy Said . . .

October, Nuku Hiva

Dear Gene,

The post office here only holds mail for two weeks so the letter tape you described in your card was sent back. I know this because the card you sent at the same time was still here after two months and wasn't sent back. *C'est la vie!* as they say here.

Peace,

We were enjoying the Marquesas. How could we not be dazzled by towering volcanic islands with names like Hiva Oa, Fatu Hiva, Ua Pou, and Nuku Hiva. Even Cristina seemed to be more relaxed and calm, as she had opportunities to go ashore and take walks in the lushly-flowered tropical foliage. Nuku Hiva was where Melville had jumped ship and hidden out for months. His experiences ashore became the basis for his novel *Typee*. We also started to meet a few more cruising boats. BLACK WHALE, a converted 23-foot Pearson Ensign with singlehander Tom Laginess aboard, and QUINTET, out of Portland, Oregon, a beautiful Swan New York 48, sailed by Fred and Gayle Bieker along with their three teenage children, Kris, Paul and Katherine, and family friend and crewmember Dale Nordin, became familiar sights.

In sharing anchorages with QUINTET, we discovered that Paul and Celia shared the same birth date. We planned to rendezvous for a big party in Ahe, the Tuamotus, at the end of October. Our departure from Nuku Hiva was scheduled in company with QUINTET to allow time to arrive in Ahe, meet the locals, and get ready for the party. We had 495 miles to sail, with a forecast of fair skies and reaching winds in excess of

15 knots. Little did I know that we were setting off for a passage that would culminate in near disaster. Disasters or near disasters always seem to start simply, and although we always recognize the potential we can never predict the occurrence.

The Tuamotu group is the largest and most farflung group of islands in the world. Lying between 14 and 25 degrees south, the chain stretches over 1,000 miles. The archipelago is made up of atolls, which are made up of islets called *motus*. Like shells on a necklace, *motus* are banded together in an encircling reef; some are pierced with passes that permit entrance into the central lagoons. At their highest, *motus* are about 25 to 30 feet above sea level. But most are lower, and the connecting reefs lurk menacingly just below the water's surface. Some of the larger atolls contain lagoons of extraordinary size, up to 10 miles wide and 30 miles long.

The Sailing Directions warn mariners away. "Navigation among these islands," read the Directions, "is dangerous because of the uncertain set of the current and the still imperfectly charted reefs and islands. However, there is little inducement for vessels to visit these groups, as the only trade with the natives consists in the purchase of coconuts, which grow on the islands, and a little pearl shell, the natives subsisting mainly on the fish they catch in the lagoons." The original name for this archipelago was *Paumotu*, which meant literally "islands destroyed." In 1851 the locals, unhappy with the name the French had given to their island group, petitioned successfully for a change, and the new name *Tuamotu* was adopted. A literal translation is "islands under the horizon." They are also more familiarly known as the "low archipelago," but to sailors far and wide the more awe-inspiring label "dangerous archipelago" takes precedence.

Being faster than TAKU, QUINTET anticipated a passage of three days; we conservatively figured on four and a half to five. QUINTET departed several hours ahead of us and radioed soon after that she was making between seven and nine knots in a grand downhill slide. On leaving, we found the same conditions and with everything hanked on were soon doing over six knots in pursuit. Two and a half days later the strong wind died and our progress slowed.

By this time, QUINTET was almost to Ahe, and the last wind carried them in, as they expected, in just over three days. With the help of their SatNav their landfall had been spot-on. TAKU was 190 miles out and moving slowly, but with luck we expected to arrive on the upcoming Friday, five days after our departure and two days before the big party.

As we progressed south our navigation became more difficult. I was shooting sun sights with my sextant and working out lines of position and running fixes. This had served us well from the Galápagos to the Marquesas, but now I was having problems. The sun's declination (the angle below the Equator) and our latitude were almost identical and my sun lines began to plot as meridians. The advancing of a line of position for a running fix was too long to be accurate. Noon sights seemed impossible until someone on the radio referred me to a passage in Eric Hiscock's *Come Aboard*, which we indeed had aboard, where he details a workable procedure for taking a high altitude sight (when the sun's declination above or below the Equator is nearly identical with your own latitude). Thursday ended with clouds on the horizon, a dead-reckoning fix that put TAKU some 90 miles out of Ahe, and hopes for a safe landfall in the dangerous archipelago the next day.

During the night the wind increased and the light overcast conditions became heavy. At 5:30 A.M. the weather signaled a bad day ahead, but I managed to catch the moon, Venus, and some early sun lines, which put us some 35 miles out—within a few miles of our DR plot, but somewhat to the east. We altered course for Ahe, and on our morning radio contact I confidently predicted that we'd be anchored by early afternoon.

By 8 A.M. the sky was completely overcast and squall lines had begun to appear on the horizon. A series of wave disturbances that kicked up the seas and gave us 180-degree wind shifts every 30 minutes with the wind strength skipping from 0 to 25 knots followed. Undaunted, we pressed on, anxious to get into the pass at Ahe and into a calm and safe anchorage.

At 10:30 A.M. I caught the faint edge of the sun in a 30-second break in the clouds and with an RDF bearing on the island of Manihi figured we were approximately due north of Ahe. We adjusted course again, and as it was still early in the day I thought confidently of the landfall soon to be made.

We were now motorsailing in variable wind conditions and had turned on the radar to aid in making contact with Ahe. By 12:30 P.M. visibility was down to less than a quarter-mile and the seas were building. We were less than five miles from our destination based on our mileage logged from Nuku Hiva. After conferring on the radio with QUINTET, we decided to continue southward. The weather was getting worse, and we hoped to sight the island momentarily and duck into the pass and out of what was obviously becoming a bad situation. Our continued checks on the radar revealed nothing, as did our peering into the limited horizon ahead.

By 3:30 P.M. we were 20 miles past our destination according to our dead reckoning, that not-always-reliable estimation of position based on course steered and known speed made good. Ahead there was nothing; around us were confused seas and towering black clouds. With reduced sail we were doing just over three knots in the lumpy water. I decided to continue until 5:30 P.M. and, if we sighted nothing by then, to run off to the northwest overnight for Rangiroa, another Tuamotan island about 90 miles from Ahe. My concern was that if we had missed Ahe in the poor visibility (a real possibility), but were still close, we could be in serious trouble heaving-to at night with no idea where we were.

The several boats we had communicated with by radio were as concerned about our location as we were. The many reports of the Tuamotus' arbitrary currents running up to five knots are not without foundation. I began to rationalize, reasoning that if we'd had a current of only one and a half knots on the nose the past 15 hours it would have kept us from making our DR position. We kept on, the radar screen still blank.

At 5:25, five minutes before our deadline to run off, land appeared out of the mist—a low smudge on the starboard bow. We cheered and clapped and called on the radio as our nerves relaxed. As is always the case, once the visual contact is made the radar becomes easy to use and tune, though the return from the low atoll was very weak. At least now we wouldn't run aground on an unseen reef. Since it was almost dark we radioed our intention to stay in visual contact with the island until the next day, when we would enter the pass to the lagoon. The prospect of a night of standing off was unappealing, but bearable when compared to the anxiety we had felt while looking for land.

By 1 A.M. the storm, such as it was, had abated and the seas were flattening. Stars began to appear, and we tacked leisurely along the coast until sunrise. It was now Saturday, and we were still a day early for the party.

By 8:30 A.M. we were off what we thought was the pass. Just to be sure, we called QUINTET and also the yacht CATSPAW. Both were already in the lagoon, out of sight at the far end.

"Did you go southwest until the island turns south?" asked Russ aboard CATSPAW, sounding like an air traffic controller guiding in a stricken plane.

"Affirmative."

"Then you have sighted the pass?"

"Affirmative."

"You should be okay then. Just come straight in."

Like the reprieved pilot who knows that the runway, the touch-down, and the end of the ordeal are mere seconds away, we swung TAKU's bow into the sparkling sunshine, set her on a course between two small *motus* and headed for the lagoon within.

Suddenly Russ's voice came over the radio again.

"Say, can you see the hut?"

"What hut?"

"There's a conspicuous hut at the inside starboard side of the pass. You can't miss it. Can you see it?"

When someone tells me I can't miss something, it invariably means that not only will I miss it but that I have missed it.

"Uh-uh Russ, no hut." We altered course and made two more crosses in front of the pass, but none of us could see a hut.

"Don't come in," Russ advised. "You're probably someplace that isn't the pass."

"This is definitely a pass." These last words were spoken from the pilot who knows he hasn't found the runway but is trying to will it to become one against all odds.

Russ verbally reviewed our course step-by-step along the motu: Sail approximately eight miles, turn the corner, spot the pass, see the hut. We had everything except the hut. About this time came the sink-ing feeling that we were not at Ahe. ("Toto," Dorothy said, "I have the feeling we're not in Kansas anymore.") With the unpredictable currents and storm conditions of the day before, an examination of the chart revealed several places we might be.

Someone on the radio guessed Manihi. Another voice replied, "No, they'd see the village." Looking at the chart again, I stabbed my pencil on Apataki, which lies 35 miles due south of Ahe, is similar in configuration and coastline, and, coincidentally, has the same relative pass location.

"Guys," I radioed, "I think we're at Apataki."

A chorus of "no" and an "impossible" came back. I reread the Sailing Directions and decided to fix it for sure. Pragmatically, I got out the sextant and the stop watch, got a good sun line and plotted it on the chart. It was 10:30 A.M.

"The problem is solved," I radioed again. "I took a sun line, plotted it, and it goes *right directly* through the pass at Ahe."

This declaration was greeted with a chorus of "hooray" and "way to go."

"And guys," I continued, "it also goes *right directly* through the pass at Apataki." (The wonders of navigation never cease to amaze me.)

The radio voices checked their charts and returned with another chorus of "no."

"Affirmative, so we are going to run south along the coast of the motu for awhile. If we are at Ahe we'll run out of island after about five miles and we'll come back. If we're at Apataki, we will keep going to the next pass and the village some 15 miles farther on. Catch you at 12:30."

"Good luck," the choir sang, followed by a solitary, "Look for the hut."

At 12:30 we hadn't run out of island. By 3:30 we were moored to the quay at Apataki, although how we missed both Ahe and Manihi escaped us. At least the weather was beautiful, the people friendly and the moorage tranquil.

12

Keystone Cops

Sunday . . . 5:30 . . . dawn . . . blue sky . . . the day of the party . . . We are all awake early, having gone to sleep at sunset the previous night. I am full of energy. I announce that we are leaving immediately for Ahe and I go on deck, start the engine and begin casting off the lines that hold us to Apataki's quay. We have about 60 miles to go: 15 for the coast of Apataki, 35 to Ahe, five up that island's coast, and four down the lagoon to the village. I figure, optimistically, that if we can do six knots we'll be in by 5 P.M., well before dark. We have clear skies, an early start, and a fantastic day. Who says sailing in the Tuamotus is difficult?

At 8 A.M. we make our scheduled radio with QUINTET, and we hear: "One, two, three: Happy birthday to you, happy birthday to you, happy birthday dear Celia, happy birthday to you. Over." They've gotten *everybody* to the mike since they think we are going to miss the party. We are motorsailing at over six knots and announce that TAKU is underway for Ahe, ETA late afternoon.

By 2 P.M. we are headed by the wind and the seas are building, cutting our speed through the water to just over five knots. I expect to sight Ahe at about 3:30, when we should be 10 miles out. At 3:15 I climb into the rigging, and an island is there, low and green on the horizon ahead. Ahe seems so large that I can't believe we missed it the day before. I feel momentarily better about my navigation. Surely the reduced visibility of the previous day, coupled with the low elevation caused the problem. We were probably only a mile or two away as we passed by.

Returning to the cockpit, I increase our engine rpm, as we still have a total of 19 miles to go and a little over three hours of daylight left. We're doing well over five knots, but something tells me we won't make it in time. I have learned from hard experience that trying to make an anchorage as the sun is setting seems to have two contradictory effects. One: the sun goes down faster than usual; two: the faster the sun goes down, the longer the distance to go seems to become. Now is no exception.

At 4:30 we radio that we expect to be off the pass at 6:15 and ask if is possible to anchor just inside. I know we won't be able to cross the lagoon and make the village before dark. Fred, on QUINTET, says that if we come in someone will meet us with a native pilot and bring us to the village. Russ radios that slack water is at about 7 P.M. and that the pass is a piece of cake even if we can't see the hut.

At 5:30 we are off Ahe and can see the lights of the anchored yachts less than a mile away at the village. Unfortunately the barrier reef separates us from the calm waters of the lagoon and we have to keep going until we can round into the pass. Celia sticks her head up and reports some smoke coming out of the engine compartment. I reply that it must be some old spilled oil and check the engine operating temperature gauge. It's high, but safe. When I drop 200 rpm it cools to normal levels. The radio reports that the yacht TIMBALINA, sailed singlehanded by a Frenchman we know named Thierry, is getting underway. On board is Tom from BLACK WHALE and a native pilot; they plan to meet us inside the pass and guide us to the village.

As we proceed northward we count off the motus; there are, according to the chart, 11 between us and the pass. Daylight is fading. We set our running lights, and Cristina and Celia drop and furl the sails in the fast gathering dusk. As we pass the gaps in the motus we spot TIMBALINA's masthead light paralleling our course. Two miles to go. Then one. Celia is on the radio chatting with Tom about the plan once we get in, but she yells out that the smoke is getting bad. I decide to check and duck below. My chest heaves involuntarily as I see all the smoke. It billows from the engine hatch, and I am afraid to shut down. I go quickly back to the port cockpit locker through which our exhaust passes. I hope that we've got a rag or piece of line or even a life jacket smoldering on the exhaust pipe and nothing more. I open the locker and flames leap up toward me.

Instinctively I slam the locker shut. Inside I am torn with fear and tension, but I try to remain calm and say, "Pass up the extinguishers.

Then call them and say that we have a fire on board." I feel the anxiety in my throat and hear the tension in my voice.

Celia passes out our three extinguishers and goes to the radio. I shoot one off in the locker and the flames disappear. The second one fails to go off. The third, and final one I take below and fire off in the engine compartment. We are barely idling the engine, just off the pass. I can see TIMBALINA less than 1,000 yards away, but we are still outside. There is a great deal of smoke but the active flames seem to be out. The engine is diesel not gas, so there is no immediate danger of explosion, but we are out of extinguishers.

I remember our deck washdown, switch it on, and begin pumping five gallons per minute of salt water into the cockpit locker to cool the exhaust.

The automatic bilge pump works constantly to remove the water we are pumping below. Things seem to be under control. I decide that we'd best get inside the pass so that if the fire re-erupts we can beach the boat inside or get help from TIMBALINA. It is now pitch black. (Time flies when you are having fun.) Cristina mans our spotlight, and as we move into the beginning of the pass I realize that we've missed slack water. I also discover that our Morse throttle cable has either jammed or melted and we cannot increase or decrease our engine speed from 1,200 rpm, the equivalent of about two and a half knots. While Celia steers I try briefly to disconnect the cable from the back of the engine, but this entails lying on the engine, and the heat and smoke are too much. We remain calm but edgy and decide to continue.

"Tom," I radio, "we're all right and on our way in."

"I hoped so," is all he replies.

With our strobe light on to pick up the edges of the pass without totally depriving us of our night vision we continue in. I become tense as I see the water that is rapidly passing the hull. Three-quarters of the way in I suddenly realize that we are barely moving. The ebb is underway, and we are getting caught. We are nearly at a dead stop and frustration is mounting. We imperceptibly edge forward, and finally we cross the opare—the dividing line between the pass current and the calm lagoon; we are inside.

TIMBALINA roars up like a carload of Keystone cops and throws us an unwanted and unneeded line. Cristina shines the spotlight in their faces and momentarily blinds our would-be rescuers. The tension has been great for them as well. Tana, the native pilot, who speaks Paumotan and French, has forgotten his French. Thierry, the captain, who speaks French and English, has forgotten his English. Though we are now inside, we are being rescued by a boat that is lost and on which communication has come to a halt. For a few moments things stay tense. Then we are all laughing, and the missing languages begin to reappear.

Once we are out of the current we decide not to anchor but to wait for the moonrise, which is supposed to occur at 9:15, and pick our way through the coral heads to the village. The moon, though, never comes up, as the clouds reappear. Tana, who has relaxed, gets his bearings and finds the missing mark. At our maximum speed of two and a half knots we trail within 10 feet of TIMBALINA's stern and wind our way through the lagoon heading for QUINTET's strobe light, which beckons us from four miles away.

Sunday, the birthday, the party day, ends at midnight as we sight the dock and slide alongside to be made fast by two elderly Ahe gentlemen who have been waiting patiently for the pilot to bring us in. TIMBALINA rafts outboard of us. The engine is shut down, the deckwash is secured, and the bilge pump finally gurgles to a halt. The boat smells of smoke, charcoal, and wet wood.

We make glasses of Tang and peanut butter crackers and sit on the coach roof and talk and try to relax. Fred rows over in the darkness, bringing some gin to add to the Tang. I decline, but the others say it is the most delicious drink they've ever had. The camaraderie is intense and special. I satisfy myself that the fire is out and that TAKU is safe. It's 1:30 A.M. We learn that we are only the fifth boat to ever enter the lagoon at night and, as far as anyone can remember, the only one to have crossed it at night all the way to the village; the others prudently anchored just inside the pass. I know we are most certainly the only boat ever to come in on fire. We also learn that Tana isn't really a pilot but a charming local resident who volunteered to help out the poor confused yachties. I ask him if he's ever brought a boat across the lagoon at night. His eyes twinkle mischievously; he laughs, and pointing to TIMBALINA and TAKU, he replies in his fast-growing English vocabulary: "Two!"

We realize that after all of this excitement we still missed the party. Someone says, "With all the entertainment TAKU provides, who needs a party?" At 2:30 A.M. people say good night and drift off to bed. We say thanks again to Thierry, who risked his boat, and to Tom and Tana. We start for our bunks. Celia announces that as long as she lives she doubts she will ever have another birthday to equal this one, nor does she ever want one. I climb into my bunk, but even before my head hits the pillow, I am fast asleep.

Searching for Ahe's conspicuous hut. C. Lowe

TAKU with Armen on the bow locks through the Panama Canal
behind the Russian ship MAXIM GORKY. D. Degnon

New Zealand's northernmost point offers some directions.
D. Degnon

Neiafu harbor, Vava'u, Tonga, provides an ideal spot for some windsurfing. D. Degnon

On a Down-Under February (mid-summer) excursion to
Mount Cook, New Zealand. C. Lowe

Catching up on repairs in Opua, New Zealand.
TAKU is on a grid next to a boatyard dock. D. Degnon

Another "adventure in paradise"—Kavieng, Bismarck Archipelago, Papua New Guinea. C. Lowe

In the Solomon Islands, Peter finds a souvenir from World War II too big to take home. D. Degnon

In Papua New Guinea, a local trader and son offer us a kitten and/or grass skirt. D. Degnon

Photo op time on the tiny island of Sim Sim, Papua New Guinea. TAKU was the first yacht to call in over four years. C. Lowe

Celia tours the world's largest open-pit copper mine in Kieta, Bougainville, Papua New Guinea. D. Degnon

Rafted up in the "busy" harbor of Madang, Papua New Guinea. C. Lowe

"Port Moresby? That way, maybe." Taking advantage of local knowledge. D. Degnon

Stretched out on top of the Volvo, I find the water pump is just as far away as I can possibly reach—plus one-quarter inch. C. Lowe

TAKU and SHEARWATER have their bottoms quickly painted between 25-foot tides in Darwin, Australia. C. Lowe

Time out for spinnaker flying aboard TAKU,
Cocos Keeling Island, Indian Ocean. D. Degnon

VAGABUNDO draws a crowd out of the desert in North Yemen. D. Degnon

13

Coconuts

TAKU stayed six weeks in Ahe. In retrospect these weeks have to rank as some of the most wonderful of the whole seven-year trip around the world. Tied safely to the small quay, we were free to come and go to the village of eighty people who had clustered their homes on a motu at the southern end of Ahe's lagoon. We spent days snorkeling in some of the clearest and most brilliant water I've ever seen, or walking the wind-swept and sea-pounded beaches of the seaward side of the motus.

Each night there would be a volleyball game with the locals or a church service or a gathering on the beach for music and singing. The villagers had beautiful voices and loved to sing for hours; in church they sang traditional hymns such as "Onward, Christian Soldiers," the tune recognizable but the words in Paumotan. On the beach they would put their voices to traditional Polynesian rowing and working songs and chants. Sitting out under a full moon with a sky full of stars on a warm tropical night surrounded by singing voices was magic beyond belief.

"*Ah-oh-ey, ah-oh-ey*," one voice would commence the beginning of my favorite, which was an ancient Polynesian canoe paddling song. The men, who were sitting, would begin to sway and move their arms in a strong paddling motion and take up the chant. "*Ah-oh-ey, ah-oh-ey; ah-oh-ey eetai vai ta.*" Then the women would take up the song, blending their voices antiphonally with those of the men. "*Ah-oh-ey, ah-oh-ey, ah-oh-ey eetai moana, ah-oh-ey eetai vai ta.*" At the end of each beat imaginary paddles would be dipped in unison. I could picture the ancient war canoes with 60 paddlers or more moving smoothly through the oceans to the same chants.

Coconut palms were everywhere. The low sandy islets made a per-

fect home for them, and their green fronds swaying in the steady
tradewinds fringed the lagoon. Why there was trade in coconuts was
easy to see. Evidence of the copra trade was everywhere. The nuts were
harvested and husked, and the inner meat was stacked in the sun on
racks to dry. At some point in the drying process the pieces would be
gathered into burlap sacks, each containing about 50 pounds of dried
coconut. The bags would then be stacked on the small village dock to
await the arrival of the monthly copra boat, which would chug into the
lagoon, belching black smoke from its stack, and exchange dried goods
and supplies for the copra that had been collected.

The smell of drying coconut was everywhere as well. It wafted
across the lagoon to TAKU, and brought memories of days at the beach
when people on neighboring towels would anoint themselves with
suntan lotion made, perhaps, with coconut oil from these very same
trees.

The production of copra was not a taxing business on Ahe or, for
that matter, on many islands in the South Pacific. The worldwide price
was down due, in part, to an increased use of synthetics to replace the
oil that was the final derivative of the harvested coconut. The trees grew
randomly, the coconuts matured and were picked, opened, and left to
dry in the warm tropic air before being bagged for shipment. We were
told that when the price went up, villagers spent a bit more time har-
vesting, but with the worldwide price depressed not much time was
required to fill the small quota the village was allotted.

Consequently, coconuts were everywhere. They rolled in the small
waves that the wind stirred on the beaches of the lagoon; they sprouted
in the sun and put down feelers to anchor themselves for the beginnings
of new trees. And they lay rotting under the grown trees and on the foot-
paths around the island. If the sea surrounded and enveloped the shores
of Ahe, the coconuts enveloped the land. One day we were all invited
ashore for another evening of festivity.

"There will be a big party," Tana, the village spokesman and now
my Ahe friend, told me. "Everybody come; we have coconut auction
and then cake!" All of us were months from our last major resupply.
TAKU's had been in Panama. The promise of cake was too good to pass
up—especially for Tom from BLACK WHALE. His boat was so small that
his storage space was limited to absolute essentials. He had made it to

the South Pacific, but by the Tuamotus he had used up most of his food.

"I've got to get on my way to Tahiti," Tom would say every day when I saw him. "I'm really low on food, just about out of cigarettes, and feeling guilty for staying here so long. Do you know I have been here for two months? But this place is just what I always dreamed the South Pacific would look like. Tana keeps giving me gifts of fish, and I don't know—it's hard to leave."

I knew exactly what Tom meant. In planning TAKU's voyage, I had given little notice to either the Marquesas or the Tuamotus. They were small dots on the map of the world. I thought that, at most, we would spend a day or two in either place before heading on to the fabled Tahiti. After all, how much could there be to do and see? They looked so tiny on the map. But like BLACK WHALE, TAKU had gone on to "cruising time." Instead of a few days, we had spent two months in the Marquesas; now, in no hurry, I hoped to remain in Ahe until the coming cyclone season (in the Pacific, I was to learn, hurricanes are called cyclones) propelled us on to the big city of Papeete in Tahiti.

Tom had become friends with Louisa, who ran what could only be loosely described as Ahe's village store. Louisa, a buxom maiden whose gapped smile reflected the lack of dental care in this faraway island compounded by the ravages that "civilized" refined sugar had brought to Polynesia, kept shop in a small shed next to her house. It was open when Louisa wanted it to be and carried staples such as rice and flour, small tins of pineapple juice, cigarettes, and occasional notions. At this particular juncture, the store was about out of everything, as the copra boat had failed, not unusually, to show the previous month, and supplies were dwindling.

We all kept telling Tom that Louisa was looking for a husband and that if he didn't watch out he'd be the permanent Ahe shopkeeper. Tom would smile and laugh and tell us how he was being careful. We'd remind him of the Marquesas where he had anchored by himself at a small village and had met a most beautiful Polynesian woman. He had sat in the village for hours flirting with her in English that she didn't understand. With expansive gestures, he had described the wonders of America and told her that he would take her there.

That night there was a knock on the hull, and Tom, expecting the beautiful maiden, was startled to find her father climbing into the cockpit from a canoe carrying most of his worldly possessions. The father pounded Tom's shoulder with friendship and kept pointing at Tom and then at himself and then at the boat saying "America, America" over and over and smiling broadly. Hours later, after much one-sided conversation, Tom managed to get the disappointed father back to shore, and the now-chastened Tom had quickly hauled his anchor. A few days later Tom arrived in Ahe, where, licking his linguistic wounds, he had remained.

"I'm six-foot-three," Tom would state, recounting the incident yet another time. "I need a four-and-a-half-foot girlfriend because that's the only bunk space available. And I wasn't getting her; I was getting her father." We would all laugh and remind Tom of this incident whenever we saw him at Louisa's. Louisa had taken to baking since Tom had started coming around. She would concoct what looked like doughnuts but what were, in reality, a form of baked dough with no sugar in them at all. These went by the Polynesian name of *fri-fri* (free-free). Louisa, with her generous Polynesian spirit, would offer *fri-fris* to any of us who happened by. Washed down with a tin of pineapple juice purchased at her store, they were a treat we all enjoyed. Now, with some sugar borrowed from one of the yachts and eggs scrounged from one of the local chickens, Louisa was baking a real cake for the coconut auction to be held that evening.

"What do you make of this coconut auction?" I asked Tom.

"I'll tell you this," Tom replied. "There's no such thing as a free *fri-fri*. The number of cigarettes I've gone through would buy coffee and doughnuts at Dunkin Donuts at home for quite a spell. You can imagine what the trade-off for a cake may end up being."

We were not burning out on paradise, but merely reaffirming to each other that paradise definitely had some subtle, and sometimes unseen, price tags attached. There was no reason to complain. We were anchored in one of the most beautiful spots in the world; the people opened up their lives and their hearts to us. However, we had begun to discover a *quid pro quo* was often attached. I could, indeed, imagine what the trade-off for a cake might be. I pictured a handful of yachts anchored in the Ahe lagoon setting sail with a deckload of coconuts somehow purchased at the coconut auction out of guilt or innocence, but purchased nonetheless.

At dark we all went ashore and entered the small white wooden building that served as a combination town hall and dispensary. Old wooden folding chairs had been set up, and most of these were now taken by the local villagers. We all had debated on the proper attire for a coconut auction and had arrived at the consensus of long pants and a (the yachtie's definition of formal) clean shirt for the men and a skirt or dress for the women. The locals were smartly turned out. The women wore brightly colored and intricately printed long cotton dresses; the men of the village were attired in dark suits, with accompanying white shirts and neckties. Most everyone, including the men, however, were barefooted or wore thongs or sandals.

Murmuring greeted our arrival, and it was apparent that rather than being under way, the proceedings were awaiting us. On a table at the front was Louisa's promised cake, and beneath it on the floor was a wheelbarrow full of green newly picked coconuts, ready for auction. Taking a seat in a row near the front that had obviously been reserved for us, we waited for the proceedings to begin. Papa Toa, one of the elders from the village and the former chief, was the auctioneer. In his conservative dark suit, he looked like a distinguished banker except, of course, for his feet in their rubber sandals. His eyes smiled at everyone, and a warm grin spread itself across his wrinkled bronze face.

Papa Toa held up three coconuts, and the bidding began. At first not much was heard, and Papa pointed, first to one side of the room, and then to the other, as a spirited bidding war went on between two of the villagers. Finally the bidding ceased, and Papa handed the coconuts to the winner while a number was chalked onto a board next to a name. Tana slid over and sat next to me.

"This is how we raise money for the church," he explained. "Instead of giving money we bid on the coconuts, and that is our pledge to the church."

This information was a help to me, as I was having difficulty trying to figure out why anyone living on an island where coconuts abounded in such profusion as they did at Ahe would possibly want to attend an auction to buy more. The next bidding was under way, and Papa kept staring at the row of yachties.

Obviously we were there to help raise money by buying coconuts and were, indeed, expected to bid. I wondered in my mind whether this kind of affair was put on every time a yacht or group of yachts arrived.

Then I chastised myself. Obviously we should participate. Hadn't these people opened their island to us? Hadn't they extended hospitality to all of us and made us feel welcome here halfway around the world? What were a few dollars spent for coconuts after all? I admired the enterprise of the whole thing and decided to bid and get my contribution over with.

Papa Toa was looking at our row again. I raised my hand and joined the bidding. Papa's face glowed and another large smile spread across it. A sound of laughter echoed in the room. Obviously, I, at least, had caught on. I could feel the spirit in the room picking up. The other bidder, Dufty, one of the younger men in the village, also smiled broadly and shouted out a bid. I raised my hand again; again there were loud murmurs of approval. The battle had been joined. Back and forth we went, each pausing as though to drop out of the bidding, until Papa Toa would count "*Un, deux*," which was obviously his equivalent of "going once, going twice." Each time he got to "*deux*" we would up the bid and continue.

"I think you are up to about fifty francs," Celia whispered during one of the pauses. Fifty francs was about ten dollars U.S., a lot of money for coconuts in an already oversupplied market.

"I'd better stop or I won't be able to afford much more of the evening." It was my turn; Papa started his *un, deux*, and I said "*Non, merci; fini.*"

"*Fini*," said Papa, pointing to Dufty and bringing down his hand to indicate that Dufty had won the bid. There was much laughter and a big round of applause.

Dufty went up and got the hotly contested coconuts, and rather than sitting down again, he came over, gave me a big Polynesian hug, and presented them to me. Everyone applauded and cheered, and the auction resumed. "What's going on?" I asked Tana.

"He gives you those as a gift, as he has more coconuts than he will ever need. Everyone is happy because you have bid. Each time we have always the same people bidding to give their money to the church. Now we were happy to have someone new to bid against. But you are our guest, and we cannot let you give money. That would not be right."

"You mean we are here to just be bidders, not to buy?"

"*D'accord* (of course)," replied Tana.

Warming to the occasion, we all added our bids to the auction as it went on, but we made sure not to run the prices up too high. One could see by Papa Toa's expression when he expected the bidding to stop. Each time the coconuts would be presented to the yachtie who had taken part in the bidding. Finally we were out of coconuts, and Papa Toa was holding up the cake Louisa had baked. The cake was the last item up for auction.

After more spirited bidding, Tana bought the cake; it was clear that he was expected to do so. Cake in hand, Tana indicated that it was to be cut and served to all present. Obviously this was expected as well, for although everyone applauded, no one seemed surprised. Mama Fana, Papa's wife, appeared with a large bowl of fruit punch. "Looks like the end of the pineapple juice from Louisa's store," I remarked to Tom. We were up and mingling with the crowd, and soon everyone had a piece of cake and a cup of punch. It got quiet, and Papa Toa said a prayer, and then everyone sat down again. "What next?" I wondered.

Suddenly Papa Toa was making a long speech. He went on and on in what I was discovering was the Polynesian oratorical fashion. He pointed frequently to all of the yachties and smiled his broad smile. When he was finally finished, he received an enthusiastic burst of applause from the villagers. He beckoned to Tana, who gave us a rough translation of the speech,

"Papa Toa," Tana said, "is thanking God that we are all here this evening, that everyone is well and that our village is prosperous. He says that we are especially grateful for our friends who have come from over the sea to be here with us and who bring much happiness and love with them. He wants us all to always remember this evening."

At this, Mama Fana reappeared. She was carrying an armload of beautiful shell necklaces, each handmade by one of the villagers. Each of us, individually, was asked to stand while Mama put a necklace around our necks and kissed us, in the French fashion, on each cheek. Mama had tears rolling down her cheeks as she did this, and I found myself choking up at the combination of tears and smiles that were everywhere in the room.

With an armload of coconuts and a beautiful shell necklace around my neck, I headed outside to return to TAKU. I fell into step with Tom, who also had an armload of coconuts; he was smoking a cigarette someone had given him.

"Real cake," he said.

"Yeah, I know. It was good, too. Coconut auctions aren't nearly as awful in reality as they are in anticipation. I thought it was really fun."

"I guess I'll have to take back what I said," Tom went on.

"What's that?"

"About there being no such thing as a free *fri-fri*." I watched Tom flick his nearly finished cigarette out over the water in a high arc. The red glow of its tip traced a path and disappeared in a sputter, lost among the myriad stars whose reflections seemed to float in the calm waters of the lagoon.

"Probably not a bad idea to take it back," I agreed. I shifted my grip on the coconuts and called goodnight to everyone. We made our way down the beach to the waiting dinghies; they floated placidly at anchor in the shallows waiting to take us home.

Soon after we were to leave Ahe and head for Tahiti. Each day Tana would take me aside and whisper: "You cannot leave today."

"Why not," I would ask him.

"Because today it will rain. It is bad to leave when it will rain."

We were in the middle of the dry season, and it never rained. Finally I said to Tana, "Why do you tell me it will rain, when it never rains?"

He smiled and hugged me around the shoulders. "Because," he explained, "we do not want you to leave." We put off leaving as long as possible, but finally our departure day was there. Tana told me again that it would rain, but the only rain was in the form of tears from all of us on the dock. Almost the entire village came to bid us farewell. We were presented with necklace after necklace of shells until our necks were weighed down. Tana explained that the necklaces were to ensure that we would return again.

We motored slowly away from the village, all the time waving and shouting goodbye. Then we were out the pass, setting sails, and pointing our bows west again, this time toward Tahiti. Cristina disappeared below. Celia took the first watch, and I sat below at the chart table and thought of our weeks in Ahe. I doubted that we would ever again have such a wonderful experience. Sure, we would meet other people, visit other islands, but Ahe was special.

I could feel TAKU lifting to the swell as we moved out from the lee of the island into the open sea. Written on a piece of scrap paper was a

Polynesian prayer. I had noted it down while we were ashore. Now I copied it into my journal for safe keeping and as a permanent reminder of the spirit and warmth of the people of the small atoll of Ahe.

Ia pue e te moana
I rara A'e ite ra'l
Ite vahi otahi ia
Hea ke repo maro
Oia hoi o Ahe

I read the words over to myself and listened to their melodious sounds in my head. As TAKU made her way toward Tahiti, I penciled in the translation:

Let the waters be
Gathered together into
One place and let
The dry land appear
And let that land be Ahe.

14

Guns

And then we were in Tahiti. Fifteen months after departing Marblehead, TAKU lay anchored in the harbor of dreams, Papeete, Tahiti. Paper work completed, bonds deposited, Cristina packed her bag and with an *arrivederci* departed TAKU at long last. We were jubilant; the strain of the past few months evaporated away as though it had never been there. We had a celebration.

"No more humming."

"No more midnight walking."

"No more 'I am so depressed'."

"Even so," added Celia, "it still cost three hundred dollars to have her gone."

"Five hundred," I replied. "She had no money, so I loaned her five. Three hundred for the bond, and two hundred for food, lodging, and clothes till her money comes in. She said she'd pay me after January first." Celia just stared at me. Her eyes glazed with a familiar vacant look. "I am so depressed," was all she said.

New Year came and went, as it is wont to do. We were enjoying French Polynesia and especially Tahiti to the fullest. Cruising boats from all over the world were arriving on a regular basis, and we were making many new friends. Celia's parents and brother came for the Christmas holidays, and we sailed them to Mooréa and back. They enjoyed basking in the tropical warmth and exploring the islands of Tahiti and Mooréa. The day of their departure my aunt Kate arrived from New Jersey.

In her seventies and an inveterate traveler, Kate had spent a week on board TAKU in the Virgin Islands and another week in Martinique. She announced that she wanted to go to Bora-Bora, which was over 100 miles away. In 1944 she had been aboard a troop ship that had called at Bora-Bora, but she had not been allowed ashore; now she was determined to rectify what she had considered for years an injustice. So off to Bora-Bora we went to spend a few days and then returned to Papeete. The summer cyclone season was now upon us and TAKU, along with many other boats, decided to remain in the Tahiti/Mooréa area until the season ended in May.

One day I was returning to TAKU in one of Papeete's infrequent drizzles. I had two loaves of warm French bread under my foul-weather jacket. The aroma was tantalizing, and I could hardly wait to get back aboard. I heard someone call my name. From out of a nearby café came Cristina. At first I didn't recognize her. She had lost weight, and had acquired new clothes, a new hairdo, and obviously a new comb as well. She looked substantially improved and was much more animated than when I had last seen her.

"Dom," she said, "I was just coming to TAKU to see you." She handed me five crisp one hundred dollar bills and leaned up and kissed me on the cheek. "I have a new diet now and feel much better; also I have made many new friends and I'm cruising with them on a local boat. I love it here. I am sorry for all of my depressions. I thank you and Celia for putting up with me for so long. I don't know what it was, but it is over—see you!" She flashed me a smile and disappeared back into the café.

I went back aboard TAKU with the still warm bread and put it and the $500 on the table. "Guess who I saw?"

Celia was incredulous. "She paid it back?"

"Yep, and she sent you her best and her thanks. She's changed and seems really okay."

"Wow, the whole $500," exclaimed Celia. "I wish to announce that I am no longer depressed."

"You just never know," I said, as I got out a knife to slice the bread.

One of the major debates that raged, and still rages, among cruising boats concerns the issue of guns. There is no right answer to this question, and ultimately the issue turns out to be one of personal preference and the feeling of security you can have with or without a gun on board. We had all heard of yachts being boarded in the dead of night and of sometimes horrible consequences to unsuspecting and innocent yachties.

Different people developed different strategies. One boat had a policeman's billy club in a bracket by the hatch. Another had a Louisville Slugger bat at the ready to ward off intruders. A German boat had rigged an electric fence around the lifelines on deck and plugged that into the boat batteries at night. But many boats, including TAKU, carried guns. I am not by nature a gun person. I know there are those who feel more comfortable around weapons and with them than I do. We had, however, obtained a single shell shot gun before leaving the Caribbean.

The idea was that if the boat were ever menaced by intruders who threatened to come aboard, we would only need to produce the gun to scare them away. Hard-core gun people said that I needed to be prepared to shoot. I thought I could if I had to, but debated that possibility in my mind whenever guns were mentioned or discussed. We had made it through the Caribbean without needing the gun, and in the tranquil and, thus far, peaceful islands of Polynesia, it hardly seemed likely that one would ever need a weapon.

The French authorities apparently agreed with that philosophy, and required that all weapons on board be declared and turned in to the gendarmes for safe keeping while in port. Ironically, there were no marauders in the vast open reaches of the Pacific, and once in port where incidents with potential troublemakers were likely to occur, the weapons carried for protection were locked safely away ashore.

Turning in weapons was to be the protocol throughout the rest of the trip around the world. Arrive in port, clear customs and immigration, hand in the weapon and ammunition, and then collect them again upon departure. What this procedure really meant was a great deal of paperwork. It also meant that one couldn't depart on a whim or on a weekend. "When are you off ?" I would ask someone who I knew was preparing to leave.

"As soon as we can arrange to get our gun and ammo back from the police," was often the answer. The authorities took a dim view of any yacht hanging around once the weapon(s) were back aboard. Say you wanted to leave on a Tuesday. On Monday you would go to the various offices and complete the paper work clearances. On Tuesday morning you would arrange to have your gun delivered to the boat. The weapon arrives; so does a front with strong wind and rain. You decide not to

leave for a day or two. You either turn the gun back in and go through
the whole thing all over again, or you hope the authorities don't see you
still at anchor or moored to the dock.

Guns quickly became a bureaucratic hassle. We all heard supposed
horror stories of yachties who neglected to turn in weapons and, in turn,
had their boats seized by the authorities or were ordered to leave the
country immediately. It was enough to ruin your day. And it was a pretty consistent rule wherever TAKU went.

Tom on BLACK WHALE had been persuaded by some friends, as he
was a singlehander setting off from crime-heavy California, to take along
a rifle. His 23-foot boat had little enough storage space, so he buried the
rifle under one of his bunks beneath a stash of clothes and some extra
canned goods. "If anyone ever attacks me," he told me, "I will ask them
to hold on a minute while I rearrange everything down below and
retrieve my gun. Then, once I have it in hand, I'll tell them to come
ahead. Makes sense doesn't it?" We had laughed at this and, after some
months in Polynesia, had laughed about the whole notion of having a
gun aboard at all.

Tom's passage from Ahe to Papeete was a long and exhausting one
for him, and he was feeling tired and irritable when he finally cleared
customs and immigration. While signing the form on which he was to
make a declaration of weapons, he thought about the mess on board
BLACK WHALE and how tired he was. He didn't want to go back just for
a stupid gun; he'd have to tear the whole boat apart to get it. And then
he would have to bring the gun back to the gendarmerie and that would
take forever, and all he really wanted to do was get some sleep. So on his
declaration form where it said weapons, he wrote "none."

A few days went by; then a few weeks. Tom's gun stayed buried.
Then the rumor started going around that customs had boarded a yacht
unannounced and had searched it completely for contraband. This
rumor quickly grew to speculating that the authorities were planning to
search other boats. Tom couldn't relax. What if they found his gun? He
couldn't actually say he didn't know it was there. He asked us if we
would believe him if he told us that he forgot he had a gun. We said,
"No."

He thought about taking his gun to the police station and telling
them he forgot to turn it in, but decided that since he had written
"none" on the form, they weren't likely to believe that. Tom agonized

and agonized. He pictured himself getting arrested and deported, getting his boat seized and taken away, all because of a gun he didn't want in the first place. One morning he sat in his cockpit trying to enjoy his breakfast and his first cigarette of the day. As he looked out over the harbor he saw a powerful outboard boat with two men in uniform speeding in his direction.

He was sure they were from customs doing surprise searches. The powerboat roared out to a boat anchored a few hundred yards from Tom, and the two men quickly jumped on board and disappeared below. Tom felt that he was next. He dove down his hatch and began frantically ripping into his storage space. Clothes and canned goods flew in every direction. Finally he had his rifle in hand; he climbed over the pile he had created and back into the cockpit.

He was just in time, for the two men had returned to the outboard and were now speeding rapidly in his direction. Without another thought, he slipped the rifle over the side and watched a trail of bubbles spring to the surface as it disappeared to the bottom of Papeete harbor. Was he in time? He thought so. The outboard boat was slowing to pass right by him. Tom realized they were throttling down so that their wake wouldn't rock his boat. He looked again.

On the side of the outboard boat was the following painted sign: *VOLVO REPAIR*, and the two men were in matching green Volvo repair coveralls. They smiled and waved at Tom, and then, once past BLACK WHALE, they sped up again as they headed back to their shop. Tom was able to see that the one not piloting the boat was holding a starter or an alternator that they had obviously gone out to pick up for repair. He looked over the side. The bubbles were gone; his rifle was gone, now some 30 feet down, resting on the muddy bottom of the harbor. Tom sat down and smiled to himself.

When he described all this to me later, he said, "My anxiety was gone as well. I never liked having the gun in the first place. My worries about guns were over. I felt that I had finally *arrived* in the South Pacific as I wanted it to be."

Let the record read that TAKU's shotgun grew rustier and rustier but was turned in everywhere it was necessary to do so until the Mediterranean. One sunset, on a short passage from Rhodes, Greece, to Kös, Turkey, I finally gave up on the constant turning in and collecting at every port in Greece and Turkey. As the sun dropped to the horizon,

I threw the shotgun astern as far as I could into the blood red water that held the sun's reflection. It was a belated peace offering to the gods of the sea. As the gun sunk from view, I experienced a feeling of relief similar, I thought, to the one Tom had tried to describe to me in Tahiti when we had been there together five years before. Some things just take awhile to learn.

15

Tom Neale

For us aboard TAKU months in Tahiti and Mooréa passed quickly and before we knew it they were behind us and we were cruising in the spectacular *Iles-sous-le-vent* (islands under the wind) of Huahine, Raiatea, Tahaa, Bora-Bora, and Maupiti. Days anchored in sparkling lagoons with some reading, snorkeling, walking on the beaches, visiting the villages and always the inevitable boat work blended one into another. I was lulled into a sense of timelessness. For the most part, the weather was always beautiful, the temperature neither too hot nor too cold. One could easily see how the fabled South Seas had captured the hearts and minds of so many.

May was upon us, and the class of 1980, as we called ourselves (we being the cruising boats from all over the world who had arrived in Tahiti and remained for the cyclone season that year), began to gather in Bora-Bora for the next leg of our individual journeys around the world. Now it was time to push westward once again. The route to take was an object of some discussion. Samoa, approximately 1,200 miles westward, seemed to be the principal destination for most.

American Samoa promised, from what we had heard, U.S.-style supermarkets with stateside prices. Prices on foodstuffs in French Polynesia were high; everything but locally grown produce had to be shipped from France and was prohibitively expensive for most of us. The French government paid a subsidy to the local people that permitted them to purchase the imported merchandise. Even the wine, that French specialty, was, to us, out of range. The yachties had discovered one cheap French wine—cheap being a relative term—that was sent from France in plastic liter bottles to save weight. It certainly wasn't going to win any prizes or end up in any wine cellars for special occasions. We had dubbed it *Chateau Plastique.*

With a few liters of this questionable vintage stowed away and fresh provisions aboard, it was time to go. We said temporary farewells to those boats who were taking a more southerly route and planning to stop at Rarotonga in the Cooks before heading on to Tonga or Samoa. The northern route (which actually looked almost straight west) skirted the Bellingshausen group (a small collection of uninhabited atolls some 150 miles west of Bora-Bora) before passing close by Suwarrow, an additional 450 miles farther on. Suwarrow lay about halfway between Bora-Bora and American Samoa. It had been the home of the legendary Tom Neale and looked like an ideal stopping place to break up the passage.

Tom Neale had lived alone on Suwarrow atoll, in the Cook Islands, for years. He was the definitive beachcomber; he had built himself a small hut and later a small house. He enjoyed the solitude and seemed to always have something to do to occupy his time. He chronicled his life on Suwarrow in a wonderful book entitled *An Island to Oneself*, first published in 1966. Occasionally yachts crossing the Pacific would stop and be treated to Tom's warm hospitality. He kept a few chickens, a small garden, and an equally small boat for fishing in the lagoon. Over the years word filtered back to those cruising to stop and see Tom. It was something I had wanted to do.

But Tom had succumbed to cancer a few years before I arrived. His house was still there, passing yachts still called, and a new tradition had arisen. Each yacht calling at Suwarrow would do a little work around Tom's place: repair the house, weed the garden, clear the underbrush from the paths. Although Tom was no longer physically present, memory of him lingered and his hospitality to world cruisers was not forgotten. Suwarrow atoll, though not exactly a shrine, became a necessary pilgrimage stop on the way around the world for many cruisers. How could you sail by without stopping?

Glen and Dan, on SEAVENTURE out of San Francisco, had come up with the idea of having a *luau* complete with a roasted pig for the group that would call at Suwarrow. A date was set some ten days in the future to allow for different cruising speeds and styles. Some ten yachts agreed that they would meet at the appointed time. "But what about a pig?" we all asked. "Do you think there will be pigs running around left over from Tom Neale?"

"Not to worry," Glen assured each of us in turn. "We have Mortimer!"

Mortimer turned out to be a live 30-pound pig that Glen and Dan had purchased from a family in Bora-Bora. They had made him a home in one of SEAVENTURE's oversized cockpit lockers. They intended to sail poor Mortimer to Suwarrow, and once there, to butcher him for the feast. However, by the time Glen and Dan, and we, had arrived, they had become quite fond of the little pig, who had turned out to be a companionable shipmate on the 600 mile passage. Mike Heeg, sailing aboard the trimaran ISHMAEL, had grown up on a farm in Canada, and agreed to spare Glen and Dan the butchering of Mortimer. He went off in the bush to dispatch Mortimer and to prepare him for the meal that was to come.

A fire was built, a spit erected, and in due time Mortimer was roasted and provided excellent fare for all except Glen and Dan who, for the occasion, became vegetarians. All manner of hors d'oeuvres, salads, desserts, and beverages, including a supply of *Chateau Plastique* which did not seem to travel well in a small boat at sea, were brought forth, and some 25 of us from all around the world sat under the palm trees outside Tom Neale's house and ate and talked and ate some more. While the food was being prepared volunteer work crews had collected all of the dead palm fronds around Tom's house and cleaned up everything inside and out. The white sand paths were groomed with an old rake that was found among Tom Neale's tools in a tiny shed.

As evening came on and it grew darker, some portable lanterns were lit, and the visiting logbook from Tom Neale's desk was passed about so everyone could sign it and enter the various yacht names and homeports represented. It grew dark; the lanterns were extinguished. People sat in small groups and talked quietly or sat alone and watched the reflections of the stars in the lagoon and listened to the booming of the surf on the windward side of the island. Finally we gathered up our belongings, loaded the dinghies, and after making sure the fire was truly out we all returned to our boats to sleep and to dream of Tom Neale and his island home.

A few more days of relaxing and it was time to head for Samoa. Awnings were struck, boats prepared for sea. One by one the anchors were hauled, and with shouts of "See you in Pago Pago!" yachts headed out to sea again.

A week later, while the class of '80 was settling in to the well-protected harbor of Pago Pago, on the island of Tutuila, American Samoa, an unseasonably late cyclone developed and its edge swept through Suwarrow. A new group of yachts were anchored in Tom Neale's lagoon. The storm came through late at night without warning. Three boats were swept onto the reef. One, moderately damaged, was refloated the next day. The other two, a boat from California with a couple aboard, and a French boat with a family aboard, were damaged beyond repair or salvage. Their crews survived; with what belongings they could salvage, they sailed to Samoa on one of the yachts that survived the blow. On the dock in Pago the American couple offered winches, sails, pieces of line, and anchors at bargain prices. Two days later, with most of the gear sold off, the owners flew out of Samoa, their cruise over. How close we come.

16

Pago Pago

July, Pago Pago

Dear Gene,

The box of books that you mention in your letter that you sent me care of my mother was forwarded by her, but the man at her P.O. told her she had plenty of time to send it by sea, which was a lot cheaper so she did. We're off to Tonga (the Friendly Isles) and then on to Fiji; thanks for the thought and the books, wherever they are.

Peace,

Pago Pago! At last! I think that I had always wanted to go to Bora–Bora and Pago Pago ever since I had first seen their names in grade school geography books. Some places just sound exotic whether they are or not; there is something in their names that seems to promise adventure and excitement. I had been to Bora and had not been disappointed; its beautiful mountains and lush vegetation bordered one of the most beautiful lagoons in the world. What was not to like?

And now here TAKU was in Pago Pago. And then someone said, "Welcome to Pongo!" I didn't understand. For years I had read the words Pago Pago in books and on maps and had pronounced them "Pay-go Pay-go" in my mind. "Pay-go Pay-go" was where I had always dreamed of going. "Pay-go Pay-go" was where I was and where I intended to enjoy myself. The local radio station played the newest local hit over and over again. You couldn't go anywhere ashore without hearing it—not that there were a whole lot of places to go. The song went, "I've got the Pongo Pongo blues," and described how awful living on an island in the middle of the Pacific was with not much to do.

After a bit of inquiry, I learned that in Samoa (which was pronounced Sah' mo-a) the word Pago, which was half the name of the principal port and village, was pronounced Pongo! Pongo Pongo it was, like it or not. It seems, according to one version of the story, that when missionaries first arrived, they brought with them a small printing press and set out to print a copy of the Bible in Samoan. However, when they went to set the type, they had lost or broken the "n", so Pongo was transliterated to Pago where it worked its way into books and onto maps and all the way back to my third-grade classroom in Philadelphia. All those years of thinking of Pago Pago merely got me ready to be surprised and disappointed.

Pago was a bit of a disappointment for other reasons as well. The harbor was dirty, as it housed two large fish canneries—StarKist being one—that pumped the effluent of their processing plants into the water. The U.S. government had pumped endless dollars into American Samoa. Inflated wages, low subsidized stateside prices, and an attempt to create a little America abroad had resulted in a local population that had lost much of its individual pride as it attempted to emulate life in the States. There was a TV station, and most of the *fales* (native houses), although they lacked modern plumbing conveniences, were able to pull in the daily "soaps" from the States. There was also an overabundance of cars, many of them four-wheel-drive behemoths with nowhere to go but up and back the 20 some miles of flat paved road that ran along the coast of the island. And there was litter everywhere.

Pago Pago had two famous landmarks. One was the Rainmaker Hotel, a quite swish establishment that hugged a corner of the harbor entrance and sported tennis courts, a swimming pool, a coffee shop, and an up-to-date, real hotel restaurant like one finds at any of the chains back home. The other attraction was a cable car ride that went from downtown Pago, such as it was, across the harbor to the top of the 1,700-foot-high mountain that made the rain that gave the Rainmaker its name. Somerset Maugham had written a story called "Rain" that took place in a small seedy general store/hotel in Pago Pago. The tale was later turned into an early movie that cast Joan Crawford as Sadie Thompson, the tragic heroine. Now a full-time grocery store, the building was a far cry from the elegance of the current Rainmaker.

There was only one catch. The previous Fourth of July there had been a real American Fourth celebration. Part of the celebration included a sky diving exhibit from a U.S. Navy plane over the harbor. At the appointed time the vast majority of the island's inhabitants had converged on Pago, clogging the major (only) road. They gathered along the shoreline to see their first live exhibition of sky diving. The plane appeared on time. The chutists leapt out over the harbor, and their colorful chutes popped open one by one. While this was going on, the pilot, who was looking back to count the chutes, flew into the cable that stretched across the harbor. The cable, ripped from its moorings, plunged down, and the plane, out of control, crashed into a wing of the Rainmaker Hotel, which then promptly burned to the ground. The pilot was killed, as was a Japanese tourist who had returned to his room to get a camera. The remainder of the populace were all in town for the festivities and were spared.

I hold many clear memories of the time in Pago. One is of going to a small shop with Mike from INOA. Mike is about six-foot-two, weighs about one hundred ninety pounds, and is in great shape. He jogs and works out. (He's from California.) He wanted a new pair of sweatpants. The Samoan clerk, who could have played guard on any team in the National Football League, asked Mike what he wanted.

"I want a pair of sweatpants, size extra-large," said Mike.

"I think you are probably a medium," replied the clerk, as he reached for a box behind the counter.

"I always wear extra-large," replied Mike. Since he was from California, he had probably never been accused of being medium at anything.

"I'd suggest a medium," said the clerk, putting a pair of sweatpants on the counter.

"I always buy extra-large. I'll take extra-large," Mike insisted.

"It's up to you," replied the clerk, handing Mike a pair of 52-inch-waist Samoan sweatpants.

Mike held them up in front of him. They were enormous. Two Mikes could have gotten inside and left some room to spare. Mike got a little red in the face, swallowed hard, and putting the extra-large pants on the counter, said, "I guess I'll take the medium."

"As I said," replied the clerk, "it's up to you." The transaction was done.

At some point in the 1960s a number of Peace Corps volunteers had spent time in Samoa. There was a serious attempt to improve health conditions in the territory. The Lyndon B. Johnson Medical Center was built to provide more complete medical care. And a way to improve sanitation was developed. Most Samoans live in open-sided, thatch-roofed houses called *fales*. Before the arrival of the Peace Corps, sanitation was, at best, primitive. The nearest bush or tree served as an outdoor toilet facility. The Peace Corps volunteers went on a major education and building campaign to create outhouses in an attempt to make conditions more sanitary and healthy. This they did. However, the Samoans had no word in their language for outhouse, and so today outhouse buildings are still called as they were then named: *fale-peacey-corpsy*.

I had my own encounter with the Samoan language. And it had nothing to do with the pronunciation of Pago or the definition of extra-large. We had visited customs on our arrival in Pago to get our clearance and to have our passports stamped in. The customs and immigration agent was another NFL football player type. Large size was a physical characteristic of many of the Samoans that we were to meet. The agent asked me the name of my boat.

"TAKU," I responded. He had burst out laughing. If you can imagine an individual who might have worn a pair of extra-large Samoan sweatpants rollicking with laughter, you get a good idea of the scene.

"TAKU?" he had inquired, bursting into laughter again. His cohorts in the office joined him.

"Does that mean something in your language?" I inquired, as I thought of the word TAKU painted on the transom, on the life rings, on the weathercloths in large blue letters, on our letter paper, and on the very shirt I was wearing. I slid my arm casually across my chest in an attempt to hide the logo that until that moment I had worn without a second thought.

"Well, yes, it does."

He stamped our clearance, and saying "TAKU" and bursting into laughter again, he returned to his work. Only later was I to learn from a Samoan friend that *taku* in Samoan means *fart*. And there we were with it emblazoned everywhere. I had actually named the boat after a glacier in Alaska near Juneau. In Alaska *taku* is a native word that means *north wind*!!

With July upon us, it was time to push on. It was hard to believe that a year had passed by since we, with Armen aboard, had transited the Panama Canal. TAKU had been hauled in Pago, and I had sanded and scraped the bottom and given her two coats of antifouling paint. We had a fair distance to go and wanted to make stops in Western Samoa, a separate country administered under the protection of New Zealand, in the Kingdom of Tonga some 400 miles to the south, and then in Fiji and its myriad groups of islands before heading down to New Zealand for the start of the southern hemisphere's summer and the accompanying cyclone season.

Apia, Western Samoa, some 90 miles to the west of American Samoa, is the last resting place of Robert Louis Stevenson, who had sailed throughout the South Pacific in the course of two cruises, on the yacht CASCO (1888) and the schooner EQUATOR (1889). He had journeyed to the Pacific in the hope that the tropical climate would benefit his poor health. He resided for a time in Hawaii, and then settled in Apia and built a house there called *Valima*, high on the slopes of Mt. Vaea above the village. He was famous in Samoa and known as *Tusitala*, the teller of tales. When he died he was buried, according to his wish, on Mt. Vaea. He wrote his own epitaph:

> *Under the wide and starry sky*
> *Dig the grave and let me lie;*
> *Glad did I live and gladly die,*
> *   And I layed me down with a will.*
>
> *And this be the verse that you 'grave for me:*
> *Here he lies where he longed to be;*
> *Home is the sailor, home from the sea,*
> *   And the hunter home from the hill.*

Perhaps the love of the Samoan people for Stevenson is best seen in the lament voiced by the High Chief Tuimaleali'ifana to express his people's grief on R.L.S.'s death in 1894. *"Tatou moni Tusitala. Ua tagi le fatu ma le eleele."* ("Our beloved *Tusitala*. The stones and the earth weep.")

Stevenson's simple tomb, with its bronze plaques, is still preserved on the peak of Mt. Vaea. His account of his travels to the Pacific, *In the South Seas*, is still in print today. In the thriving port town of Apia, the capital of Western Samoa, we went to the *Tusitala* Hotel and had a *Valima* beer (the national beer of Samoa) in the bar.

17

Stamps Shaped Like Bananas

"That's ridiculous. There's no way I'm paying any bribes." My back was up. On the radio my voice sounded angered, yet confident. We had left Apia behind, and passing out of the lee of Upolu Island we were now bashing into 20-knot winds and big seas as the two principal islands that comprised Western Samoa gradually sank below the horizon behind TAKU. We were headed south for a change, this time for the Vava'u Group in northern Tonga. I had figured it would take about three days for the passage.

With two days left to go, the sky was leaden and totally overcast, the seas were steep, and the boat's motion was uncomfortable. I had been seasick about once an hour ever since we had rounded the tip of Upolu and hit the slop. The initial 20 knots of wind had freshened to a good 25 to 30, and the seas were wild and confused. We were burying the lee rail, an unusual occurrence for TAKU, which has above average free-board. The resulting spray in the cockpit was keeping us wet and miserable. In addition, we had just learned, on our regular radio schedule, that boats arriving in Tonga, some 250 miles ahead of us to our south, were being hit up for some form of gratuity upon clearing in. The combination of the weather, my unremitting seasickness, and this unfortunate bit of information merely served to drive me into a mean and irritable state of mind. If the voyage conditions were mean, well, I was prepared to be meaner.

Celia, who was feeling somewhat better, and I had a powwow and decided to shorten sail to try to reduce the boat's motion. We were hoping to get to Vava'u in jig time, as there were several other boats ahead of us and some leaving behind us, and we knew about the inevitable comparison of passage times that would ensue.

"So it takes three and a half days," said Celia. "So what? At least we can be comfortable, and maybe you can stop hanging over the rail." Having just returned from this less-than-comfortable position, I agreed without debate, and we went forward and wrested the main down and got the boom securely fastened in the gallows. Under reduced canvas of double headsails and mizzen, TAKU forereached, smoothly clicking off the miles and bringing us ever closer to Tonga.

"What do you really think about this bribe business?" Celia inquired.

"No way are we going to pay anything," I responded. I was determined not to give in to this petty larceny.

"Even if they won't clear you or let you go ashore?" she continued, following up. "Besides they haven't asked for money so far, just booze and shotgun shells. Don't we have a bottle of *Chateau Plastique* anywhere that we could pawn off?" We had spent considerable time on the radio, the yachtsman's form of the fabled coconut telegraph. If the locals had their ways of speeding information along, so did we. We had discussed at length clearance procedures with boats already in Tonga. All had been hit up for some sort of "present" for the customs officer.

Apparently the strategy the officer used was varied. In one case he had asked to see the ship's liquor supply and upon inventorying it picked up a full bottle and placed it in his bag, saying "This is for customs." In another instance he had asked to count the ammunition, and having done so, he asked those aboard if he might have one or two shells as he had a gun and ammunition was difficult to obtain. The sailors in question, feeling backed into a corner, had said certainly and watched incredulously as the man slid a dozen shells into his bag. Each yacht that had checked in with this particular official had been caught in some manner or other, and now the word was filtering back to those of us on our way.

For me, one of the delights in sailing in the South Pacific was getting away from the custom of tipping. Country after country, island after island, the people were gracious, warm, and open. Printed advice to travelers usually included the following admonition: "Tipping is not customary in our culture. It is not expected, nor should it be offered for service. Service to visitors is a pleasure and offering reward for this would reduce that pleasure and offend. Please do not tip." Until now, Polynesia had been a refreshing change from the mercenary hands-out tactics of home.

We had been well received everywhere in the Pacific. Although we had not been inundated with storied canoeloads of gifts as in the books of old, we had certainly garnered an abundant share of coconuts, bananas, and other tropical fruits, shells, and necklaces as we cruised our way across the Pacific. We had reciprocated whenever we could, by having local people aboard for visits and tours and by serving coffee, tea, cookies, cake, and refreshments of all sorts. The last week in Ahe we had sailed seventeen villagers from Ahe to nearby Manihi for a sports competition when the weather was too rough for them to cross in their own boats. On our return we had been feasted to a fare-thee-well, and despite all of our efforts to reciprocate, the balance sheet was greatly stretched in favor of the Polynesians.

"Perhaps if we thought about it as a gift?" Celia asked. "After all, look at all the wonderful times we've had and the wonderful things we've been given."

"You'd probably say the same thing after you were mugged," I responded testily. "Look, we've never had any difficulty with officials anywhere asking for anything. If I want to give someone a gift, let me choose the person and the gift. When someone in uniform comes aboard representing his country to grant me *pratique*, he should damn well do it. Port charges are one thing, but taking things is another. It's legalized stealing. Every time a boat succumbs to that sort of pressure and pays out, it just makes it harder for those that follow. I, for one, am prepared to draw the line." I was pontificating, I knew, but I was truly annoyed.

The last day and a half to Vava'u passed swiftly. The wind moderated. We hung up the main, caught a couple of sights, ate, and kept down some of the food while TAKU sailed swiftly on. We barely noticed the passing water under our keel as we were busy discussing the up-and-coming clearance and canvassing our fellow yachties behind us for their opinions.

Then suddenly there we were. The Kingdom of Tonga. Since Tonga straddles the International Dateline, the country refers to itself as "the land where time begins." Vava'u was picturesquely perched on the side of a hill overlooking the harbor. A few local boats plied to and fro about the dock, where a large inter-island copra boat was taking on

cargo. Tonga (or the Friendly Islands as it is known) consists of a widely scattered group of more than 100 islands and islets that spread for
more than 175 miles north to south. Boat traffic is a normal part of the
people's everyday lives and is what links these widely scattered islands
together into a kingdom.

The sky was a brilliant blue with a few scattered tradewind puffers.
The air was so dry that it seemed crisp; the green of the foliage ashore
was vibrant and inviting. The overcast, rough weather that had plagued
our passage had blown on its way. We worked our way up the harbor to
Vava'u proper, and the rattle of our chain as the CQR sought the bottom
and the snap of our Q flag at the starboard spreader immediately below
the red-and-white Tongan courtesy flag announced our arrival. We were
prepared, we thought, for whatever courtesy Tonga had to offer.

We inflated and launched the dinghy, and after hooking on the outboard, Celia went ashore to seek out the officials, as we had been told
they had no means of transportation to the yachts, and if the dock was
occupied, as it now was, a boat could wait for days for clearance. Within
a few minutes she returned with three Tongans. They were all wearing
valas, the traditional skirts worn by almost all the inhabitants. Watching
them come aboard I had the feeling, which I had experienced on other
occasions, that I was somehow in the middle of a glossy travel article of
the sort I used to read at home as I dreamt of far-off places. One of the
pictures had come alive, and here I was.

One official wore an overskirt of woven pandanus leaves, which we
found out later were called ta'ovala and are worn on formal occasions or
when in mourning. The man in the ta'ovala also sported a navy blue military tunic with silver buttons, crossbelts, and a large badge. They all
were barefooted, and each incongruously carried a briefcase.

All three climbed formally below and squeezed their way around
TAKU's table. Briefcases were opened; we produced passports, ship's
papers, and our outward clearance from Western Samoa. There was little conversation and much filling in of forms and stamping of papers.
Finally one of the officials looked at me and spoke, "If you would be so
kind, could you drop two of us (he indicated one of the others) to the
other yacht that has just arrived so that we can facilitate its entry. Mr. __
will finish up here."

Off we went. By the time I had delivered the two to the other yacht
and shaken hands and exchanged amenities and returned, Celia was

accompanying Mr. __ to the ladder. I ferried him to the other boat as well and rushed back to see what had happened. "Well?" I asked before I was even halfway aboard.

"He's the one," said Celia. "He asked me for shotgun shells."

"Did you give him any?" I asked.

"Are you kidding? I'd rather face the King of Tonga in all his enormous glory in a rage than you anytime. No, I told him we had only a few and that we needed them all." She paused hesitantly.

"C'mon," I said, "what happened?"

"So he said, 'Oh,' and gave me our clearance."

"All right . . . way to go . . . hang tough I always say . . . the hard line works every time." I was overjoyed.

"Back off," said Celia. "You don't understand; he cleared us in, but he gave us only a week."

A week! I couldn't believe it. Everyone we had spoken to had received a month, which was renewable upon application. "How are we going to see anything of Tonga in a week? That's ridiculous."

Celia continued: "He said we have to bring a list of all of the anchorages we wish to visit for his approval. But he did say we could probably get a week's extension if we come in before the week runs out."

The ploy became clear. Tonga was a big country to see by water; the Vava'u group itself had over 30 excellent anchorages, but at a distance of 5 to 25 miles from Vava'u itself. If we wanted to see anything, we would have to rush about and return within the week to Vava'u to go through more bureaucracy. "Did you ask him about a one-month permit?"

"Yes, he said sometimes they give that, but in general the rule is for a week at a time."

"You mean that for a few shotgun shells or a bottle of booze they give you a month."

Celia went on: "I guess that's it, or at least that's it with this one official."

"Well, we made our choice; we'll just have to make the best of it or find some way to appeal."

The allotted week sped by, and we remained in Vava'u trying to decide what to do. Other boats came in. Some were hit up, some offered on their own, and some weren't asked. All received a one-month clearance and pulled anchor to enjoy their cruising in Tonga.

As our week ended we wondered what would happen when we

went for our renewal. We were determined to ask for a superior if we couldn't get a month. We went ashore and up the dusty road to the customs office. Celia had prepared a list of anchorages for approval, writing down every one she could find on the chart. We decided she would go to customs while I, the more annoyed and potentially more volatile, would buy stamps and mail letters. Part of the Tongan economy depended on stamp sales, and the country's stamps came in all sorts of odd shapes like bananas and pineapples in an attempt to capture some of the worldwide philatelic market.

"How can a country that sells stamps shaped like bananas make such difficulty about cruising permits?" I had asked as I went off to the post office. I was going to wait there and if Celia needed me for appeal, she would come and get me. She seemed to be gone a long time. Finally she reappeared. "Well?" I asked.

"The same guy was there. He asked me again about extra shotgun shells, and I said no, and he read over our anchorage list and crossed several out, saying we couldn't go to them." I felt my temper rising. "But then he got called away to the phone, and another official came to help me, and when he found out why I was there he said that that was wrong, as the one-week permits had gone out several years previously. He said all yachts got a month. So he stamped our papers and gave us a month, renewable for a second month if we want."

"Hooray for the telephone; let's get out of here and go cruising before they change their minds."

So there it was. We got our time, and we didn't have to pay any type of bribe. The issue is not very serious when you look at it closely, but somehow we felt relieved and vindicated. Principle has to be worth something, even if it is only self-respect. We especially enjoyed going to some of the more remote anchorages where many of our fellow yachties had already gone. We were able to answer their "Don't you TAKUs have to check in with your probation officer?" with a smug look.

Later we met Bob from New Zealand, who was to become a good friend. He was a white-haired, mustachioed, debonair man with a mischievous twinkle in his bright blue eyes. "Bloody hell I was going to give those scoundrels anything," he roared. He went on to recount his experience. He, too, had received a week. On his way to town for his second week he jotted down a list of things to do on a piece of paper. It read: "beer, cigarettes, bread, post office, customs, veggies"—a typical yachtie list with a certain identifiable set of priorities, one that will keep you from forgetting the essentials as you wander about. On the way to customs he remembered he had to furnish a list of anchorages he wished to visit. It was too far to go back to the boat, so as he walked in the door to customs he was busy jotting down anchorages on the paper in his hand with the intention of transcribing them to a fresh sheet in the customs office.

"What do you want?" asked our "friend" the official.

"My week is up," replied Bob politely, determined not to lose his temper. "You told me to come in and furnish you with a list of anchorages."

Before he could continue further, the official snatched the list from his hand, slapped it on the counter, and stamped it with several rubber stamps. "You have a month," said the official, pushing the papers back, "and then if you wish you may have another." Bob scurried from the office, a smile spreading across his face. Obviously the word had gotten out, as it sometimes has a way of doing. Yachts arriving later cleared without difficulty. Sometimes the good guys really do win.

The time in Tonga went by quickly. We feasted with new Tongan friends and bought *tapas*—the beautiful and intricately decorated cloth hammered by hand from the bark of the coconut trees—and bunk loads of Tongan baskets. The workmanship was exquisite, and the prices were so low that we couldn't say no. The sky stayed blue and the air remained crisp and clean. Winter in the southern hemisphere tropics is wonderful.

I forgot about the business of bribes. We wouldn't meet it again until Indonesia and the trip up the Red Sea to the Middle East where bribes are a way of life. One pays them there in the form of *baksheesh*. But that was over the horizon of the future. Sitting comfortably in Tonga I ruminated on the joys of the South Pacific, where, with the exception of the one Tongan official, service was always given willingly without the thought of reward. My recollections of Tonga always include Bob and his list, which he kept and which read: "beer, cigarettes, bread, post office, customs, veggies, Kapa Island, Port Morrell, Kenutu, Hunga." Overstamped on it was the word "Approved" and a large circular official stamp that read, "Kingdom of Tonga, Vava'u Group, Customs and Immigration."

18

Across the Dateline

September, Suva, Fiji

Dear Mom,

The surprise package you sent to Fiji arrived. I thought at first it was the missing books. They have a 30 percent import duty on everything, including (if you can believe it) incoming postage. After I paid $23 duty I opened the box and discovered two white rubber mermaid fenders. I'm sure they'll be very useful. I have seen pictures of them in catalogs but had never thought to get them for myself.

Love,

One of the most significant revelations that comes from extended cruising cannot be discovered by chartering for a few weeks or even making a long passage. Once the ties with shore and home are severed, the cruiser discovers that among the many joys and pleasures awaiting are the comradeship, warmth, and generosity of fellow sailors. This humanizing aspect of cruising is often overlooked when thinking about the proper boat to buy, where to take it, what to do once there, and ultimately, how to pay for it all.

The close feeling does not happen immediately but develops gradually, until one day you find yourself surrounded by a large extended family of cruising folk, all with similar hopes, ideals, goals, and experiences. Ideas, information, and meals are all shared, as are anchorages, adventures, books, spare parts, labor, hard work, troubles, comfort, and respect.

With similar destinations on the water highway around the world,

you stay linked by radio between ports and in person at the various
stopovers that make up the itinerary of a circumnavigation. The
International Dateline marks one halfway spot for those sailing around.
Although it may not be the geographical midpoint for most people's
cruises, crossing the dateline, like crossing the Equator, marks a milestone of sorts. For those of us who live in the western hemisphere, the
movement into eastern longitudes is exciting. No longer do we mark the
familiar "W" on the chart, nor do we use it in our calculations. We abandoned north when we crossed the Equator and have accustomed ourselves somehow to being on the bottom of the world. Now we are faced
with "E" and the fact that we have to pay closer attention to what day it
is. The intellectual exercise of recognizing that in different parts of the
world the day of the week is different captures our imagination as we
cross the line.

For those of us cruising the South Pacific, this event occurs somewhere between Tonga and Fiji. It makes us more careful of our navigation. We are essentially unsettled as we reduce our sights. The currents
around the Fijian islands are fierce, and each year unwary yachts are
caught and wrecked. Sometimes it is just the current; sometimes it is the
inattention to detail that takes place in reconciling the shift in day and
longitude that occurs when the dateline is traversed.

The voice on the radio asking for help during the morning radio
schedule caught everyone's attention. Each day on the passage to Fiji
someone had gotten confused about navigation and long explanations
ensued in which those who felt they knew what they were doing talked
to those who were feeling unsure.

"Can someone please help me with a dateline question?" came the
woman's voice over the radio.

"Sure. Go ahead." The male voice answering was confident sounding, almost cocky. Obviously he had managed the dateline crossing with
ease, and now that his coordinates were south latitude and east longitude, he was anxious to help others to make the mental transition.
"What's your question?"

"Well, we just crossed the dateline," the woman's voice tentatively
rejoined, "and I want to know whether I should take one birth control
pill, two birth control pills, or no birth control pills. I'm confused." So,
too, was everyone else, but not for the same reasons. Here was a new
navigational issue with which the basic tomes had never dealt. Silence

on the airways. Then finally the same male voice that had offered help was back; it sounded less friendly, more irritated. Obviously, this wasn't the dateline question that Mr. Navigator was planning on answering.

"Lady," came the voice on the radio, "forget about the dateline. Don't even try to figure out what date it is. Each morning when you get up, take a pill. You know, after it has been dark and the sun comes up— that's a new day. When you see that sun come up, take a pill. One a day, just like at home. Every day. One."

"Thank you," came the female voice. "I think I understand now." Those of us listening in hoped she did.

While TAKU was in Fiji, two female cruisers on different boats found themselves pregnant when they arrived. They had both suffered from chronic seasickness, and each time they were seasick had thrown up their birth control pills. Whatever protection there might have been went to the fish. Ultimately what each believed to be chronic seasickness turned out to be a form of morning sickness exacerbated by the motion of their boats. There are more than navigational hazards that await the unwary.

Fiji found us all mentally keeping watch on the seasonal clock. September was not the start of autumn that we remembered, but here, down under, marked the slide into the southern hemisphere's spring. With the end of that spring would come the cyclone season, and it would be time to find a snug berth for the southern hemisphere's summer. The unwritten rule suggested that one could find relative safety either near the Equator, as cyclones were virtually unknown in the band that stretched out to 10 degrees north or south of the Equator. Or, if the equatorial region was out, one should seek safety in the mid-latitudes, away from the volatile and explosive tropics.

Temperature differences between the warm tropics and the cold waters of the Southern Ocean set things in motion, and the violent cyclones that occasionally plagued the tropics were born. The idea was to get south to New Zealand, outside of the cyclone band. The cyclone season started in mid-November so it was important to be there and have passages out of the way before then. Spring in New Zealand presented another set of problems; cold weather and gales could be expected. So we all elected to sit tight, to cruise the extensive and varied waters of Fiji and to let spring proceed for a month or two before starting south.

Some yachties had fallen in love with Tonga, and one, having done some research, announced that Tonga had only had one mild cyclone in the past thirty years. The climate was warm there; Tonga was only five days back eastward. We all knew how beautiful the anchorages were. Why go to New Zealand? The passage there was long, and some rough weather was sure to occur. He managed to convince a few to return, and when the time finally came for us to head south, they departed Fiji and headed east to Tonga to spend the cyclone season. While we were safely tucked away in New Zealand's Bay of Islands, they, anchored in Tonga, were hit by only the second cyclone to strike the Friendly Islands in thirty years. Several of the boats were wrecked; almost all of them were beached and had to be refloated and repaired. So much for statistics or for going against the odds.

We bring our social lives along with us as we cruise. For us, Fiji was no exception. The need to strike a balance between insular, isolated, self-oriented cruising and an abundant social calendar full of community activities came into sharp focus at the anchorage we all shared in front of the Royal Suva Yacht Club. Some 100 boats from all over the world converged there as September wore on. Many were old cruising acquaintances, while other "new" boats with new friends to be made also arrived on almost a daily basis. The farther afield your cruising takes you, the larger your social circle becomes. On the "highway around the world" each additional stop seems filled with more and more people that you know.

You also discover that too much interaction can create other sets of problems. Balance is necessary. You begin to long for your own space, your own uninterrupted time. With the veranda of the yacht club beckoning with cheap beer, inexpensive meals, and friends to spend time with, the lure of socializing is difficult to resist. Fiji turned into a round of sightseeing, movie going, souvenir hunting, shopping for electronics and boat work. We went to firewalking ceremonies. We shared the rental of a car with Dave and Marcia from MAÑANA and Dan from SEA-VENTURE and spent two or three days circumnavigating the island of Viti Levu by car. Finally Celia went off on RUNAWAY, a Hood-Maas 58 footer, as part of an early season delivery crew to take the boat to New Zealand. I settled in to have time alone, to read, to write, to try to put things into perspective.

After a day alone working on trying to rectify a stubborn shift lever on TAKU's engine that I had thought would take me only an hour, I ended up aboard MAÑANA for an evening of popcorn, munchies, and beer. I was feeling particularly low, as I had spent the best part of a magnificent day down below working on a mechanical problem. English majors, for the most part, keep away from mechanical problems, and for good reason. The topics of conversation drifted for a while as we watched the sunset. Finally the conversation settled—with a thud—on engines and mechanical problems others have come to know and to remember. In a fit of momentary frustration and anger I berated the group. "Can't we talk about anything else? I wish I was back in the classroom. At least there an occasional idea worth thinking about was exchanged. All we talk about is motors, engines, and boats."

This, of course, is not exactly true. Yachties are as interesting as they are diverse, and their broad spectrum of experiences and passions ensure that their lives and conversations are anything but dull and routine. My frustrations with the others was unfounded; at the same time we all need to be reminded to vary our conversations, to open our discussions to new topics. Cruising permits that, but like anything, the exotic and the unique can, if not valued, become commonplace all too soon.

A few nights later I was at a dinner party on another boat with many of the same people. I had long since apologized for blowing off steam, and generously they were still talking to me. As the dinner wound down one of them said: "I've been thinking about what you said the other day about the classroom. You taught *Hamlet*, right? I've never understood why he doesn't just kill Claudius when he finds him kneeling at prayer."

Before I could say anything a spirited discussion erupted, and all present were swapping opinions and quoting from the play to back up their points. But as the discussion only seemed to go so far, I gradually realized that something was "rotten in the state of Denmark."

Warming to the group, I suggested some other motives for Hamlet that sprung to mind, with references from the play to support them. The group was lively and interested, and I got caught up in the conversation and was enjoying the spirit of the moment. The discussion went on for an hour. Finally, someone said, a bit shamefacedly, "I guess I'll have to read the play." They all agreed. "We hope you aren't mad anymore," another one offered.

Marcia of MAÑANA explained. "We wanted you to have a good intellectual discussion so we tried to find copies of *Hamlet* but could only find these quickie notes up at the University of the South Pacific bookstore here in Suva. We've all been reading them, meeting secretly and practicing. That's why you haven't seen us around. I hope we fooled you a little."

They looked at me expectantly. What a bunch! I pictured them using up their time in Suva to work on *Hamlet* so that I could be cheered up. "Yeah," I said, my voice halting, "you sure did. Thanks."

There was an awkward pause, and someone said, "Let's go ashore to the Yacht Club and see if Billy is there. Maybe he'll show us his new tattoo."

All the way to shore Glen made dueling motions and shouted "a rat, a rat; dead for a ducat!" He continued to quote this line for months to come. I realized I had completely forgotten about wasted days doing mechanical things.

19

Protocol

Picture, if you will, the return home of one of Captain Cook's crew after a long three-year voyage under harsh conditions: a voyage of excitement, adventure, and romance that took him to the Pacific and back.

"Henry," (let's suppose that's his name) "where have you been? Haven't seen you around ye olde *Silent Unicorn* for quite awhile."

"Oh," says Henry, "been sailing out and about with Captain Cook. Went through the Strait of Magellan to the Pacific, stopped a bit in *Otahite* (Tahiti) where we set up an observation post to record the transit of Venus. Then we were off to Alaska to do some charting, and then we went to the Sandwich Islands where Cook went and got himself bashed and killed so we had to come home. You know, a bit here, a bit there. What's new with you?"

Is it possible that someone could have sailed to the uncharted waters of the world with Cook and thought of the voyage merely as a job? How did a sailor, unschooled, bring back impressions of the world that lay floating in the Pacific to those who had never been outside of the villages and pubs of rural England? Can we even imagine what it must have been like to see the paradise islands of the Pacific, to meet the friendly Tongans, the fierce Fijians, the moody Sandwich Islanders? What was it like to be in Tahiti before modern conveniences, before the European encroachment, before the ubiquitous tourist?

In many ways cruising replicates those earlier days. We go to out-of-the-way places. The peoples and cultures are different from what we have known at home. My mind is crowded with memories of a Pacific that could be as far away and as distant as the moon; the images of color and smell and sound crowd my senses as though to burst them.

Practically everyone out cruising looks for some memento to mark having been somewhere. Like the miniature Eiffel Tower that tourists bring home from Paris or the countless china plates seen in flea markets and yard sales everywhere with *Columbus, Ohio, Jamboree* or *Souvenir of Pensacola, Florida,* written in large orange script across a green croc-odile, we accumulate items that verify our travels, that validate our real-ly having gone.

"Been there, done that, bought the T-shirt," we quip, but the fact remains that we have been there, wherever there is, we have done that, whatever that is, and we sometimes buy a T-shirt to record the event.

For Bill, the young skipper of SINTRAM, a T-shirt wasn't enough to record his voyage from New England; he wanted something more per-manent. In Suva he had found a full-fledged tattoo parlor, and like sailors of old, he now sported a full-rigged ship tattoo. With more dis-cretion than his earlier counterparts, he had chosen to have this memo-ry inscribed on his hip. With the experience still fresh, he could, after a beer or two, be persuaded to tug down the waistband of his shorts and show it off. He was having his Andy Warhol "fifteen minutes of fame." I, on the other hand, have only words to mark my experiences.

Perhaps the following will help. Some say the only difference between a fairy tale and a sea story is the beginning. Fairy tales tradi-tionally commence, "Once upon a time," while sea stories begin, "Now this is no lie." There is only one thing worse in the world than a roman-tic, and that is an incurable romantic. Fed on fairy tales, sea stories, dreams, and visions, the incurable romantic floats through life on a com-posite view of the world that is occasionally near, but often far from, reality. Most boatowners are incurable romantics. Certainly all cruisers are. It is what brought us all from so far away to find ourselves anchored off the Royal Suva Yacht Club in Fiji.

This is no lie. I had always wanted to get a boat and to sail to the South Pacific. And here I was. I had been fed by books in which I read about great sea adventures, and I had been captivated by the movies. For ten cents you could adventure on the high seas. And, years ago, there was the newly arrived and limited television show. Delivered right to the comfort of your home in a plain box on a pint-sized screen came adventure, intrigue, and "romance" on a weekly basis. All you had to do was turn the dial.

But before television made its inroads into my life, I would go (repair we used to say in those days) to the theatre and settle in to the comfort of a padded seat; the lights would dim, and I would watch awe-struck as the quasi-historical pictures grew larger than life on the silver screen. The ones I liked best always opened with a shot bow-on of a marvelous square-rigger, sails full and by, bearing directly down upon the audience. As the ship came nearer, we were drawn magically aboard, and there was Errol Flynn or Clark Gable or someone equally dashing. He was always dressed in a clean, loose-fitting white shirt, his hair blowing casually in the breeze, whether Force 2 or Force 9, and he was never at a loss as to how to handle the ship or what to do with the hundreds of friends he always had aboard for company. One of these friends would, if something went wrong, be able to repair the entire wardrobe of sails in a few hours, or produce a steaming cup of coffee that remained unspilt on every angle of heel, or staunch a wound, cut off a limb, erect a new mast, or (and this was best) watch the boat in port while the hero went off to woo beautiful maidens, right wrongs, overturn injustices, and spend inexhaustible supplies of gold coins.

They were never seasick, these heroes. They never took a sight; rarely, if ever, looked at a chart; they didn't seem to worry about provisions or cyclone seasons or clearing customs or finding a place to haul out to scrape and paint or to do laundry. Nor did they have problems with their outboards as they always had six or eight willing friends to grab an oar and ferry them back and forth to shore whenever they needed to go. As I recall, the heroes never rowed. If they were unfortunate enough to lose their ship, some king or queen or grateful government would usually give them another within minutes of hearing the news, with, of course, the inevitable bags of gold necessary to enjoy themselves to the fullest.

"Wait a minute," I can hear you say. "Not even the most incurable romantic would fall for that." But, and this is no lie, they would; we did.

A day or two after Celia returned from her delivery trip to New Zealand a storm blew through the Suva anchorage. I was awakened in the middle of the night to the sound of airhorns coming from other boats. The airhorn is the yacht's equivalent of "Bugler! Sound the charge!" Its penetrating screech will wake even the most hardened sleepers. Yachties use it to warn each other of imminent dangers.

The wind had picked up, and TAKU was rocking and straining to her chain in the formerly calm anchorage. I was on deck in a moment and saw searchlights from other boats pointing off toward TAKU's bow. A large barge had apparently broken loose and was drifting down through the anchorage and threatening the yachts moored in its path. All around us boats were desperately hauling anchors in attempts to clear out of the way before they were hit and possibly sunk. We were directly in the barge's path.

"We can't get our anchor up in time," I screamed above the wind at Celia. To pull in the anchor would have meant moving us forward, closer to the barge that was looming larger and larger some 50 yards ahead of us. "We'll have to slip our chain and run for it."

We quickly tied some fenders to the chain to buoy it so that we could recover it later and began paying it out. Unfortunately we had only about 60 feet out and had almost another 440 feet remaining in the chain locker. As fast as I could, I hauled the chain up the pipe and let it run. Unfortunately the barge was shielding us from the wind and we were, consequently, drifting more slowly than it was. It would soon be upon us.

"Get a sharp knife and a flashlight," I instructed Celia, "and get ready down below; once all the chain runs out, cut the line that holds the bitter end to the boat. Don't get your hands in there until it is all out. It's going to be close." We had, of course, fastened the chain to an eye in the chain locker to prevent an inadvertent loss of the whole piece overboard. Celia disappeared down below.

The barge was just about on us. Its topsides were so high that it blacked out the sky in front of us. Armlength by armlength, I hauled chain as fast as I could and let it fall to the deck. I felt a bump. The barge was pushing on our bowsprit, and as it did, we started to move faster and the chain started to run out on its own. I moved to the bowsprit and, pushing as hard as I could, managed to turn us partly sideways to the bulk of the barge. The chain continued to run out. The barge was sliding down our port side. Suddenly a corner snagged the port shroud of the mainmast.

I could hear the wire scraping on the metal hull of the barge. Sparks were starting to pop from the point of the contact. The shroud was being pulled like a bow string. Any second we would lose the mast. Suddenly I didn't hear anymore chain running out, and Celia was back on deck. We were free, except for the shroud that was hung up on the side of the barge. We ran to the port rail, and together pushed as hard as we could against the side of the barge to relieve the strain on the shroud.

There was a sharp "pop" as the shroud came free, and miraculously the mast was still up. I started the engine and moved us slowly ahead; the barge drifted on by and through the anchorage to ground eventually in the shallows across the harbor. We had been lucky. Clark Gable never had problems like that. I rigged our spare anchor and dropped it, and once TAKU settled, we went below for an uneasy sleep.

The morning brought bright sun and blue sky. The only evidence of the difficulties of the night before was the grounded barge far across the harbor and a large "hole" in the middle of the anchorage where boats had been before they were forced to vacate in the unplanned and untimely move.

We hauled our spare anchor and motored slowly forward to recover the chain and primary anchor that we had slipped during the night. As we came alongside one of the fenders and hauled it aboard and began the long and laborious process of recovering 500 feet of chain, a newly arriving boat motored quickly by us, Q flag flapping at the spreaders. The captain couldn't believe his luck. There, right in the center of a very crowded anchorage, was a large open spot with plenty of swinging room. He wouldn't have to anchor way outside the pack as each new arrival usually did. Here was a spot close to the dock, and he wasn't about to miss it.

"You can't anchor there," I shouted as loud as I could. He was three or four boatlengths ahead of us, readying his anchor to let it drop. He looked back to where we were, with our chain disappearing over our roller into the water. I shouted again. "You're right on top of our anchor. Don't anchor there."

He looked again, measuring the distance in his head. He was several boatlengths ahead; I was clearly one of those fussy skippers who liked a lot of space around his boat. He went ahead and dropped his anchor and, satisfied that it was holding, disappeared below.

"He'll be sorry," I told Celia, as we continued to make chain and haul our hastily abandoned ground tackle back aboard.

In a while we were close on his stern, and I hauled chain until our bowsprit was peeking over his pushpit and partway into his cockpit. I went forward and yelled again.

"Hello! You can't anchor here. You are right across our chain and

on top of our anchor and you will have to move so that we can get it up."
A head popped up, and I smiled to myself to see the startled look on the
man's face as he saw our bowsprit looming into his cockpit. "I asked you
not to anchor there; now would you please move?"

Anchoring protocol requires that later arrivals must always defer to
boats that are already anchored and set. If boats get too close, the one
who was last to anchor must pick up and move. It is an inviolable rule.
The man stared at me and at TAKU, and I could see him trying to figure
out how we had gotten from three boatlengths behind him to right in his
cockpit. He looked at our chain; it still tended down and disappeared
forward under the stern of his boat. He grumbled something and then
went forward and began to pick up his hook.

I continued to make chain, and TAKU slid along behind him like a
large puppy on a leash. The man got his anchor up and prepared to
motor away, to find some spot outside the pack. He looked across at me
and then at his depthsounder and then at me again.

"How much damn chain do you have out?" he yelled.

I looked back. "Five hundred feet," I replied, holding his gaze. The
normal anchoring procedure calls for a scope (or length of anchor line)
of about seven to one, line to depth of water. If you anchor with all chain
as TAKU does, a scope of three to one up to five to one is usually more
than enough in calm protected waters.

"Five hundred feet!" The man's voice was incredulous. "But it's
only ten feet deep here."

I wasn't about to give him a sensible explanation, to tell him about
the barge and our near disaster of the night before. His rush through the
anchorage and his unwillingness to listen had lost him that.

"We like to sleep securely at night. We don't like to drag," I shouted as pleasantly as I could. I saw him shake his head in wonder as he
motored off to find another spot. The world was full of damn fools. And
I, to him, was certainly one of the biggest. *Five hundred feet of chain in
ten feet of water.* And he thought he had seen it all. *Wait till the guys
back home hear about this!* Our anchor was up; it was time for us to
leave Suva and the crowd for a while.

20

Gardner McKay

We headed up the coast of Viti Levu to do "a few days on the hotel circuit." The hotel circuit consisted of day-hopping around parts of Fiji and anchoring off the splendid palm-lined sand beaches of that country's leading hotels. All the cruising boats indulged at one time or another as they passed through Fiji, but we all, in turn, spoke somewhat disdainfully of doing the hotel circuit, albeit it meant having a series of beautiful, excellent anchorages, nice sandy beaches, and easy access to shore and fresh water, showers, swimming pools, poolside bars, evening discos or movies, and meals out if you wanted them—in short, all the comforts of the tourist world.

Our disdain, when we voiced it, was usually tongue in cheek, for after months of cruising in out-of-the-way isolated areas, a little pampering was, however expensive, good for the soul. Whatever meager benefits we derived from the hotels were returned in kind, as there, anchored a mere stone's throw from the hotel, would be one, two, or more "world cruising boats" for the hotel guests to photograph and gawk at. As the hotel brochures sometimes even said: "Enjoy our marvelous beaches, pool, and water sports and view cruising yachts from all parts of the world." The hotel got its quid; we got our pro quo.

A few days later we dropped anchor off Nadi, Fiji. Nadi was another one of those places like Pago. It was actually pronounced *nan-dee*. I had heard people describing a fabulous anchorage off *nan-dee*, but I could never find it on the chart. After spending time in Fiji, I discovered that *nan-dee* and Nadi were one and the same.

To be exact, we were anchored off Fiji's magnificent (as those things go) Regent Hotel, 100 miles up the coast from Suva. As we dropped the hook I noticed that we were anchored near an old schooner. She had obviously seen better days. Shabby, with streaks of rust from her chainplates weeping down her topsides, she had shortened masts and a gigantic permanent framework on her decks supporting a spread of faded blue canvas that shaded her whole deck. The schooner was a ghost of what she once must have been; only her lines hinted at her earlier majesty.

After we watched her come and go for a day or two, her function became clear. She was the "head" boat for the hotel. So much a head and the old girl, without a visible name, would belch black smoke from her exhaust, raise a ratty and much too small sail or two, and lug tourists out in the harbor for "an authentic sailing ride" and a chance to snap pictures of the hotel, the world cruising boats, and each other.

One day, while watching her depart, I commented to Tim who, with Mike of the sweatpants fame, was anchored there on their Westsail 32 INOA. "It seems so sad. That must have been a magnificent schooner once; look at her lines. Even all that junk they've built on her decks can't hide them. I would love to have seen her under sail in her prime."

"You probably did," replied Tim. "Don't you remember Gardner McKay?" Remember Gardner McKay? My eyes practically misted at the mention of his name.

"You mean . . .?" I was speechless.

"Yep," said Tim, "you're looking at what remains of TIKI."

"Who," you might ask, "is Gardner McKay? And what was TIKI?" Find people at least in their forties who are ocean cruising and just ask, "Do you remember Gardner McKay?" Sometimes the name is momentarily lost to them, but if you get a flash of recognition you will know that you have come upon true, pure, incurable romantics. It was Gardner McKay who rescued me from despair and who propelled along my dream of cruising to distant places.

For a while—it seemed like years—in my youth, Gardner McKay starred in a weekly television series called "Adventures in Paradise." The show was based loosely on a James Michener collection of stories by the same name. Gardner, under the character name Adam Troy (what else?), sailed a magnificent schooner around the South Pacific, stopping at various islands (usually unnamed), anchoring in crystal lagoons, trading with local natives, carrying occasional mail, passengers, damsels in distress, and malcontents (whom he quickly contented), and just having a good time. TIKI, a magnificent schooner of about 60 or 70 (or was it 100?) feet, always opened the show.

Gardner's sole assistance on these adventures was a local islander who never said much but who seemed to take care of everything. A steaming cup of coffee or a cold drink was always available, and Gardner never had to row himself anywhere. Gardner's mate, as I will call him, must have done all the cooking, all the boat work, and all the laundry (for Gardner always looked great wearing a set of freshly pressed khakis and one of those billed captain's hats with the crossed anchors set rakishly on his head).

From the time we would first see TIKI, all sail cracked on, till the time she would appear in port, a scant five minutes later, all sails down, neatly furled, covered, and bagged, and all lines coiled, Gardner never seemed to leave the cockpit.

I do remember that when TIKI nosed her way into the lagoon (she never had any problems with the passes, even though they weren't marked and Gardner never looked at a chart), there were always people to greet her, a convenient anchorage (10 to 15 feet, sand, excellent holding), or more than likely, a gigantic wharf, fendered perfectly, unused. Without a cross current, cross wind, or cross word, TIKI would come alongside. Several willing and able line handlers were always ready. They never missed and tied perfect bowlines every time, and they didn't have to recite to themselves that the rabbit went up the hole, around the tree, and back down the hole again.

With TIKI safely moored, shore was a mere step away. The tide was always right. There were no ladders or barnacled pilings to scale and no crowds of local children and gawkers to wade through. There was no customs man, no representative from immigration waiting to grab his passport and check his visa and ask him if he had extra shotgun shells. There was no man from agriculture, like the one we were to meet in New Zealand, to take away his popcorn or other "undesirable" foodstuff. Perhaps Gardner didn't have a "Q" flag, or, more likely, they hadn't been invented.

There were occasional dusky maidens to be contended (or was it contented) with or seemingly prim but usually vivacious missionaries or schoolteachers or daughters of planters home on vacation. Remember, this was before the sexual revolution, before marriage, before "relationships," divorce, E.R.A., minimum wage—before almost everything. This was *paradise*, and to an incurable romantic like me it seemed perfect.

But I grew up and discovered, as others had before me, that the world was round. It wasn't a question of two charts (one for the top and one for the bottom of a flat world) or six (in case you pictured the world as a cube). There were catalogs full of them of various shapes, sizes, projections, scales, prices, and ever-changing numbering systems. And there were all those books on how to cruise, and there was such a choice of boats; it boggled the mind to think of it. I grew up to discover that if, as they say, all thought is sorting, all cruising is compromise and choice.

I couldn't find a 40-, 60-, 80-, or 100-foot schooner, so I got a 41-foot ketch instead. When people asked me why I named her TAKU I replied, despite what new knowledge I had garnered in Samoa, that she was named after an Alaskan word for north wind, but if you think about it, with a couple of vowel changes TAKU could become TIKI easily enough. Now I know why Gardner wore plain old khakis and kept things simple.

At some point I discovered that the available feast of cruising information, books, magazines, and articles as well as the number of boats, amount of equipment, and choice of clothes was so rich that one could metaphorically and ironically starve to death while trying to choose among them. I was learning that "adventures in paradise" (lower case) was a full-time, seven-day-a-week, 24-hours-per-day occupation. One had to work at getting to those lagoons.

Most of the time life aboard a cruiser is routine: there's boat work to do, letters to write, books to read (I was working my way through the complete works of Charles Dickens and had finally finished *Bleak House*, a book that I had tried several times to read in earlier years), food to buy, meals to prepare, dishes to wash, and at sea, navigation. On top of all that you can add meeting people, exploring and seeing where you are, and preparing and planning for where you want to go. As in Gardner's time, the weather is usually beautiful, but, we were about to find out on our passage to New Zealand, it is not always so. In "real life," as the folks back home prefer to call what they do, there is a work time, a play time, a rest time, and something called a weekend. In the cruising life the days start early, usually with the sun, and often end early—and go on seven days a week. Cruisers frequently have to ask each other the day of the week so they can integrate themselves into the world of opening and closing hours of the villages, towns, and cities they visit.

As we moved from island group to island group we had all begun to discover changes in geography, in scenery, in people, in problems to be solved, and in ourselves. Rather than one experience repeated infinitely, as many of the folks in "real life" assume, cruising is an infinite series of different experiences to be savored and enjoyed. We were not, as some of the "real life" people had thought and said, going "troppo." No sitting under a palm tree in a straw hat listening to the coconuts fall for us.

I was beginning to realize that the notion of what I was doing, what life was like out here in "paradise" to those back home, stems in part from some of the same factors that got me and most of the rest of the yachties out here in the first place. The image must come in part from those who remember Errol and Clark and their hundreds of friends, swashbucklers all, and from those who remember Gardner McKay and TIKI and the endless, unvarying lagoons, each with the inevitable girl.

Out cruising we read *Time* and *Newsweek* whenever we can. We read articles on government waste and mismanagement and whatever the current world crisis happens to be. That news seems as unreal at times as Gardner McKay's world. At times it appears that the folks back home are the ones who have gone "troppo."

The season pushed on. We left TIKI to her destiny at the Regent Hotel and sailed to seek our own farther south in New Zealand.

21

A Cup of Tea

Six days out of Lautoka, Fiji, bound for New Zealand, and we are still sailing hard. The wind, which has been over 20 knots since we cleared the pass at Lautoka, is still strong, and the reef we tied in the main some five days earlier remains undisturbed. TAKU has been moving upwards of seven and a half knots under her 150 percent genoa, working staysail, single-reefed main, and mizzen. The passage has been dry and fast, and the old Aries windvane has been holding TAKU to her course with a minimum of fuss.

We had detoured north from Nadi to spend a few days in the Yasawa group, a chain of volcanic islands that stretched about 50 miles north-northeast some 22 miles off the coast of Viti Levu. The group is virtually unspoiled, rarely visited, and has some beautiful white sandy beaches and protected anchorages. The Yasawas are the home of the fabled Blue Lagoon. Our stay there was short and after a provisioning and birthday bash (could it have been a year since Ahe?) in Lautoka, we were on our way.

We had departed Fiji 24 hours behind LA NUI, a William Atkin-designed 36-foot African Star with a cutter rig. Her crew, Amy and Mickey Searle of Honolulu, Hawaii, are sailing her well and fast. We have shared anchorages with them since Pago. We had also departed within an hour of MAÑANA, Dave and Marcia Reck's Fuji 35 ketch out of Seattle, Washington. We have been together, on and off, since Tahiti and consider ourselves fast friends.

We are all staying in touch by radio. The previous worries and concerns of a difficult passage to New Zealand melt away as we abandon the tropics and sail into the somewhat higher latitudes of the southern hemisphere. A New Englander at heart, I can't help feeling upside down as we move farther and farther south.

As of this particular morning's radio contact, TAKU is, according to our dead-reckoned position, about 60 miles behind LA NUI and gaining and more than 100 miles in front of MAÑANA, which is having a wet ride and losing ground behind us. I have never thought of TAKU as a particularly fast boat, but the winds and sea seem, on this passage, to be ideal for her, and she fairly skims along under her press of sail. I decide that a cruising ketch is designed for these conditions and sit back to enjoy another day, excited by the prospect of arriving before, or at least within hours of, LA NUI and a day or so ahead of MAÑANA. Cut a cruising sailor and watch the racing blood run out every time.

As we close with New Zealand, the weather changes. The early November cloud cover this day reminds me that although it is spring, winter, at least in this part of the world, is not too long past and that thus far we have been lucky not to run into any heavy weather. Tim and Mike aboard INOA skipped the trip to the Yasawas and departed Fiji ten days before us for the 1,100-mile trip. Our regular radio contacts with them indicate that they are now only 100 miles ahead of us. They have been enroute for sixteen days in a nasty variety of wind and weather, ranging from awful to atrocious. We, fortunately, have picked up a different weather system and hope to ride it all the way to Opua in New Zealand's Bay of Islands. In my happier moments I reflect on completing the passage in less than eight days and being at the dock to greet INOA, MAÑANA, and LA NUI as they straggle in. I can see myself, devil-may-care, smug, and all-knowing, the boat put to bed shipshape, greeting the stragglers. This passage is a piece of cake.

With these thoughts dancing through my head, I chance to look astern and see a very dark, menacing line of clouds that appears to be moving in our direction. I yell down the companionway to Celia to come on deck. She replies testily, "Be quiet a minute, I'm listening to the weather. There's a line coming through somewhere near here this morning. Just a minute, and I'll be up." We are far enough away to be out of any immediate danger, but the dark line is definitely heading our way, so I work my way forward and hand the staysail and lash it securely to its club-footed boom. That way there will be less sail to worry about should we have to shorten. In the time it takes me to secure the staysail, the dark clouds have obscured the horizon, and the line has gained on us appreciably.

"Celia, get up here!" I yell again, putting a bit more urgency in my voice.

"They're still giving the weather," she yells back.

"I'm living the weather! Grab the rain gear and get out here, quick." We are going to be hit, and there is no way out. Mysteriously my rain gear flies unaided out of the hatch, followed by Celia's face. She is looking aft behind me. "Oh, my God," she says. "Why didn't you tell me?"

I pull on my rain jacket, throw my rain pants on the cockpit sole behind the wheel, and yell: "Hurry up, will you? We've got to get the mainsail down."

I work forward to the mainmast, and while Celia eases the mainsheet as much as possible from the cockpit, I release the halyard. Things are coming down on us too fast to round up; the pressure of the wind is holding the sail against the spreaders, and for a moment it won't come down. Old gaff-riggers had a procedure for an emergency dropping of their mainsails. It was called "scandalizing the main" and consisted of throwing off the peak halyard that held the heavy wooden gaff boom aloft at the top of the sail. The weight of the gaff dropping would pull the sail down in quick order. Sometimes the sail was damaged, hence the term "scandalizing," but it saved getting caught with a large press of canvas up in a strong wind squall.

Our triangular-topped marconi rig main has no weight aloft to pull it down. With the wind blowing hard from astern, the released sail merely pastes itself onto the mast and the shrouds. The line squall is right behind us now, and I can feel the wind starting to pick up. I brace myself as best I can and claw at the sail near the track; with my weight pulling it, it inches down clear of the spreaders. The squall line is traveling far faster than we are, and it is obvious that we can't get the main furled fast enough and certainly not before the advancing line catches us. By now we are both tugging the sail down the track, and large billows of it are snapping about the deck like angry dogs. It starts to rain and howl as the stronger wind catches us. The sky grows completely dark.

"Get the boom into the gallows . . . anywhere, and sheet it home tight," I scream. The boom, responding to the pulling sail, is gyrating wildly back and forth. Jamming two flapping sail ties between my teeth, I throw myself into the writhing mass of Dacron on the deck in an attempt to subdue it. The Aries vane seems to be holding us on course, and with the reduction of sail to just genoa and mizzen, the boat will balance and hold her own for a while.

Carrying armloads of mainsail and pushing more before me, I hang myself over the boom on top of the sail while Celia gets some ties around it. The wind has risen to about 30, and it is raining hard. As I cling to the now placid mainsail, Celia yells through the rain that according to the weather report from Norfolk Island it's a small disturbance, with maximum winds to 40 knots, that will pass through in a few hours.

"It shouldn't get much worse," she says.

With the main secure, I climb back behind the wheel and check the course. We are still holding well. Fruitlessly I pull my puddled rain pants over my wet jeans and prepare to wait out the system. The anemometer reads 35 knots plus, and the knotmeter shows us doing eight and a half, with an occasional nine for inspiration. The 35 grows to a steady 40, and I realize that the big genoa is much more than we need or want. Normally we use rollerfurling and can quickly reduce our headsail, but I had taken it off for the passage to permit more flexibility of headsail changes. As a consequence we have gotten caught.

The rain pelts down as we put on safety harnesses and then go gingerly forward to hand the genoa and reduce sail. The seas have picked up considerably, and I am surprised and impressed to see how big they have become. I think to myself: "At least it isn't the middle of the night." Out on the bowsprit the motion is decidedly worse, and I find myself hoping that I won't get seasick. "We'll have to try to round her up. You bring her into the wind; I'll throw the halyard, and you dump the sheet and come forward to help me."

Celia returns to the helm and releases the vane while I get the halyard ready to run. At eight and a half knots, a boat TAKU's size rounds up in a hurry. I wave to signal that I am ready, Celia puts the wheel up, and around we come. The sails start to thunder as we come into the wind, and I realize that the 35 knots we have been seeing was apparent wind, as we have been moving away from it. The full force of what has been really blowing hits the sails, the boat, and me all at once. The genoa snaps and cracks, and the sheets jump as though they are alive. I throw off the halyard, and the big jib viciously works its way down the forestay. I know we won't stay bow-to-the-wind for long, so dodging the flailing sheets, I work forward with my harness, now uphill, now down, to where I can pull in and sit on the sail before the boat pays off and the sail blows out of control. I can see Celia throwing the sheet loose from the primary winch and working forward with her harness to help me.

With the forward motion of the boat stopped, TAKU bucks and plunges, and the comforts of the bowsprit, minimal at best, become nonexistent. One moment inches from the water and the next high above it, I sit on the jib and proceed to unhank it. As we plunge, part of the now-loose sail is caught by the sea and fills. It starts to drag the rest with it. "We'll lose the sail," cries Celia. "Don't unhank anymore. Let's get it aboard and get some ties on it first." Laboriously, an inch at a time, we haul the heavy sail back aboard. As the bow rises, we feel the weight pull against our fingers and hands, and as it drops we gain a few more inches as we change and reinforce our grips. I have tried to imagine what it must have been like on a square-rigger rounding the Horn—80 to 100 feet above the deck, swaying crazily on the foot ropes, one hand for the ship and one for yourself. Those guys must have been crazy. Sitting on a little bowsprit four to eight feet above the water trying to get a genoa aboard in wind and rain is more than enough for me. With the sail back aboard and tied in stops, I finish unhanking it, and we drag it slowly toward the forward hatch. TAKU is pitching violently now, and we have to crawl up and down the ever-changing slope of the deck, dragging the waterlogged sail—one hand for the boat, one hand for ourselves.

We open the hatch and together shove and cajole the reluctant sail below. A great deal of nonreluctant water goes enthusiastically with it. The feeling of relief that floods over me when the hatch slams is immense. It is blowing hard and raining steadily, but once again we are close to being back in control. Celia crawls her way to the dinghy chocked on deck and, untying the cover, works the ever-ready storm jib forward to me. "Let's get this up. This motion is awful. We've got to get some way on." Back to the end of the sprit I crawl and slowly hank on the storm jib and attach the sheets. I notice that the seas have increased even more and are now coming at us from the side. A particularly large sea smacks us. I hear a loud crack and watch as our port trail board floats away; it has been literally torn from its mounts. How easily that could have been one of us and how impossible it would be in these conditions to get someone back aboard. Celia and I exchange looks. Obviously we have had the same thought.

We work our way back to the mast and raise and secure the storm jib. With a headsail on the boat we can once again get moving. I am feeling awful from the constant pitching, and I am soaked through to the skin. "Are you okay?" I ask Celia.

"Fine," she replies. She has disconnected the vane again and is getting TAKU back on course.

"I'll be back in a minute." I go below. I am greeted by a shambles of books, clothes, and equipment piled in the greatest mess imaginable. I strip off my wet rain gear and my wet clothes and, finding a towel, dry myself. I pull on a wool sweater and wool long johns and replace my wet gear. I feel appreciably warmer and more relaxed. Wool next to the skin will keep you warm even when wet.

I search for and find the seasick medicine. Half a Phenergan tablet, my usual dose, often makes me sleepy, but since I have the feeling that things are far from over, I take an ephedrine tablet as well. This combination had frequently been recommended in books and articles, but I have never tried it. In more than two years of ocean cruising, discounting our first troubled passage to the Virgin Islands, this is the first heavy, heavy weather we have hit. I hope that I can keep the medication down.

Back on deck the wind is howling, and the rain is continuing to pelt. "I think we'd better hand the mizzen; we're going too fast," says Celia. The knotmeter reads 11 knots. One of the advantages of the split rig boat is that when you are down to the final shortening of sail, the mizzen, you can drop it from the relative safety of the cockpit rather than having to venture forward where we have already spent far too long. Celia holds the helm while I pull and claw the mizzen down and secure it. The boat slows and steadies, and we race on under storm jib alone. The seas seem enormous. What has been a vast plain of water is now one approaching mountain after another. As these mountains come toward us, they blanket the storm jib and the boat rolls horribly. We rise to the crest of the waves that pass harmlessly under us while the jib fills with the press of the wind and TAKU staggers forward like a drunk.

"This is ridiculous. We need a bit more sail to keep moving. This weather system should be just about by." I work my way forward and raise and set the storm trysail. We keep it hanked on and ready in its own track resting at the base of the mainmast. With it up and drawing, the rolling abates, and the boat once again picks up speed. I relieve Celia at the helm. "We'll do a half hour on, half off till this blows over." The seas are too large and too erratic to trust the windvane any longer, and when we are in squalls we feel more in control if one of us is steering anyway. Celia crouches under the dodger out of the wind and most of the rain, and I hook my harness on and settle in to working the boat.

The helm is easy, and we seem to be moving well, but the seas are the biggest I have ever seen and look almost square. Walls of water rush at us from the port side, and each time TAKU waits and then, at the seemingly last possible minute, rises to the top and rushes down the other side. With her normal 1,100 square feet of working sails reduced to a mere 150 square feet, in a 75-square-foot storm jib and a 75-square-foot storm trysail, we are fairly flying along at a steady ten and a half knots.

I find that I am avoiding looking to starboard as we rise to the top of each wave; the knot in my stomach that comes when I involuntarily glance that way confirms my fear. Each time we rise to the crest, the seas fall away abruptly beneath us. They seem almost vertical. I feel as though at any moment we will plummet off the top of one and crash on our starboard side some 20 to 30 feet below in the here-again, gone-again troughs. I have read of boats falling off waves and being severely damaged. Peering across the top of the starboard weather cloth each time we get to the top of a crest, I can imagine all too well how it might happen.

Although I saw many big seas in Alaska when I was in the U.S. Coast Guard and many confused seas while running inlets in New Jersey in small powerboats, I can recall nothing anywhere like these. What's remarkable is their disproportionate size for the wind strength, which has settled to between 35 and 40 knots. I feel the cold rain running down my neck and back. In addition to everything else, my foul-weather gear obviously isn't doing the job. "We've got to heave-to," I shout to Celia. "I'm afraid we may broach."

"What do you want me to do?" she asks, shouting above the wind.

Somewhere on the top of one of those square seas my confidence oozed away, and now when I want it, I find it has truly departed without a trace. "Go get the book, and see what it says about heaving-to."

"Get the book! What book? You know how to heave-to; we've done it before." Celia is annoyed. There is nothing like a good storm and a little uncertainty to brew up an argument. I grip the helm as we race down the upper face of yet another wave. The knotmeter touches and passes 11. "Slocum didn't need a book," shouts Celia. "He just hove-to and went below and made himself a cup of tea."

"Take the wheel," I yell back, "and hold on; don't broach us—I'll go read the book. Besides, Slocum probably couldn't read." I feel like a traitor as I say it since Slocum wrote voluminously about his own solo circumnavigation, and I take my storm below, leaving the other one outside.

One of the real dangers in a storm is having your boat travel too fast. As the waves get steeper, the boat tends to accelerate as it travels down their slopes. Imagine, if you will, a large tractor trailer rig driving speedily down a steep hill. The front end suddenly slows appreciably or stops. The back end is still moving, trying to pass the front. The trailer slews around and the truck rolls over. So, too, with a boat. As TAKU surfs down the waves and becomes hidden in the troughs below the force of the wind she tends to slow. My fear is that the stern will overrun the bow. When this happens on a boat there can be serious consequences. The first, broaching, occurs when the boat slews around on its side, much like the tractor trailer. This broaching leaves you broadside to the oncoming seas and in danger of being rolled or inundated by a following sea. Pitchpoling, where the yacht goes end over end (usually only once), is a more serious possibility. This occurs when the seas are very steep, and as the movement of the boat accelerates, the bow is depressed and the stern, rather than passing to one side or another as in a broach, lifts instead up and over and the boat turns upside down. Precipitous seas and too much speed can be a lethal combination.

The first course of action is to slow the boat speed by reducing sail area to reduce speed. In really extreme weather one can run along under bare poles propelled solely by the windage of the mast and rigging aloft. Even that can be too much and one can then stream warps (heavy lines) astern to create some drag. Or one can set a sea anchor, a large parachute device that helps to slow the boat and to hold her at a comfortable angle to the wind. Or, most easily of all, one can heave-to, turning the boat to the wind, backing the jib, and lashing the helm down so that the boat is almost stopped and wiggles its way slowly, slowly through the water until conditions improve. Conditions is the operative word, and there have been countless books and articles written about heavy weather, expressing all sorts of opinions as to techniques to use.

Of course I know how to heave-to. We've done it before on other occasions, although never with a trysail. What is gnawing at me is *the book*. The day before we left Fiji, Glen from SEAVENTURE had given me a copy of a book called *This is Rough-Weather Sailing* for my birthday, with the admonition to read it carefully on the way to New Zealand. I, of course, had ignored his admonition. While at the helm I had remembered the presence of the book below and recalled my disdain upon its receipt. So here I am, sopping wet, wedged in the corner of the galley sole, looking to see if some new, marvelous, miraculous technique for heaving-to has been developed and hidden away inside its pages. It hasn't. Things remain the same. I slouch back on deck, trying to appear calm and indifferent.

"Let's heave-to; I'll take it." I relieve Celia and once again dance TAKU along the crest of the seas. Surprisingly we have now been in the storm system for over five hours. "I think we're just traveling with it. We've got to stop and let it pass. Are you ready?"

I put the helm over, and TAKU rounds up. One look at the huge wave bearing down on us over the swinging bowsprit is enough. I put the helm back, and TAKU wheels and tears away down the face of the wave as it passes beneath us. "We'll never get around. The seas are too steep. A wave will catch us and push us backwards down the face, and we're liable to fill the cockpit, or break the vane, or worse." Inside I am shaking. The times we hove-to or practiced heaving-to the seas were always much slighter, and we did it with ease. I realize that I am suddenly cold and tired and running out of energy.

"We'll gybe around," I yell, trying to sound confident. Rather than spinning our bow into the wind to turn and risk the possibility of being suddenly pushed over backwards, I have decided to turn away from the wind, to spin the stern through, which, I hope, will minimize our risk. Watching the waves for a bit, I pick mine, and as it comes up under us, I spin the helm, and TAKU races down its face. As we tear along, I push us past the gybe point, the jib and the trysail slam back as the wind comes to their other sides, and we don't broach. In a moment I have the helm lashed. Although facing back the way we have come, TAKU is riding comfortably, taking each sea in stride as they come at us. We take a quick look around and go below.

"Cup of tea, Joshua?" asks Celia. I grimace. I climb out of my wet clothes again, get a dry sweater, and grabbing my sleeping bag, wedge myself into a corner of the cabin sole.

At 1800 we make our radio schedule. MAÑANA hasn't had any change in weather. INOA is on Day 17 of her voyage and has just a bit of rain. They are anxious to get to New Zealand. Mickey on LA NUI states that he is under way again, as he hove-to as soon as he saw the heavy black clouds approaching. He says that it "blew like stink" but after two and a half hours the sun came out, he put away his book, which he had been reading below in the dry comfort of the cabin, and got under way. He asks how we are doing. I look outside. It is still black, pouring, and blowing. "Oh, we decided to run with it for a while to catch you guys. We were doing 10 knots or better for more than three hours. Now we're hove-to. Just about to have a cup of tea," I lie.

"Those seas looked big," says Mick, his voice crackling through the radio speaker. "How was it?"

"A piece of cake," I lie again. "See you guys in Opua."

A day and a half later, eight days and one hour out of Fiji, we tie to the customs dock to clear in with INOA, nineteen days out of Fiji, and LA NUI, which has arrived the night before, some 15 hours ahead of us. MAÑANA arrives safely some 30 hours later. With everyone now in port, the saga of our "cup of tea and piece of cake" gradually slips out and is revealed to all. In retrospect we would have done better to heave-to earlier, but the decision to run with a fast-moving system wasn't a bad one in itself. It did, however, mean a lot of work, energy expended, anxiety, and a long, miserable, wet day. Why do we rush? What racer's urge propels us?

22

Land of the Long White Cloud

Two years after her arrival in the Virgin Islands, TAKU swings to her anchor off the small former whaling town of Russell, in New Zealand's Bay of Islands. Subtropical New Zealand will be home for the coming tropical cyclone season. It is November, the beginning of summer in New Zealand. The *Kiwis*, as the New Zealanders call themselves, are changing over from long trousers and woolen socks to shorts and sandals. They are packing campers for their summer vacations, opening up and provisioning their boats for a summer of sailing. It is a time to mail Christmas cards, to get ready for a summer season of fun. The sense of what is happening seems discontinuous, paradoxical. New England seems far away here in Aotearoa, "the land of the long white cloud," as the Maoris called New Zealand.

I loved New Zealand. That's all there is to it. Plain and simple. In many ways it was like being back in the 1950s. With some three million people and 23 million sheep, the North and South Islands that comprise New Zealand have a lot of open space. The pace of life, the clean air, the lovely scenery, and the friendly people can lull the unwary visitor into a sense of timelessness. Getting places was easy; getting things done was also simple. Therefore why hurry?

For the cruising yachtsman, New Zealand is a major milestone on a trip around the world. Emerging from the long white cloud that appears before the land itself comes into view, the country is an oasis to the cruising sailor. After months, or years, in the islands of the South Pacific, which, though full of culture and interest, often lack the conveniences the industrialized world has come to take for granted, New Zealand is a place where one can relax, feel at home, and yet still experience the uniqueness of a foreign country. Although the Kiwis speak

English, New Zealand is not England or the U.S.A., but rather a distinct and wonderful place all its own.

TAKU's work list was extensive. One cannot sail for more than two years and for thousands of miles without having maintenance to be done. The average boatowner in New England launches in late May or early June and keeps his or her boat in the water until sometime in late September or early October. During this four-month period, if he or she were to sail the boat both days of every weekend (highly doubtful given the New England climate and probability of rainy weekends), it would be used for a total of thirty-two days. Add to that a two or three week vacation period and another fifteen days maximum are tacked onto the usage column. That gives a maximum utilization of forty-seven days; the actual average usage is probably thirty days or less.

TAKU, in New Zealand, had been under way from home for more than two years, or some 750 days. No wonder I felt like there was a lot to be done. Most boats had arranged long-term haulouts in Whangarei, some 100 miles south of the Bay of Islands. Whangarei boasted a full-service yard, and the town also offered the necessary ancillary services that a boat on the hard might need. There were hardware stores, ships' chandlers, sailmakers, machine shops, and electronics repair services. One advantage to spending time in a land that has such a vast coastline and an intense interest in the sea was the ability to get things fixed or replaced with comparative ease.

The big debate ranging among the yachties concerned travel. We all wanted to see the country. New Zealand had mountains, fjords, glaciers, hot springs, national parks, sandy beaches, rugged coastlines, interesting cities, subtropical rainforests, and flora and fauna of all sorts to suit every taste. We all intended to get out and see as much as we could. Should we do our boat work first and then go sightseeing? Or should we set aside a time for sightseeing and then come back and do the boat work? There were advocates for both approaches.

For me, with a list of jobs to do in Panama that said "finish in Tahiti," a list of jobs from Tahiti that said "try to get these done in Pago," and a long list from Pago that is arrowed through and says "to be finished in New Zealand if possible," the decision was clear. I had not sailed almost halfway around the world just to do boat work. I could do boat work forever and still have more left to do. Of course, there were essential jobs to be done, but they could be completed with some planning and organization. And wouldn't a relaxed, happy sailor just back from a few weeks ashore do a better job, have more energy to put into the work?

TAKU's crew would join the long pilgrimage of yachties heading out to see the country while the few people with troubled consciences would stay and get all their jobs done (if possible) before venturing forth. We did, however, spend a fast week at a small yard in Opua where we tied up alongside the dock at high tide and sat on a grid at each low. The tide would rise and fall and we would ride up and down the well-fendered pilings while work was going on. The secondary winches were moved from the bridgedeck to aft and outboard on to newly fabricated stainless mounting bases; a loose weld in the bow pulpit was strengthened, and some other stainless fabricating was carried out. The main hatch was removed and freed up; long swelling with salt water had made it sticky. A hole was cut in the deck and a deck prism installed over the galley to emit more light. Some carpentry modifications and additions were carried out below. Any job that I thought I couldn't fix, that took either a skilled craftsman or a specialized tool (like the welding), was completed in short order. Now we could go away and leave the boat for a month or so and then come back with ample time to carry out the routine maintenance jobs on my list. The difference between a 35-foot boat and a 41-foot boat is really simple. The 41-footer allows you to carry more maintenance problems along with you.

TAKU went on to a mooring in Opua, and we went off in a 1963 four-door, right-hand-drive Triumph that we had purchased in Whangarei for the princely sum of $2,300. The poor old car had over 200,000 miles on it, and was, at the time we combed the used car lots, the cheapest vehicle available. To preserve their currency against depletion by foreign exchange, the Kiwis have imposed a terrifically high duty on all imports. Unlike home, things in New Zealand are repaired and kept rather than discarded. Ours was not the only old car on the road. Most of the other yachties were similarly fitted out with rolling stock from the used car lots of Whangarei or Auckland. So, too, were a great many New Zealanders themselves. My sense of living in a past time came about in part from the number of vintage cars that plied the roads of this wonderful country. There were ample panel beaters (body shops) to keep them repaired and on the go. With the demand for cars exceeding the supply, we all felt we could buy vehicles for our six-month stays, use them, and then resell them for what we paid or for only a slight loss and thus avoid high public transportation charges. In almost every case this proved to be true.

How can one understand New Zealand without having been there? The pictures in books do not do justice to this spectacular and wonderful country. From Cape Reinga on the northern tip of the North Island to wonderful, windy Wellington on the north edge of Cook Strait, which separates the North from South Island, to Christchurch and Queenstown on the South Island, all the way south to Invercargill perched on the southern edge of the country, the scenery is extraordinary. Yachtie crews used to lapping up sea miles at the snail's pace of five or six knots sped from one end of the country to the other. Fifty miles an hour in a car allow one to cover a lot of territory. We all took in all the sights from Milford Sound and Mount Cook in the south to Ninety Mile beach in the north. From the hot springs to the caves, from the coast to the mountains, we all saw as much as we could.

Late summer in New Zealand had arrived, and the roadside stands were filled with strawberries, kiwi fruit, apples, plums, and vegetables of all sizes, colors, and descriptions. The weather continued stable and warm. Driving in a car one started to forget about reefing sails, taking fixes, putting on foul-weather gear, eating on a slant, bathing in cold water, and sleeping in odd patterns. New Zealand rejuvenated our bodies, re-invigorated our souls. We were refreshed, energized, and content. We had rendezvoused at various campgrounds with Mike and Tim, Dave and Marcia, and a host of other boat crews that were out on the road. We shared museum trips, gondola rides, trail rides, hikes, and thoughts and ideas about the future. And suddenly it was the end of March, and we were back on our boats getting ready for the next leg of the journey around the world.

TAKU couldn't have done it without Kim and Merv U'ren. They were Kiwi friends of another pair of yachties, Red and Ruth Brooks, a couple in their sixties, on their second circumnavigation aboard their lovely sloop TUFFY. By chance I met Kim and Merv on the dock in Russell and gave them a lift out to TUFFY in my dinghy. By the time we completed the 10-minute trip we were fast friends, and I had been "adopted" by this warm-hearted couple.

Celia had arranged to work at Hood's sail loft in Auckland in exchange for the loft building TAKU a new main and mizzen at a substantial discount. I planned to sail the boat to Half Moon Bay, south of

Auckland, haul out there, and get as many jobs done as time would permit. Before we knew what had happened, Kim had taken Celia home with her to live until TAKU could make the trip down to Auckland, and Merv had come aboard to help me for the four-day sail down the rugged coast.

Merv was a recently retired mechanic and not much of a sailor. But he was a good companion and could hold the wheel while I put the sails up and down or lowered or raised the anchor. He was a quiet and soft-spoken little man. (I seemed always to tower above him.) He raised orchids in his spare time, and with his recent retirement he suddenly had more spare time than his orchids needed. We had long talks on our way to Auckland about TAKU's travels and all the work that had to be done. "I have some spare time," Merv told me. "Maybe I could give you a hand?"

"Why not?" I thought, sensing that after a day or so of giving a hand Merv would be delighted to get back to his orchids. This was not to be. Every day for the six weeks TAKU was in Half Moon Bay, Celia would leave by eight o'clock for her job at the loft, and shortly thereafter Merv's lime-green Escort would trundle into the yard and park under TAKU's bow. "Good-day mate," Merv would smile up at me. "Let's get at that list."

We did everything. The alternator went out for repair. We took the chain to be regalvanized. We pulled the engine and sent it to the machine shop in the yard for some repairs while we engineered new mountings. We sanded and painted the bottom. We replaced hoses and hose clamps. We got the refrigeration up and running. Each day the list grew a bit shorter. Whenever we hit a snag, Merv would push his glasses back on to the top of his head and think and then say something like, "C'mon, let's go. I have a mate who works for a mob over in Ponsonby. He'll know how to fix this (or where to get this replaced)." And the mate would, or the mate would have a mate that would. Round Auckland we would buzz in the lime-green car, gathering up necessary bits and pieces for the next job.

My interaction with Merv didn't stop at the end of the work day. At quitting time, Merv would force me quietly into his car. We would drive across Auckland and the Auckland bridge to his house. There Kim would have a multicourse dinner ("It's just leftovers") waiting. "Take a shower first, Dom. It looks like Merv has done you in again. Did you bring your laundry. No? Well, you must bring it tomorrow; it will give me something to do."

Celia would arrive from the sail loft, and we would have a family supper at the U'rens, ending always with a massive special New Zealand dessert. "It's only a *pavlova*," Kim would say as she produced a magnificent equivalent to a fantastic strawberry shortcake. Over dessert and coffee we would sit and look out the enormous sliding glass doors toward the city of Auckland and the islands of the Hauraki Gulf. Then it would be back to TAKU for the night.

"They are too generous," I would say to Celia. "Merv is giving up all of his time to work on the boat. He shouldn't do that. I'm going to speak to Kim." The next night after dinner I did so.

"Kim, I am concerned that Merv is working so hard on my list. I'm fully prepared to do as much as I can; he needn't feel obligated to do so much. And neither should you. You have treated us wonderfully, but surely we are getting to be a burden."

Kim took me aside to make sure she wasn't overheard. "If Merv is a bother, please tell me. You don't know how good it is to have you here. He was very depressed after he retired and sat around the house feeling glum all day. Even his orchids didn't cheer him up. Now he bounds up every day full of energy. His health has improved, and I am so happy to see him act like his own self again. He is happier than I have seen him in years. We love having you, and if you don't mind having Merv around, it is doing him, and us, a world of good."

"We didn't have this conversation," I said, as Kim gave me a hug. The next day it was business as usual at the boat. Celia didn't work at Hood's on Sundays, and on those days the lime-green car would arrive with both Merv and Kim.

"You can't work seven days a week. We are off on an excursion," Kim would say. "I've packed a picnic." We would be taken to an orchid show or to a hot springs for a therapeutic soak. Sometimes we would go for scenic drives along the Coromandel peninsula. Or we would visit one of the many vineyards that produce New Zealand's excellent wines. We saw as much of the greater Auckland area as the Sundays available permitted.

Our chain was back, as was the engine, reinstalled by me and Merv. It was running well. Celia and some fellow sailmakers came with the new main and mizzen and bent them on and then took them off again to make last-minute adjustments. TAKU was gradually coming back into shape. A new, full–sized dodger was installed, replacing the small companionway dodger that had given scant protection against spray and wind. By the end of April we were back in the water and doing sea trials in the Hauraki Gulf. We took Merv and Kim sailing whenever we could and whenever they would come.

The Triumph went back to a used car dealer, and TAKU, along with the cruising boats that still remained in the Auckland area, moved to Marsden Wharf in the heart of downtown Auckland. With Merv's continuing help, provisions were brought in and stored aboard. Fall, in New Zealand, was well under way. The days were crisp and cold. I found myself wearing my down vest as I moved around outside. We fired up and used the charcoal cabin heater that had been unused for over two years. The time had arrived to move north, back to the tropics.

23

New Destinations

June, New Zealand

Dear Gene,

Your tape just caught me, as we are a bit late getting away. Delighted to hear the Christmas party. Seems like Christmas gets a bit earlier each year. The weather here has gotten cold so the tape seemed quite seasonal even for June. We're off toward Japan via New Caledonia, Vanuatu (I know, "Where's that?"), and the Solomons.

Peace,

MAÑANA and INOA had already left for New Caledonia, and we tracked their 1,200-mile passage by radio. LA NUI and SEAVENTURE had departed for long trips, the former to Hawaii and the latter to San Francisco via Hawaii. Mickey had told me not to go too fast. "You guys go bop around in the Solomons for a bit and then cruise up to New Guinea or Japan. I plan to sail back to Honolulu and put my business in order and then backtrack out here again. We'll catch you before you get across the Indian Ocean. We'll stay in touch by radio." We were to do that, but within a year Mickey Searle, good cruising friend, had died of cancer at the age of 33. His unexpected death was a sobering loss that affected all of us who knew and loved him.

The time came to depart. Customs brought our gun. The last possible bottle of New Zealand wine had found a place below. On a cold, raw, early June day, we bid farewell to Merv and Kim, who had come down to the wharf in the now familiar lime-green Escort. They planned to drive out to a bluff overlooking the harbor and watch TAKU leave. We were off for New Caledonia with deadlines to meet. Marcia and Dave on MANAÑA had reported by radio that the weather there was wonderfully warm and tropical and the anchorages were safe and comfortable; we were in heavy sweaters and down vests as Auckland's winter was setting in. We wanted to catch up with them since we planned to sail together with them and Mike and Tim on INOA toward Japan.

On the chart table was also taped the time of arrival of a flight in New Caledonia. My 14-year-old son, Peter, was coming in ten days' time to spend his summer vacation. We had a rendezvous to make.

Merv threw our lines aboard, and after backing out of Marsden Wharf, we raised the sparkling new main and mizzen. They set beautifully. The staysail went up and started to draw. Then the yankee was unfurled, and TAKU, her bottom clean and her gear shipshape, stood out through the Hauraki Gulf bound for New Caledonia. "It's nice to be under way again," I told Celia. I thought about the letter that had arrived the previous day that was tucked safely in the chart drawer. I had sold my first article to *Cruising World*. A magazine was paying me money for something I had written. The prospect of doing more excited me, but writing would have to wait. Down below the new SatNav updated our position. My navigation chores were reduced and I felt as though we had an extra crewman aboard. The shoreline became less distinct. The details of New Zealand were blending back into a long white cloud. The land was no longer New Zealand, but rather had become *Aoteaora* again. On the highest bluff I could make out, with the aid of binoculars, the lime-green shape of Merv and Kim U'ren's car. Every few minutes I would wave my arms over my head in their direction. I could not see Merv and Kim, but I kept waving long after the car, and then the bluff, faded from view.

The trip to New Caledonia took us back to Gardner McKay land. As we sailed into Noumea, the capital, after a nine-day bash, we looked far from my remembered vision of *Tiki*. Dressed in full foul-weather gear, harnesses, and boots, we had completed what was certainly a forgettable passage from New Zealand. I was beginning to believe that most passages were of the forgettable sort. After all, if I had wanted just to go sailing I could have stayed home in New England, which has some of the best sailing waters in the world. Or if I had wanted to combine cruising with sailing, I could have remained in the Virgin Islands which boasts endless anchorages and warm tradewind weather.

Ear wafers, the current talisman against seasickness, were stuck behind our ears. The patch (*Transderm Scop*) that had been "invented" for the space program had become available to the public while we had been in New Zealand and was now in general use on most yachts. It worked for me. One of the nicer attributes of the patch was that you stuck it behind your ear, which meant that if your stomach was upset, you didn't have to swallow medication or keep it down. The patch also lasted for three days, and if that wasn't enough time to get your sea legs you could then put one behind the other ear for another three days and so forth.

I was now managing to read and to do tasks below that I had not been able to do during the first two years of the voyage without some degree of discomfort or outright nausea. I would speculate, of course, that it wasn't the patch, but rather I was becoming acclimated to the motion of the sea after all this time. Nonetheless, it was nice not to feel queasy; I wasn't about to try passage making without the patch. Most yachties get seasick at some point or another. There are very few who can say truthfully that they have never been seasick or felt queasy whatever the weather. Feeling unsettled was a hazard of the "job" to which we had become resigned. For some, the ear patch had uncomfortable side effects: nervousness, dry mouth, anxiety. But for me it worked fine. In the ensuing years of using it I have never had any problems. I have also discovered that I can cut the patch in half and apply only half for a short trip; half a patch still works for me, but not for as long.

Bleary-eyed, fatigued, and anxious for a harbor, we presented a far different view from the one in "Adventures in Paradise" I remembered. We were missing one horseshoe ring with man-overboard light that had been washed overboard from its bracket when we had been boarded by a large sea off the quarter. The sea had merely picked the horseshoe from its bracket above the pushpit and taken it away. We did not feel too bad about this loss when friends on MARAMA, a large Australian ketch that departed New Zealand at the same time we had, reported the loss of both their horseshoe rings while enroute to Fiji. We felt even better later when we read that WANDERER V, the Hiscocks' famous boat, with its new owners aboard, also lost a horseshoe en route to Fiji at about the same time and in the same sort of weather. Somewhere, either floating in the Pacific or on a beach or in a hut on a tropical isle must be quite a collection of horseshoe rings. No matter. We still had another. The surviving horseshoe ring, however, leaned rakishly (the only rakish thing about TAKU) at a 45-degree angle into the cockpit along with a bent stanchion (also at 45 degrees), a damaged pushpit, and a torn and frayed weathercloth, all caught and rearranged in a tableau by a heavy pounding, early winter, boarding wave at sea.

We motored to the wharf with our sails still reefed and tied loosely to their booms. No line handlers came to meet us. One of us shinnied up the five feet necessary to reach the wharf and made TAKU fast. After we waited patiently under our Q flag for several hours, the officials arrived, and after filling out reams of forms for customs and immigration officials who spoke only French, we were finally cleared to anchor in the crowded harbor. There, surrounded by boats we knew from New Zealand, and with a good meal put away, we felt as though we were back in Paradise again.

Peter arrived safely the next day, and with his gear stowed aboard we set off for the next leg of the journey, which would take us through the Loyalty Islands, to Vanuatu, and up through the Solomons to Papua New Guinea. Most of the sailing, with the exception of one or two short two to two and a half day passages happened in daily hops. Navigation took place by eyeing the next island on the horizon and setting sail. There was time in the various anchorages to go ashore and explore or just to enjoy the peace of this less explored area of Melanesia. A half-dozen or so other boats were making the same basic trip: INOA, MAÑANA, JANE, SHAMMY, FLEETWOOD, and BROWN PALACE, all saw one another regularly, and a night's anchorage would often find TAKU next to one or more of these friends. The company was usually welcome.

Day to day was routine. Up early, a good breakfast, a look at the weather, stow for sea, a look at the chart, up anchor, up sails, another look at the chart and then establish the course for the new destination. The sailing was usually brisk and fun. We would choose destinations that were not overly long or stressful. We would arrive early enough to set the anchor, put up the awning if necessary, and have enough time remaining to swim and then to go ashore to walk on the beach or to the local village (if there was one). Gradually we worked our way up the island chains. Everything was routine, or so we thought.

24

Captain Blood

Force 2, brilliant clear blue skies, flat seas, and TAKU is making a good five knots under genoa, staysail, main, mizzen staysail, and mizzen. The world is a combination of blues and greens. The bright rich blue of the sea contrasts with the paler blue of the sky and with the varying shades of green that are distinguishable on the surrounding islands. We are sailing through history, having left Honiara, the present capital of the Solomon Islands on Guadalcanal, to cross Iron Bottom Sound for Tulagi in the Florida Group, a bit north and within sight some 24 miles away.

History, we've learned, has brought many people to the Solomons since they were first recorded by the Spanish explorer Alvaro de Mendaña: the British, who took over and ruled these islands for many years; the Japanese, who drove out the British; the Americans, who drove out the Japanese; a variety of soldiers-of-fortune, traders, merchants, freebooters, missionaries, voyagers, and us. The Solomon islanders, descendants of the local inhabitants that Mendaña must have met, have managed to survive despite the various occupations, which grew to a wild crescendo in World War II.

We try to imagine convoys, air bombardments, P.T. boats, capital ships, and the rest of the war disturbing this tropic sea, but all is quiet now. The only noise is TAKU's bow wave as she moves closer to the Floridas. Below us Iron Bottom Sound seems peaceful and serene. If we could see far into its 300- to 400-fathom depths we might distinguish the rusting hulks and wreckage of the worst defeat suffered by the U.S. Navy and the Allies in World War II. In a 50-minute engagement Australia's CANBERRA was sunk, as were America's ASTORIA, QUINCY, and VINCENNES. Critically damaged were the CHICAGO and RALPH TALBOT.

Japanese losses were limited to one ship torpedoed while returning up "the slot" to Rabaul, Papua New Guinea.

We are about nine degrees south of the Equator, and the sun has been direct and hot overhead for a large part of this late October day. I figure we have about two hours of daylight left, ample time to thread our way through the fishing nets and into mangrove- and coral-encircled Tokoyo Bay.

Celia, chart in hand, climbs the maststeps as we motor along at about four and a half knots. She sits relaxed on the port spreader, one arm about the mast, and shouts above the engine, "It's okay; I can see the reefs. Come a bit to port—good!" For all their beauty, the Floridas have some treacherous coral reefs and heads, often inches below the surface of the otherwise 200- to 300-foot-deep water. Some are well charted, and others aren't. We have a local Solomon Island chart produced on blueprint paper, the Sailing Directions, and a local cruising guide written by Australian cruising guru, Alan Lucas, to assist us. (We will later meet Alan in the Med and share many excellent and happy times with him, his wife, Patricia, and son, Will, aboard their boat TIENTOS.)

Even armed with all of this back-up assistance we prefer to have someone in the spreaders to "read" the water. All three of us have mastered this valuable technique, and the distinguishing blues of the deep water contrasted with the greens and pale greens, whites and browns of the shallows appear to the one aloft like a giant colored chart beneath the boat. In part we are now anxious to get in and get anchored, for the late afternoon sun makes the water difficult to read, and the area we are in is hazardous.

As we move into the final channel to Tokoyo Bay, Peter goes to the bowsprit to act as an additional lookout. Extra eyes are always helpful when piloting in unfamiliar waters in close quarters. Peter has now been aboard for about four months and has become a valued member of the TAKU crew. The channel winds and twists through the fringing reefs. We are moving through 80 feet of water with depths of two to three feet sharply delineating the channel. We hope to round the final dogleg and anchor for the night in about 20 to 40 feet—mud, good holding—with fellow cruisers aboard MAÑANA and FLEETWOOD and in sight of a sunken Japanese World War II destroyer we hope to dive on. The sun has slipped lower, and the water begins to glint gold. It sparkles brightly, and

I realize that I can no longer read the water from the helm. I call to Celia: "I can't see anything now. How much farther?"

She replies, "Not too far; I can still see the reefs pretty well, but if the sun gets much lower, it'll be really hard. Come a little right." My hands turn the wheel slightly right, and I watch the land in front as it appears to slide to the left of the headstay. Peter yells from the bow, "I can't see anything anymore because of the glare."

In a few brief moments the water has turned into a glimmering gold sheet. The effect is dazzling; we float on a solid gold ocean that once was blue, surrounded by bright green mangroves and hills and occasional brilliant white patches of sand. As I marvel at the colors and the sheer beauty of the moment, the mangroves on the port side suddenly open up and there, also floating on a sea of gold, are MAÑANA and FLEETWOOD anchored near the hulk of the former destroyer. "There are MAÑANA and FLEETWOOD," I yell, glad to be at the end of the day, ready to anchor, have a cold beer, swap some stories. Within the time it takes me to have this thought, there is a loud crunching sound followed by a jolt, and TAKU comes to a dead stop from four and a half knots. I am thrown against the wheel. Simultaneously Celia screams. I jam the engine into neutral, and my whole body is shaking as adrenaline rushes here and there to replace the tranquil feelings with those less familiar, but dreaded ones of fear and apprehension.

Peter yells that he can see coral right below the water at the bow and along the port side. Celia arrives on deck shaking. She explains that when the boat stopped she was thrown from the spreader and only her arm around the mast stopped her from a nonstop plunge to the deck. She managed to swing herself around and catch the maststeps with her feet so that she could climb down. None of us knows exactly what happened. We see dinghies pulling out into the gold sea from FLEETWOOD and MAÑANA and heading our way. "We hit so hard and stopped so suddenly we may have holed." As I say this I am staggered by the implications. "We had better check before we try to get off." Celia grabs a mask and fins and splashes quickly over the side, followed by Peter, while I rush below. I pull up floorboards and open cabinets, dreading the thought of what we might be up against if water is pouring in.

My initial examination reveals no obvious holes, but the possibility of cracks in the hull and damage to the keel always exists. I remember that Airex—TAKU's hull material—is supposed to be strong and flexible, and I give thanks for that. I go back on deck to hear Celia and Peter's report. "We're right on the edge of the reef and seem to be caught on the bottom of the keel and all along the port side," Celia yells from the water. "I don't see any major damage."

"Okay. C'mon back on board, and let's see if we can get ourselves off. What a mess! I don't understand how we hit. What on earth were you looking at up there?" Fear and apprehension have given way to their less pleasant cousins, tension and anger.

"Everything, including the water, went all gold; I was about to tell you to slow down when you yelled that you saw MAÑANA and FLEET-WOOD. I looked over and bang!" Celia is obviously as upset as I am, and we take another look at the chart and the cruising guide and realize that the reef extends farther than either of them indicate. It has grown. We should have thought of that possibility. We have apparently caught the edge just before the turn.

By now Dave and Marcia are there as well as our old cruising friend Randy Brown from FLEETWOOD. "Are you guys okay?" asks Marcia. All of us have heard of groundings and boat losses since we have been in the South Pacific. Often these have been of boats with whom we have shared anchorages. We have all discussed how to avoid groundings and been through all the "what I'd do's."

The new arrivals are shaken and concerned. Dave adds, "Man, you really stopped dead! Any damage?" I reply that there is none that I can see.

Randy tries to smile reassuringly. "Just tell us what you want us to do; we're here as long as you need us. Jamie is in the middle of cooking something but can come right over if you need her as well." I feel a tightening in my throat as Randy says this. No condemnations, no hassles, just friendship, camaraderie, and support.

I realize that everyone is waiting for me to act, to generate a plan, to take charge, while I, too, am standing around hoping the situation will take care of itself. "Let me see if we can back her off," I offer, secretly hoping that merely by putting the engine in reverse we'll back away from our troubles as easily as one leaves a slip or dock. I put the engine into reverse and watch the wake as the water from the turning propeller swirls behind us. I push the rpm up, and as they climb I look to the shoreline to watch expectantly, yet vainly, for the mangroves to begin to move. Nothing happens. The engine temperature climbs, and the boat shakes from the vibrations induced by the high rpm. But we are, indeed, stuck fast. I shut the engine down and try to act enthusiastic: "No go. I guess we'll have to kedge off."

In the books kedging always sounds simple. Even the old square-riggers used to do it. Just send a hearty boat crew out in the long boat with a spare anchor, wrap the rode about the old capstan, and have the crew walk in circles, pushing on the capstan bars while the boss of the whole operation stands around in the equivalent of today's expensive striped sailing shirts singing sea chanties. I think that's how Errol Flynn did it in *Captain Blood*. The old ship moved without any troubles at all. So we get out our Danforth 22H, which we use for a kedge, and our hearty boat crew of Randy and Peter take it out in our inflatable version of the long boat (more a fat boat), and at the end of our 250 feet of rode they drop it into the now-darkening water. Dave makes it fast to our version of a capstan, a self-tailing primary winch, and starts to grind. Marcia lends Dave a hand, and we see the rode stretch tight as the anchor bites and starts to hold. Dave can barely gain on the line so we run it across the cockpit and take the tail to the other primary. Peter and Dave crank simultaneously, but we don't move. Randy and I try, but the line is stretched tight. I rev up the engine in reverse and punch it to the limit. Suddenly there is a terrible grinding and bad vibration in the engine. I shut it down and go glumly to investigate. "Errol Flynn never had these problems," I mutter as I go below.

I discover, as I suspected, that we have backed the shaft out of the coupling, and so, for the moment, we are without an engine. This uncoupling has happened before, despite Merv's and my attempts to correct the problem in New Zealand. I know I must wait until the engine cools down before attempting any repairs. Our concern, once I am back on deck, shifts to what will happen if the tide drops. Various opinions are voiced, and none of us can figure out exactly what the stage of the tide is. We use the "pragmatic experience" approach. Randy thinks that it is falling because when he rowed over the tide seemed to be way up the mangroves, as it might appear if it were high. Dave thinks it's about high, as does Celia, since we are already in the middle of a dis-aster, and naturally we couldn't expect the tide to be favorable.

Marcia, Peter, and I agree that the tide is far from high, and is, in fact, coming in. My evidence is that this is what I want it to be. Marcia and Peter offer that two weeks before when they were ashore at the yacht club in Honiara for a movie the tide was higher after the movie than it was before it. None of us think to consult the tide tables. We do all agree that there is only one high tide a day in the Solomons, which launches another round of discussions as to how this is possible. It, too, is inconclusive.

We decide to try to secure TAKU so she won't shift if the tide is dropping. Dave and Marcia go back to MAÑANA to get a 35-pound Danforth with a 300-foot rode, while Randy and Peter row out our 45-pound CQR and its 300 feet of line from its home on the bowsprit. We have the other 45-pound CQR on the sprit with 400 feet of chain attached but dread the notion of trying to row it out. It was the anchor that we had to dump in Fiji, and while in New Zealand I had shortened its chain by 100 feet, but it still had a lot of links attached. I know that we also have a 75-pound fisherman and a 45-pound Luke with rodes if we need them.

While everyone is occupied, Celia and I hold a war council. "What do you think?" we both ask simultaneously. I speak first.

"I think the tide is rising despite the vote. Whatever happens, we've got to get off." I look around. "Jeez, I didn't realize it was so dark; where'd all the daylight go? Let's proceed methodically. If all else fails we can get a government boat from Tulagi to come tomorrow and tow us off, though I hate to think what that'll cost." So much for war councils.

By now Randy and Peter are back, and the CQR has taken a strain on the bow. Dave and Marcia return with their 35-pound anchor, and we rig it off the quarter. TAKU is now held off the reef by three points, and if the tide drops we won't shift except into deeper water. We now proceed, like the Keystone Cops, with the old standbys.

With Marcia, Celia, and Peter clinging to the boom, we swing it out over the water, while Dave, Randy, and I attempt to winch us off. Nothing happens. "We've got to lighten up." We dump the remaining CQR and 400 feet of chain on the reef to try to raise the bow. We remember, as in Fiji, to buoy the end of the chain. We lift the Dyer dinghy from its place on deck and swing it out over the water and then fill it with as much gear as we can. We try combinations of the above. We alternately winch and have everyone "sally ship," running from side to side. (As I recall, Hornblower used that technique quite effectively.) We are now working under the spreader lights with pitch darkness surrounding the boat. We try everyone on the bow, on the stern, on the boom, and in the dinghy, but we are still stuck fast.

"That's it guys—go home—get some sleep; we'll try again tomorrow. If we have to, we can unload the internal ballast. We've got about ten or twelve 90-pound lead pigs and also another 100 feet of chain under the floorboards. And we can always pump the tanks. That's almost 300 gallons combined of water and fuel."

"You guys relax; we'll get you off tomorrow," Randy assures us. "We'll all keep the radio on channel 68, and if anything at all happens and you need us, just yell."

"Just call," Marcia adds. "G'night guys . . . cheer up." They row off into the dark, and we are left alone under the stars, fast to the land with ropes, anchors, and keel. What has been orderly and shipshape is now a confused mess of lines and gear.

Celia interrupts the silence to ask, "Do you want anything to eat?" I realize suddenly how tired and keyed up I am.

"Peter, put the VHF on 68, will you?" Peter goes below to comply.

Both Peter and Celia know me well enough to leave me alone at times like these. It takes a while to get over feeling foolish that you got yourself in a bad situation and feeling frustrated that you can't get yourself out. I walk about the decks checking the three anchors. The lines are stretched drum-tight. In the cockpit the depthsounder, inadvertently left on, winks four feet, four feet, four feet accusingly at me. I reach over and snap it off and feel a little better.

I reach in the companionway and push the bilgepump switch from automatic to manual. Holding the spring switch on, I pump the standing water in the bilge so that if TAKU leaks during the night and the bilgepump goes on I'll know we have started with nothing and that we are shipping water. The only sound in the darkness is the splash of the water coming out of the bilge. There is more than I thought there would be, and finally the splashing stops. The bilge is as empty as it can get. I prepare to go below for the night and take one last look, as is my custom. I always check the anchor bearings before retiring, only tonight I know it is a futile effort. As I watch the silhouette of the shore, it appears to move slightly, and suddenly it moves rapidly. I shake my head as though to clear it, and realize that the shore isn't moving, but that TAKU is sliding rapidly astern as the taut anchor lines draw her away from the reef.

"We're off! We're sliding off," I shout as I run to the bow to confirm that we have shifted. Celia arrives on deck in an instant, yelling happily, "We're off, we're off, we're off!" Down below I hear Peter on the radio calling, "FLEETWOOD, FLEETWOOD, MAÑANA, MAÑANA—we're off, we're off, we're off."

We all start taking up on the now-slackening anchor lines, and I turn the depthsounder back on: 13 feet, 18 feet, 24 feet, 37 feet, 41 feet, where it finally stops. We draw the three anchors tight as Dave, Marcia, Randy, and Jamie arrive and climb aboard. There is much laughing and backslapping and good humor. The shared prospective dread that we all had of the following day is eased. Everyone gradually quiets down. We decide to stay where we are for the night, as we are riding on three well-set hooks away from the reef. Things settle down. MAÑANA and FLEET-WOOD, shouting congratulations and goodnights, head for home again, and we watch their flashlights as they row off. Peter goes to bed. Celia is fading, too. "Goodnight, Captain Blood! You got us off."

Once again I'm left with the depthsounder; it winks reassuringly now: 41 feet, 41 feet, 41 feet. I check my watch. It's only 2200. Ten hours earlier we were broad-reaching across Iron Bottom Sound. A little over five hours earlier we were about to turn and anchor for the night. It seems like days ago. And then for five hours we have worked to rescue TAKU. There has been no storm; our lives have never been in danger. But the anxieties, tensions, and efforts have been real and intense. The moon slips up from behind a hill, and I can see the once afternoon-gold water shimmer in silver blue. I can pick out the shapes of MAÑANA and FLEETWOOD clearly now, and a bit farther I can make out the shape of the Japanese destroyer.

Overhead the stars whirl as they have for countless years. Once again cruising has illuminated one of those brief moments of recognition of mortality, of history, of the balance we attempt to strike with nature and the world as we sail—and how quickly and unexpectedly it can all shift and change. My reverie is changed as I feel TAKU shift ever so slightly on her tackle. It is a barely perceptible feeling, but one I have come to know and recognize well in the 17,000 miles of cruising that have taken place thus far. Reassuring and soothing, the motion is the best and most continual statement that a boat makes. Tonight it is a particularly welcome statement. The world is tranquil, sheened in silver. No matter that the next day it will take us seven hours to recover our three anchors, pick up our 45-pound CQR and its 400 feet of chain from the reef, lift our dinghy back on deck and restow its cargo, coil ropes and line, scrub anchors and deck, and finally spend many of these hours

hanging upside down over the engine to fix the coupling and to recon-
nect the shaft before we can motor 400 yards and reanchor next to
MAÑANA and FLEETWOOD. Tonight the world is silver, and we float, we
float!

25

A Japanese in the Garden

Back again in the islands of the South Pacific after a season in New Zealand we built on what we had learned in our previous season in Polynesia. We had learned that good visiting protocol meant bringing gifts, and we came well supplied: balloons and penny candy for the children, tobacco and cigarettes for the men, and thread, needles, and material for the women. We were given in return drinking coconuts, handmade trinkets, and freshly caught fish and lobster. I learned not to worry about the topsides of poor old TAKU; the occasional canoe bump was rare, accidental, and less troublesome than trying to chase people away to protect her. We learned that if we expected to visit ashore, having visitors from ashore on board was part of the deal. We learned that if you could relax, the whole experience was fun. And we learned about trading.

Trading was much more prevalent in Melanesia than it had been in Polynesia. People seemed to have more time on their hands, for trading was never quick. It takes a while to decide whether to trade at all. The local islander will bring what he or she has to trade by canoe to your boat and then will look carefully at the items you want to trade while you check out his or hers. Trading in the islands of the South Pacific is an age-old ritual continued in modern time. After a few trades you get the hang of it. One thing we learned was to bring out only one item at a time to offer for exchange and to be firm.

We learned these guidelines from watching Tim when he and Mike anchored INOA next to TAKU in one of Guadalcanal's many anchorages. Tim became enamored of a beautiful shell necklace. Its owner, a young man, was a masterful trader and during a long afternoon taught Tim all there was to know about trading. Tim was a slow learner.

Tim offered Jason a T-shirt in exchange for the necklace, about the going rate. Jason said he didn't like that T-shirt, whereupon Tim began to bring up T-shirts for Jason's inspection. Jason would look at them, try them on, hold them up, and reject each in turn. Tim wanted the necklace desperately, so he began bringing up all sorts of his best clothes. Jason examined each item and then asked if Tim had anything else. Out came a harmonica, which Jason played and set aside. Tim then showed him his snorkel gear, followed by a cassette tape, a Swiss army knife, and a myriad other things. By the end of the afternoon Jason had seen absolutely everything Tim owned and was no closer to trading his necklace than when he started. In fact, he had realized what a powerful necklace he had. Why, he had only to put it away and Tim would rush below and come up with something else to show him. Jason apparently decided he would reserve this new power and left Tim sitting in a cockpit full of belongings.

If Jason was Tim's trading nemesis, TAKU's was Mary. She was a delightful girl with a charming smile, and she came almost every day in her pirogue to trade with us. Mary was not a trader, though, and on top of that, she was painfully shy. Where Jason controlled the situation, Mary was controlled by it. You felt obligated to protect Mary from herself.

Worse still, Mary had some absolutely lovely things to trade. Each day she would skillfully bring her pirogue to within six feet of TAKU. The other traders, like Jason, would always come right alongside, grab the toerail, and tie up to a stanchion. They would put the things they had for sale or trade on the deck and wait while you looked them over. Mary was different. She would sit docilely in her pirogue and, with an occasional subtle and deft twist of the paddle, keep her distance from our quarter. We would call hello and try to engage her in conversation. After a few days we managed to learn her name, what village she lived in, and that she did, indeed, have something to trade. We even managed to coax her alongside.

The first day alongside she produced a magnificent string of shell money; it was one of the most exquisite we had seen. Its bands of colors were made up of tiny shells and pieces of coral: reds, whites, blacks, and yellows, each shaped and formed to match the others and then drilled and strung in intricate and harmonious patterns. In the traditional, non-cash economy, shell money was a way in which families could accumulate wealth. A young man desiring a bride would have to come up with many yards of the intricately made "money" as a bride price. Relatives would help him make it and accumulate it and then it would be given to the bride's family in exchange for the bride. Possession of strings of shell money was a sign of success in a local family.

In the modern economy, bride prices had all but disappeared and shell money was sold to tourists (the few there were) and to yachties who sailed by. The string that Mary offered was magnificent and worth $15 to $20 American money, a top price, at the going rate. Jason's goods paled in comparison. Now, normally a trade might take the better part of the day as Tim had learned in dealing with Jason. You would be shown the various items, and after looking them over you might set one or two aside in which you were "possibly" interested. We all learned that too much enthusiasm for any particular item would, with a sharp local trader, put its price out of sight immediately.

Our initial attitude had been a Rousseau echo. Here we were dealing with the "noble savage," and weren't we lucky to be doing that, and wasn't it great to acquire some local artifact, regardless of its cost? A few Jasons quickly disabused most cruisers of that notion. As we accumulated more experience and more goods, we became shrewder traders. We were able to curtail our enthusiasm for any particular item. We learned, painfully, to be able to say no when prices were too high. And we discovered the traditional trading methods: You finally select an item and ask the price. You are given the first price, usually very high, which you are supposed to refuse immediately.

Your refusal will trigger a second price, usually lower than the first but still, according to tradition, too high. With your best disparaging look you then offer a much lower price (opinions differ on whether it should be one-third or one-half the second price). The seller will then give you his or her third price, which is somewhere between your offer and his or her second and which is generally accepted to be the "fair," or market, price of the item. Getting through the items and to the final price can take a great deal of time and try even a poker player's patience. But time is in ample supply in the South Pacific, and if you want to trade you spend it or you pay. Celia, old poker player that she was, loved it. I, on the other hand, was, to Celia's dismay, more likely to pay the first price in order to get on to other things.

"Dom," she would say, "you just can't do that. Trading is an art form, a local activity; you can't disappoint these people." Peter would agree.

"What about me?" I would reply in a moment of pique. "Eating, or sleeping, or doing anything here is getting to be an art form. Every time I try to do something, another canoeload of used-artifact salesmen bang on the hull and want several hours of my time. You and Peter want to play Trader Vic and trade—you trade, but leave me out of it."

For a while I was left out of it. Celia and Peter did the trading, and our supply of carvings, shells, and artifacts grew. Occasionally I'd be called on to give an opinion or to look at something or to meet someone, and on the whole we struck a good balance. I was free to do other things, to enjoy the South Pacific in my own way, to read *Little Dorrit* at my own pace, but I was available. The others were free to trade to their hearts' content. Then we met Mary. There she was with this beautiful shell-money necklace, and I knew that buying it would take the better part of the day. Celia asked her what she wanted for it.

Mary replied, "My father say two hundred dollars." I winced, as obviously it was going to be a long day, but Mary went on, "If not, fifty dollars, and if not, fifteen dollars." She smiled sweetly. So did I! She was obviously new to negotiation. Celia produced the $15 and got the necklace, and Mary left. Each day thereafter she came, having been sent from home with something to sell or barter, and each day it was the same. "My father say . . . , and if not . . . , and if not . . . ," and we'd be at the third price and finished. Celia began to worry about Mary. "People are going to take advantage of her."

To make up for Mary's lack of expertise and finesse as a trader Celia was giving her extras in each trade. Some clothes, a box of cookies, a bracelet for herself—each time Mary left she went away with the third price and a few extra goodies. We began to hypothesize about Mary's conversations at home. "Did you ask first price, daughter?"

"Yes, and then they say no, so I ask second price. When they say no, I get third price and all of this" (showing the extra goodies of the day).

"You are a marvelous trader, daughter. Tomorrow you must go even earlier." If nothing else, we were sure Celia was turning Mary into a trader in the eyes of her family, if not in fact.

Finally, piling Mary with parting gifts, we sailed on, leaving her in her lagoon to await another yacht that might someday chance to stop there. Our new philanthropic spirit had gotten even me interested again in trading. I was happy that there were, in addition to the Jasons of the world, some Marys to balance things out. Such, I thought, was my attitude when we arrived in Vella Lavella in the Solomon Islands' New Georgia group.

The whole New Georgia group had been swarming with Japanese during World War II, and the PT 109 incident had taken place just outside of its capital, Gizo. Learning of this bit of history Peter and I had gotten into the exploring spirit, discovering old Coca-Cola bottles, wrecked airplanes, Japanese gun emplacements, shell casings, and all manner of World War II detritus.

Celia, on the other hand, had become more involved and more judicious in her trading. She would ask traders if they had any "old" things: tools, cooking implements, or whatever. She had acquired several stone axe heads, a pestle, some cutting tools made from shells, bone fish hooks, and all manner of smaller artifacts. One unusual old piece of coral she and Peter had been assured was a charm to keep things from being stolen. It had been hanging in a house in a village they had visited; they had traded for it and brought it happily home to TAKU. I had protested when I saw it, and every time I bumped into it hanging in the galley I swore. Celia pointed out smugly that since she had brought it back we had nothing stolen. I pointed out that we had never had anything stolen before she brought it back.

The traders from Vella Lavella came in the evening and brought only a small carving between them. They were pleasant young men and when asked if they had anything old to trade said that they did have two bride stones if we were interested, since now that people went to church they didn't use bride stones anymore. In fact, no one in the village made them any more, and all the old men who had known how to had died. They rowed back to shore, and one, William, invited Peter to see the village.

The other man, John, eventually returned with the two bride stones wrapped in paper. They were big and heavy, about six inches across, and carved from a giant clam shell. Worn with age, they were similar to ones we had seen in the Museum of the Solomon Islands in Honiara, and as far as we knew they were quite rare. I could tell from the look in Celia's eye that she was prepared for a heavy evening of trading. But before it could get under way I happened to notice the paper in which they were wrapped. It had Japanese characters printed on it, as well as a map. My god! What a find this might be.

I asked to see the paper and asked John if he knew where it had come from. "Oh, yes," he replied. "An old woman who lives in the village thought she saw a Japanese soldier in her garden one evening. So she told the chief, who sent word to Gizo. Then the plane came and flew around the island, calling for the soldier and dropping papers to tell him the war was over." I had read several accounts of Japanese soldiers still holding out 20 and 30 years after the war. One was right here on Vella Lavella.

Before I could enquire further, Celia asked about the bride stones. I waited impatiently, and after much negotiation she bought the two for about $10 each, a real bargain. I watched like a hawk to see whether we might get to keep the paper, but to my dismay John folded it carefully and put it in his pocket. I decided on a bold frontal approach. I got my wallet out of the chart drawer. "Look, I'll give you this for the paper with the Japanese writing and the map on it." John demurred, shook his head, and started to speak. This was going to be harder than I thought. "Look, can't you use the $10? I know you can, and I'd really like to have the map, so why don't you just sell it to me."

"But . . . ," said John, handing me the map as I pushed $10 into his hand. Celia was frowning at me, but I paid no attention.

Before John could speak further, Peter returned with William and burst below, full of excitement. "There's an old lady here who had a Japanese soldier in her garden, and they couldn't find him, and a plane came and dropped maps." (I was smiling smugly to myself as I thought of my sensational trade, and I didn't really comprehend what Peter was saying.) "And the villagers collected all the maps that fell, and they use them for scrap paper, and they gave me a whole pile of them." My contented smile disappeared as Peter produced a pile of maps. "And look what William gave me." Peter showed us a beautifully carved canoe paddle.

Peter got out his baseball hat and handed it to William. "This is for you." William refused, but Peter insisted, so William put it on, and we all told him how great he looked. His smile was worth a hundred baseball hats, but then Peter's obvious joy over his canoe paddle and handful of maps was at least equal to William's smile. I felt mortified about what had happened and what I had done and even more so when John handed me the $10 and explained, "I wanted to tell you that we have lots

ブーゲンビル島ニ残留シテヰル
日本陸海軍将兵ニ重ネテ告グル

ソロモン諸島ノ日本陸海軍在郷軍人會

我々ハブーゲンビル島ニ残留シテヰル日本軍将兵ノ安全ニ日本ヘ帰還サセルタメ日本祖國カラ來タ捜索救出隊デ曾テノ戰コンデ諸士ト行動ヲ共ニシタ諸士ノ戰友達デアル

大東亞戰爭ハ今カラ三十七年前ノ昭和二十年八月十五日ニ終ッタ南方地域ノ日本軍将兵ハ昭和二十年末カラ昭和二十一年ニカケテ日本ニ帰國シ平和國家トナッタ日本カラ來タ

キタ 現在ノ日本ハ新シイ憲法ノモトニ平和國家トシテ豊カニ榮エテヰル 我々ハ諸士ノ姿ヲ見タク今デ九回目デアル ブーゲンビル島民ノ報告ニヨリ毎年諸士ヲ探シニ日本カラ來テヰル

デリ 今回デ九回目デアル 現在ノブーゲンビル島ノ住民ハ日本人ニ對シテ非常ニ友好的デ諸士ガ危害ヲ加エル恐レハ

全クヤ昔ノ戰友ニ對シ我々ハ絶對ニウラウカナイ モ残留日本兵ハ今度ノ出デ來ルカ又ハ海岸部落ニ出テキテ諸土ガ山中密林ニ山中密林デ出デ來ルカ諸士ノ山中密林ニ永年ノ苦闘ニ對シテ國民全部デ英雄トシテ迎エニヰクノデアル

諸士ガ出テ來ル気持ニ決断ノツカナイ諸土ハ何モ心配ハ要ラナイ 國民全部モ心配シテヰルノデアル ブーゲンビル島カラ日本捜索隊ハ戰友達日本ニ在ルトモ諸士ヲ祖國日本ノ豊カニ樂シク國家ニ國民ニ帰國シテ下サイ諸士ハ出デ來ルベキデアル ブーゲンビル島ニ潜在シテヰル 我々戰友ハコレニテ人生ヲ!!

我々ハ昭和五十七年八月二十日デブーゲンビル島ヲ

昭和五十七年五月

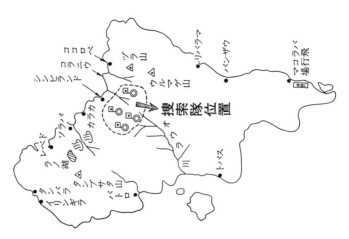

捜索隊位置

所場ル居ノ隊索捜

of maps at the village. The children collected them all when the plane dropped them. I was going to tell you that you could have as many as you wanted."

The poor Japanese soldier, if there indeed was one, never had a chance. The maps had all been collected by the people of the island as they fluttered down. The news that the war was over, that it was okay to come in, that he should give himself up, never reached him, or if it did, he ignored the summons. We'll never know.

Later, after we were all in our bunks, we talked about the day. "They really are lovely people," said Celia.

"Yes, they are," I replied into the dark, thinking of what had transpired.

"Dad? Do you really think there was a Japanese in the garden?"

"Pete, you know that coral thing you and Celia got that keeps things from getting stolen?"

"Yeah?"

"Well, I've changed my mind about it. I believe that it works. And I'm glad we have it on board TAKU. If it can work, there certainly could be a Japanese soldier still on Vella Lavella."

"Maybe we should leave him some of the maps!" Peter said.

"Somehow, Peter, I think if he needs a map he'll get one."

"Goodnight Peter; goodnight Trader Vic," came Celia's voice through the dark, ending the day.

26

Queen Elizabeth

23 December, Rabaul
Papua New Guinea

Dear Mom,

Thanks for the Christmas card and the wool hat. And for the article on malaria. We are all taking anti-malarials once a week as we are supposed to. So far no problems, although some people on other boats have had bad headaches. I called Hood's long distance, and Celia took the mizzen sail back with her when she went home to Connecticut. Hood's wants to see it. They will pay the air freight. Who knows? That's right, we really did see the Queen of England in Honiara. I told you there are lots of people out cruising. Rabaul is about four degrees south of the Equator. Today the temperature is in the mid-nineties and it's very humid. Not really Christmas weather. Peter and I are leaving in a few minutes to sail to the Duke of York Islands (about 40 miles from here) to spend Christmas. We intend to have a cookout on the beach with a couple of other boats who are also in Rabaul and who will sail there as well. Tim, from INOA, is accompanying us, as Mike flew home to California for Christmas and he is by himself. He promised to do the cooking. Yesterday Peter and I explored Rabaul. It's a wonderful little town with a splendid market. Giant avocados are two for 25 cents. We saw the underground headquarters where General Yamamoto directed the Japanese troops in this area. We also saw huge caves in the sides of the cliffs (Rabaul is in the sunken cone of a volcano) where the Japanese hid their boats so the allied planes couldn't see them. It is all very scenic and quite pretty. The drawback is all the beetle nut juice that the locals spit on the ground while chewing the nuts which they do all of the time. You remember Bloody Mary from *South Pacific*. The other drawback is the humidity, which is awful, although we do get heavy rain showers every afternoon after it builds up. Peter and I have found a solution to surviving the humidity. We discovered that there is a Coca-Cola bottling factory where you can buy Coke by the case which we do. It quenches our thirst. We also stop at Steamy's and Burns-Phillips, the two air-conditioned food stores in town, as we walk to the post office and back. We spend a lot of time cooling off in front of the meat counter. Peter has taken a diving course from an Australian dive shop here and is going on some dives next week in the harbor to look at the many sunken Japanese ships that got caught by the bombing raids. I do a lot of typing out under the awning each day. Tell Aunt Kate we will go to Finschhafen and try to find where her WW II hospital was. It's quite a ways from here. We won't be there for a few months. Papua New Guinea is a lot bigger in real life than the maps in the atlases indicate. There are over 750 different languages spoken in the country. Fortunately English, or at least pidgin English, is one.

Off to the post office to mail this, and then off to the Duke of Yorks. As they say here: "*Ssst . . .mai pren, mi laik tokim yu wanpela samting . . .* Happy Christmas!

Love,

We had in fact seen Queen Elizabeth in Honiara. She and Prince Philip arrived on the royal yacht BRITANNIA for an official visit. We just happened to be there to pick up mail and to arrange a refund for Peter's return flight to the States, as he had decided to take some time off from school and to stay aboard TAKU for awhile. There were a series of staged events for the Queen's visit: a large convocation at the small soccer stadium outside of town, a motorcade down the main street, a stop at the memorial park, and a visit to the museum. I was excited to see the Royals. Pictures in my head of Elizabeth's coronation parade with hundreds of thousands of loyal subjects lining the streets of London assailed my memory. I got Peter and Celia to hurry ashore so that we could get a good glimpse of the motorcade. It consisted of one car, which had been brought on the BRITANNIA. There may have been as many as 200 people lining the main street of Honiara; all the others had gone onto the stadium for the later ceremonies. We waved in a desultory manner as the car went by and saw a gloved hand move behind the rolled up windows of the air-conditioned car. It was over like that.

"That's enough of that," said Celia, as she departed to go back to the comparative comfort of TAKU. "They sit in an air-conditioned car, and we stand out here in the hot sun sweltering away. No wonder royalty died out." I couldn't argue.

"And look at the trees, Dad," said Peter. "They went along yesterday and cut all the coconuts off so none would fall on the Queen or her car. I bet she wasn't even waving; I bet they have a mechanical hand that does it attached inside the window." I had to admit that my first glimpse of royalty had not overwhelmed me. Still, people in London would give anything to get as close to the Queen as we had. I persuaded Peter to come with me to the museum to watch the next stop of the royal entourage.

"C'mon Pete. Keep me company. There are lots of trees around the museum so there will be some shade. And besides we won't have to watch out for falling coconuts." Peter hesitated. "I'll buy you a Coke at the Honiara Yacht Club," I added. Such a place existed with a small beachside bar and a section of strand where we all pulled our dinghies up when we came ashore. The yacht club was one of Peter's favorite spots.

"Sure. Why not? I'd love to see the Queen again." Peter was easy.

We waited about an hour in front of the museum with a mere handful of others. They were clearly the staff, as they were dressed very formally for the occasion. Peter and I, in our shorts, short-sleeved shirts, and visors were clearly underdressed for the occasion. It was comfortable in the shade, and eventually we saw the white air-conditioned car approaching. There was some scurrying as those waiting formed into some kind of receiving line.

The car pulled up to the curb, stopping almost right next to Peter and me. A well-dressed attendant jumped out of the front seat and moved swiftly to the back door and opened it. Out stepped Prince Philip, resplendent in a white military uniform, and the Queen, dressed all in fancy pink with a large matching hat. The Prince nodded to Peter and me as he and the Queen walked the few feet to the start of the receiving line.

Here we were, no more than five feet away. Who would have believed it? The Queen's make-up looked a little droopy, and both Royals looked hot and tired. I imagined the conversation that probably occurred as they were driving over. "Thank goodness. Just one more of these beastly things and then we can go back to the boat and put up our feet and relax." "You're the one who wanted to cruise to the South Seas." And so forth. They disappeared into the museum while Peter and I made our way back to the yacht club for a cold drink.

"Real hands," I said to Peter.

"Yeah," he replied.

"Maybe we should row over later and see if they want to trade some charts. We can tell 'em to watch out for the reef in Tokoyo Bay." We laughed. At the yacht club we met a member of the band from the BRI-TANNIA who was having a Coke.

"If we get drunk or in trouble we are sent back to England immediately," he explained. "It's not a bad way to see the world. The ship is over 200 feet long. One-third of it is for the officers, the crew, the attendants, the band, etc. The other two-thirds is for their majesties." He looked a bit wistful. "The only problem is that every place we put into and I get to go ashore, it's always a holiday because the Queen is there. All the shops are closed for the occasion. All I've been able to buy are a few postcards or souvenirs of the Queen's visit from vendors on the street. Not much to send home."

We told him we could see how that might be a problem.

27

Fortune Cookies

We were on a streak of bad luck. TAKU had now completed four years of almost continuous cruising. A bizarre series of unconnected, or so they seemed, events on board reduced us to the state of a character trapped inside a Poe story. "It's just bad luck," I overheard Celia saying to Peter. "We've been on a streak. It'll change."

"I'm not so sure," I countered, entering the conversation, and mentally dredging up words like poltergeist, demon, and exorcist. I recalled the *Amityville Horror*; they thought it was bad luck, too. Peter, who understands these things, suggested that perhaps we were under the influence of extra-terrestrials.

We had been cruising in Papua New Guinea for months now and for the most part we had loved every minute of it. We had moved from Bougainville in the south, north to Rabaul and on to Kavieng on the islands of New Britain and New Ireland respectively. Then we had darted across the top of New Britain on a passage of several days to Madang on the large island of Papua New Guinea itself.

The day we were to leave Madang, the intake hose came off the water pump, causing the engine to overheat. Examination showed the hose clamps, doubled for security, to be tight and no apparent reason for the separation. Further examination revealed a leak around the cooling jacket of one of the injectors. From then on it was one surprise after another. The four-day delay to effect repairs was spent under blue sky and 15- to 20-knot breezes out of the north that quit the moment we finally departed. The northwest trades had just ended early for the year, and we had the variables with showers and little wind that would move us the direction we wanted to go. We headed south for Finschhaven, the seldom-visited Trobriands, and then on to Australia.

We were on our own. MAÑANA had skipped Papua New Guinea and gone directly on to Brisbane, Australia, where Dave and Marcia had hauled her while they went to spend some time back home in Seattle. FLEETWOOD was already in Australia doing major boatwork. INOA, with Mike and Tim, had left us in Rabaul and headed up to Guam, where the two hoped to find some work to replenish their cruising kitty. The only other yacht around was BROWN PALACE, with Bob and Jane Brown aboard. We had kept company with them on and off, and now they, too, had headed off, catching the last of the trades on their way to Australia.

Our autopilot mysteriously refused to work after the first three hours underway. When we did get a little wind and were sailing peacefully at about four and a half knots, the genoa sheet parted with a crack at a place that, when examined later, showed no evidence of chafe or stress. The radar had died off the coast of Bougainville a few months before, although the SatNav was again working after some repair in Madang. What would be next, I wondered?

As we proceeded, events began to accumulate. Our eight-month-old inflatable decided, on its own, to separate its bottom from its pontoons, making it unusable. The head, which had been totally disassembled per manufacturer's instructions and had had perishable spares renewed and the remainder cleaned and reassembled, and which had worked perfectly for three months since that time, went on strike. The ham radio, our ever-reliable communication link, would cut out and go dead at odd times, but only when what seemed like "important" information was being received. Each day a new event was entered into the log or on the list of maintenance to be accomplished. Our new main continued to mildew in front of our eyes. The freshwater pump quit, but not before allowing the best part of 80 gallons of water to disappear into the bilge.

"We're just a few weeks too late for our haulout, that's all," said Celia to my posterior as I struggled to tighten the newly-leaking stuffing box one day. "Cheer up," she added, "remember your fortune." We were at the bottom of our food bins, eating up all the things we had avoided for months or years; we anticipated a big stock up in Australia. I had opened a long neglected tin of fortune cookies that we had found on sale somewhere in Vanuatu and that Peter had thought would be a good addition to the larder. I was desperate for something sweet. The first five cookies I had eaten all had the same fortune, "Develop your sense of humor." Losing patience, I had passed the tin to Peter.

"No wonder this was on sale!" I'd grumbled. Peter's first one had said, "You will go on an ocean voyage." I had grabbed the tin back and tried again, feeling a little encouraged. I could use an ocean voyage at this point. My next one had said, "Develop your sense of humor." I had thrown the tin over the side, and since that time both Peter and Celia had been encouraging me to develop it. Despite the fact that the key broke off in the ignition in the start position, that two of the four batteries died, and that our ever-faithful windvane began to act as though it had schizophrenia, we pressed south towards Australia. The closer we approached, the better I felt, and the less significant became the ills that had been plaguing us.

When the turnbuckle (actually the rigging screw, since we were in the southern hemisphere, where it is called that) failed, it exploded like a cannon shot. Normally our equipment failures had occurred when we were asleep or somewhere else. I had taken to muttering, "Rust never sleeps." In this instance I watched it transpire. We had cleared the China Straits and were two and a half days out of Samarai, Papua New Guinea, rollicking across the glorious blue Coral Sea towards Cairns, Australia, which lies about 1,000 miles north of Brisbane on the Queensland coast. We had forgotten our troubles.

Cairns had much to recommend it as a destination. For one, it was the closest port, lying only 550 miles from Papua New Guinea, and here we were almost halfway. Cairns was also an official port of entry. Reportedly it boasted good haulout facilities for yachts, which we needed, and though it lay snug inside Australia's Great Barrier Reef, it was easily accessible through deep-water, well-marked navigable passes. Lastly, a cruising friend whom we knew from way back had been anchored in Samarai outbound from Australia. He had just come from Cairns and said, "You'll love Cairns; the people are really friendly, there are all kinds of supplies, and best of all there are 48 restaurants and innumerable snack shops and ice cream places." This kind of information always picks a yachtie up.

"Are there any Mexican restaurants?" Peter had asked hopefully.

"Mexican restaurants in Australia," came the reply. "Would you believe there are three in Cairns: *The Little Elephant, El Rancho,* and

Mexican Pete's. We ate at all of them, and even though we are from southern California, we thought they were great.

Well, with three Mexican joints to choose from as well as 45 other possibilities, we would be in sailor's heaven. After six months in Papua New Guinea, the thought of a taco, even an Australian one, was something to keep us going, something to make the growing list of repairs melt away. We had spent the first half of the passage discussing where we would eat first and then where we would eat second, and so forth. I even forgot the sardonic tin of fortune cookies. With Peter's insistence that any place called *Mexican Pete's* couldn't be too bad, we had settled on that. All we had to do was to get there.

TAKU was moving well under 150 percent genoa, working staysail, full main, and mizzen. The Aries vane was behaving itself, and although the wind had freshened to 18 to 20 knots from the 10 to 15 we had had for the first three days, we had no cause for alarm. But, as sometimes happens, things at sea have a way of rapidly changing. One moment we were close-reaching for Cairns, the next Celia called me up on deck. "I think we ought to roll in the genny; the wind is a steady 20+ now." I put down my book (I was now working on *Nicholas Nickleby*) and came topside to take a look. The wind was, indeed, up a bit from what it had been, and the seas, correspondingly, had begun to build. We had talked to Steve, cruising on his Cal 2-46, CARINA, who had a weatherfax aboard. He had told us the prognosis for the next few days in the Coral Sea was for good weather, 10 to 15 knots, so we assumed our heavier winds were just a local phenomenon.

I stood in the hatch looking forward, assessing the situation. We were pressing a bit, and it did look like time to roll in the genny. Celia had been reading in the cockpit, and Peter was on watch behind the wheel. I was about to say, "You're right! Let's crank it in till the weather moderates," when there was a tremendous boom. My words never got out of my mouth.

At first I thought the headstay had parted, for the heretofore straining genoa was flogging wildly in the wind and threatening to tear itself to pieces if we didn't act quickly. "Run off, Pete," I said. Peter brought TAKU around off the wind. "I think we may have broken the headstay." Moving quickly forward, I dumped, in turn, the halyards for the mizzen, the main, and the staysail to reduce our speed and to take as much pressure as possible off the spars so we wouldn't lose them. Celia followed, pulling down and subduing the mizzen and the main in turn.

As I got to the mainmast and dumped the staysail I realized that TAKU had not parted her headstay, but that the bobstay had gone. (It turned out later that the jaws on the turnbuckle holding the bobstay to the bowsprit had failed.) With a sickening feeling I watched as the genoa flapped and rocketed on the sagging headstay, sagging because the bowsprit, once so elegant by extending almost eight feet in front of our bow, was now pointed high in the air, having already shattered one samsonpost into which it was mortised and broken the other post by ripping itself out. One inboard end was wedged perilously around the staysail stay and under the club boom, which had been fractured at its mount. Our 75-pound fisherman anchor had been moved from its chocks under the club and was, at present, acting as a weight to keep the inboard end of the bowsprit in place.

Assessing the situation as quickly as possible, I realized that we could not get the genoa down because our roller-furling halyard makes fast to the roller-furling drum (an old design); this was now eight feet in the air, and with no tension on the headstay it was impossible to roll the sail around it. I also recognized that it was next to impossible to go up the bowsprit to cut the sail loose, as extra weight might carry it completely loose, and with the still firmly attached headstay and two 45-pound CQR anchors on rollers at its end, the sprit could become, in short order, a lethal battering ram if we were not able to keep it subdued. Meanwhile, the genoa was flogging itself to death and the noise it was making was almost unbearable.

Celia returned to the cockpit and sent Peter forward with his and my safety harnesses and our rigging cutters. Peter and I both hooked on and set to work. Our most immediate concerns were twofold: one, get the flogging sail down and secured; and two, secure the bowsprit. I thought of cutting all the mess away, but the idea of trying to replace the bowsprit and the pulpit and the two anchors and rollers in Australia made me first at least attempt to save the gear if at all possible.

The seas were large now and uncomfortable, and with the redistribution of weight forward TAKU had a new and unpleasant motion. Clipped on tenuously with my harness and with Peter sitting on deck also clipped on and holding tightly to the back of my belt, I attempted to cut the wire halyard that led to the furling drum. If I could do this, the sail would drop and take some of the upwards pressure off the sprit. I discovered two things. First, I couldn't quite reach the halyard no matter how far out I leaned, and second, when I could reach it with our three-foot-long steel rigging cutters fully extended in front of me, the cutters were too heavy and stiff for me to work with my arms extended.

We devised a solution. Peter and I tied as many sheets and spare lines as we could to the bowsprit and bow pulpit. Some we just tied off around the mainmast; others we fair-led to mast or cockpit winches. We then took up all the tension we could to keep everything from shifting. Eventually we looked as though we were inside a giant bowl of spaghetti. Then, with a monkey's fist on a light line and the boathook, we managed, after several futile attempts, to get a line between the sagging and still flogging headstay and the hauling part of the halyard, which sagged off a bit from its point of attachment at the end of the sprit.

Once this was accomplished it was an easy job to fashion a slip knot and draw it tight. With both Peter and Celia pulling on the line, we were able to get the halyard close enough for me to cut it with the rigging cutters. Down slid the tattered remains of the genoa, and the noise abated. That in itself was a big relief. TAKU was now lying ahull with a broken bowsprit and the lowered genoa trailing in the water.

As we could not get safely to the end of the sprit, I cut the luff wire in the sail as far out as I could reach, and we dragged the remains of the genoa aboard and stuffed it in a bag. We quickly set up all spare halyards as additional headstays, attaching them to the stem fitting which was still securely in place. With the bowsprit jauntily sticking up and out to starboard and tentatively secure, we held a council.

"I guess we won't be getting to *Mexican Pete's* on Friday night," Peter contributed.

"I'm not sure we can even make Cairns now—after all we were fairly hard on the wind and now without a headsail and no usable headstay we'll just have to lay off a bit. We've got things under control, just." I went on. "The bowsprit can still unwedge, and I don't really want to cut it loose or to cut the headstay to get it loose if I can help it. Let's just keep heading for Australia."

We decided to motorsail with the storm trysail and the mizzen and maybe set the spitfire unhanked to leeward for a little push up forward. The staysail stay was holding, but it was one of the ingredients saving the bowsprit, so I was reluctant to put up the main with the wind conditions and no headstay. We had more than enough fuel to motor the remaining 250 miles to Australia, so we decided we'd best get on with it.

We were moving slowly but unfortunately not in the direction we wanted and needed to go. A cursory study of the chart will show anyone that the Coral Sea is not, by any means, misnamed. From the Great Barrier Reef up the coast of Australia it presents some of the potentially most dangerous waters in the world. As it narrows, the reefs of New Guinea join the reefs of Australia, and the Torres Strait area that connects the two is created. Navigable with great care, the strait is most always entered well above the converging reef area into which we were now being pushed. As the reef funnel narrows toward the north, the currents increase, the rocks and shoals become more numerous and are not always accurately charted, and the prudent navigator finds less and less room for prudence and more and more room for error. We still had a cushion of miles between us and the principal shoals, but I could see how this cushion would begin to erode away. As long as we could keep under way we were fine, since there was a navigable big-ship channel just outside the Australian side of the reef.

We knew, however, that if we should lose our mast it might possibly hole the boat and compound our problems. Were we to lose the use of the engine, our jury rig of sail alone would make a safe landfall dubious. The chart indicated that as we couldn't lay Cairns we would have to try to penetrate the reef farther to the north. We would have no trouble going in that direction, since the southeast trades were fresh and blowing well. The problem would be finding an opening in the Great Barrier Reef, and then if we were able to get inside, we would still have to get somewhere to effect repairs.

As we limped along in the rising seas, I felt some momentary communion and commiseration with Captain Cook. On board the ENDEAVOUR he had found himself being pushed north by the same strong southeast trades, but he was inside the reef with no apparent way to get out while we were outside trying to get in. With luck we would be able to make "reef fall" in two to three days on a small opening. Unlike the passes farther south that were well used and well beaconed and marked, this opening would be discernible only if we were close enough to detect the difference in the water colors and the pattern of the seas.

We were hand steering now, as the vane couldn't track the out-of-trim, out-of-balance wounded bird that was our floating home. Each time a particularly big sea came along we would watch it lift us and push us, and we would watch the lines on the bowsprit tension and the whole lash-up sway against the inner forestay. "If this keeps up we're liable to lose our rig; then we'll really be in the soup. There's no way we can even safely cut it loose now with this wind and these seas. We're just going to have to hope for the best," I said. As the wind and seas continued to increase, we began to fear more for the rig. I decided to put out a radio call so that if we did lose our mast, and with it our antenna, someone would know where we were if we were reported overdue.

Upon radioing the details of our situation we were informed that a big pressure system had unexpectedly recurved up the Queensland coast and that the revised forecast was for strong winds and very rough seas—an Australian southerly *buster*, which, when it occurs, sends all the smart people scurrying for port. We were scurrying for port, but our scurrying was so impeded that we would be stuck in this weather system the whole way. We got connected with an Australian volunteer rescue coordinator on the radio. He advised us that there was basically no available help anywhere nearby if we should need it in a hurry. He also told us that as we neared the reef we would get, with the southerly buster, an increased set to the north.

Don, the Australian, was reassuring, and we were glad to hear his voice. He set up a series of radio schedules for us with himself and a group of Australian amateur radio operators, who agreed to maintain a constant listening watch should the weather, or our situation, deteriorate further. Don's recommendation was that as the weather was going to continue to blow we should not try for the pass off Cooktown, 150 miles above Cairns, where we had been headed, but rather limp farther north. The Cooktown pass was some 25 miles offshore and provided no shelter once inside. We were advised to make for Lizard Island some 50 miles farther north.

This option would also give us some choices. "You have a choice of five clear passes off Lizard Island. There is half-mile passage, one-mile passage, two-mile passage, and on up. Once you get inside," he advised, "it is only eleven miles to Lizard Island, where there is a protected safe anchorage. And," he added, "if you should need assistance, there are usually prawn boats and trawlers in that area." Lizard Island it was. He admonished us, though we were still over 200 miles away, not to try to enter in the dark. "The reef is low and you won't see it until you are almost on top of it. If you get there during daylight you will be able to see Lizard Island and get some bearings to come in on." He also advised us that the strong southeast wind would give us a bad lee shore and that the seas would get rougher as we closed with the reef.

Two nights later we were about 40 miles from Two-Mile Opening off Lizard Island. The wind was still howling as the buster continued to move toward the north. Although we were tired, we had, by lying ahull each night, kept up on our rest. The bowsprit had shifted slightly but still seemed to be well wedged and secured. At dark we went through our usual drill. We gently eased the sails down and secured them, leaving the storm trysail up to steady us. With the wheel lashed, TAKU rode comfortably ahull. We secured the engine, and as the motion stopped, we set a riding light, established a watch schedule, and tried to sleep.

At midnight I suddenly woke up with the feeling that something was wrong. A check around showed that all was the same. I saw that the SatNav was working on a fix so I waited and then plotted it when it came through. "Celia, Peter, wake up! We've been set 25 miles in the last six hours. We've obviously gotten into the stronger currents near the reef. We're less than 18 miles from the pass, but now the course is wrong. We're going to be hard on the wind, and if we don't get underway now, we're going to be swept by the pass in the night."

Underway we went, and our track on the chart from the SatNav fixes indicated that we were indeed being swept north. "We'll never make it," I thought out loud. The next navigable opening was another 120 miles farther north, and there was no good shelter there.

Celia took over the dividers and parallel rulers while Peter continued to steer carefully in the dark. "Look," she said, "we have four hours till first light; we'll have to creep in with the SatNav and a good lookout, and with luck we should be able to pick up the last pass at daybreak. Don't forget you can see Lizard Island once it gets light, and we'll be able to take bearings."

"Okay," I agreed, "we'll stand straight for the reef as close to the wind as we can get; the current and our leeway will bring us right to the two-mile passage. We may have to creep in in the dark with the depthsounder, but with these seas we should see the reefs breaking. Besides it gets light at five; we'll pick out the pass without a hitch."

"Five forty-five," replied Celia glumly. "It gets light at five forty-five."

"Call it five fifteen," I responded with false cheer. "Don't forget we're moving west."

"Exactly," replied Celia, "don't you forget we're moving *west*."

Three hours later we are approaching the reef. It is still black; the wind has increased to 30 knots. The seas are big and more confused, probably in part because of the wind and also because of the vast amounts of water being turned aside by the reef. The sky becomes perceptibly lighter, indicating the arrival of pre-dawn. The SatNav produces yet another timely fix, which puts us only three and a half miles from the still unspotted reef. From the fix we also learn that we are being subjected to a two-knot current setting us to the northeast. We cannot heave-to and await the light, for if we do we will be swept past the reef opening and will be unable to beat into the big seas and strong current. Our blunt-nosed, bowsprit-out-of-joint boat forges on. "We're just going to make it," I announce.

Peter goes forward to the bow to keep watch. When our dead reckoning on the SatNav shows us having a mile to go, the sky lightens enough for us to see. Celia takes over the helm, and I join Peter on the lookout. Simultaneously Peter and I shout, "There it is," as we see a wall of breaking seas ahead. There is a gap in the breaking seas and farther to the right they commence again. We are right on target. We hold our course, hard on the wind, and with our leeway crab toward the gap, which shifts more and more from the right to almost dead ahead.

As we reach the gap in the reef the sun breaks the horizon behind us. We look for Lizard Island off in front of us, but it is out there somewhere in the early morning haze, unseen. Although the sky is clear and blue, the wind continues to howl. Suddenly we are in the gap between the breaking seas, and the sea flattens; the Coral Sea ground swell that has kept us company is gone. The depthsounder reads 150 feet and indicates a gradually shoaling bottom; we have escaped the turmoil and are inside Australia's Great Barrier Reef.

But we are far from safe. The whole inside of the reef is strewn with coral patches, and much of the area is imperfectly charted. We slide through the quarter-mile-long pass and prepare to set our course for the unseen Lizard Island, some eight miles away, but as we come out of the protected waters of the pass we realize we are not going to make it. We now have 35 knots of wind, and inside the reef there is a steep four- to six-foot chop coming from the direction of Lizard Island. Now in open water again we realize that inside the reef is not refuge but a place of danger. As long as we stay on the port tack we can keep our bowsprit protected, but if we are forced to take aboard the other way, to come over to starboard, the bowsprit will be jutting to the wind and all of our temporary lashings that have saved us so well so far will be vulnerable. To add to the mess, the reef to the right of us extends inward from the pass for some four or five miles, only gradually dropping off to the north.

When we have our 0700 radio schedule with Don I advise him that we are inside the reef but feel we may not be able to claw our way off the lee shore that we have found. He tells us that there is a sports fisherman at Lizard Island who is willing to come out and assist but cannot give us a dead tow; the boat, SIMONE, will take about 30 minutes to get to us. I give our latest position and ask that SIMONE step on it.

Back on deck we sheet the spitfire, still unhanked, as close as we can, flatten the storm trysail as much as possible, and crank in on the mizzen sheet for all it's worth. Even with the engine we are losing to the lee, but slowly. As our two main anchors and chain are unusable, stuck at the end of the inaccessible bowsprit, we get out our 22-pound high-tensile Danforth, and a long rode in case we have to try to anchor where we are, in 90 feet of water. "When SIMONE shows up, maybe they can help hold us off the shallows or tow us in four miles to where we can drop the hook behind one of these big coral heads shown on the chart until this blows over," I offer as I try to work out a plan.

Celia, on the helm, suddenly yells, "I see a buoy off to port." What she thinks is a buoy turns out to be the tuna tower on SIMONE, which is surfing down the chop at well over 20 knots and headed right for us. Peter and I go forward to rig a monkey's fist on a light heaving line, and we attach that to our 250 feet of five-eighths rode, which we flake out carefully on deck.

SIMONE is close enough for us to see the people on board. Up the tower is George York, a bear of a man, a veteran prawn boat and charterboat captain with 30 years' experience inside the barrier reef. On his fantail are his local crewman and Mike from CHRYSALIS, a fellow yachtie and friend who was anchored at Lizard Island. They have already rigged a bridle, and as SIMONE sweeps around us at about 15 knots and turns into the seas, George waves for our line. He maneuvers SIMONE like the expert he is, and though I throw the heaving line, had I waited a minute more I could have passed it to Mike.

As Mike makes our line fast George maneuvers away, and Peter and I feed out our 250 feet of line. Suddenly the line goes taut and there we are, moving slowly in the direction of Lizard Island. With our engine continuing to run in gear to keep some of the strain from the tow line we are able to make about five knots. We aboard TAKU have a wet ride with lots of spray to dodge. As we move along I watch our anemometer hit 45 and then 50 knots. The strong winds we had been warned about are still around.

Within an hour Lizard Island appears out of the haze. We are amazed by how big it is and understand, at last, why we were told we should be able to sight it well offshore. In another hour we round its tip, and in the lee the wind suddenly drops to 15 and the seas flatten. George tows us in, and we watch the bottom shoal; when we are in 12 feet we drop our anchor.

George swings by to tell us that he is sorry if he has towed us too fast but the strong wind warning had been upgraded that morning to, as he puts it, "Fresh to Frightening" and we had luckily come in at slack water. Snug behind Lizard Island it is hard to believe how bad it was "out there." George adds: "In another hour there would have been three to four knot current pouring out of the pass. You never would have made it in. When I heard where you were and looked at the time, I knew that I had to hurry. I think that I was almost at full throttle before the mooring line hit the water. I'll let you get settled, and we'll get together later."

We are in, we are safe, we are attached once more, however tenuously, to the land. All that remains is to clean up, get the bowsprit aboard and lashed, and work our way south to Cairns inside the reef after a rest and after the winds abate. We sit in the cockpit feeling the tensions drain out. It has been four years since we left the United States and 10 months since we left New Zealand; we have been cruising steadily away from civilization for most of that time. Now here we are in Australia at last. Down below is a mess of sails, sleeping bags, and wet clothes. Suddenly out of nowhere comes a Boston Whaler with *Lizard Island Resort* painted on the side. It comes alongside and, without a pause, over the rail climb a customs officer and an immigration official in full regalia.

"We have been looking for you in our radar plane, which is at the

Lizard Island strip now. Why have you entered here rather than at a port of entry?"

I explain that we have been cleared by radio to come into Lizard Island. Obviously no one has told the customs man. He says again, "This is not a port of entry; what reason do you have to be here?" Peter and Celia and I all look at one another, at the broken bowsprit hanging over the side, at the temporary lines running everywhere to winches and cleats, and at the piles of sail bags and clothes that raise our cabin sole to bunk level, and we all begin to giggle and then to laugh. "Why are we here?" The question is the funniest thing I have ever heard. Even after the officials have been led below and sit with their knees drawn up to their chins and grudgingly clear us in and then depart, I am still overcome with the giggles. All Peter has to do is draw himself up straight and put a mock-serious expression on his face and ask: "Why are you here?" and I dissolve in laughter. If nothing else, I have developed my sense of humor.

TWO

HOMEWARD BOUND

28

Changes

June, Cairns
Australia

Dear Mom,

We're just about ready to weigh anchor so that we can get around
to Darwin and across the Indian Ocean this season. I'm glad you
got to see Peter on his way home. After having him aboard for a
year, the boat seems empty without him. All the repairs are done,
and the sail is back from Sydney, as is the inflatable. The work was
more extensive than I thought. Didn't get to see much of Australia
except for the boat yard. Thanks for the article on the dangers of
the Red Sea. I was aware of most of them. There are a handful of
boats making the trip; the rest are opting for South Africa and the
Cape of Good Hope. Met some wonderful cruisers from San
Diego: Buzz and Maureen Hatheway on a boat called GAMBIT.
We're probably going to buddy-boat up the Red Sea together. The
only thing we really need is an American flag; could you send one
to Darwin? We expect to leave there in August. Tell Aunt Kate that
those were pictures of Finschhafen; a cement dock remains as the
only sign of WW II. The rest is a giant copra plantation now.

Love,

TAKU left the South Pacific behind when she rounded the tip of Cape
York. On the map, Cape York stands out as the peninsula that juts well
up from the upper righthand corner of Australia. For me, that besting
of Cape York on a glorious July morning represented psychologically a
change of attitude as well as a change in direction. The former was real,

while the latter was solely imagined; we were still headed west. The psychological change was a realization and tenuous acceptance of the fact that TAKU was headed home. Until that time we were merely on an extended cruise of the South Pacific, the armchair sailor's dream come true. Leaving the Pacific was a definite closure, a finite marking of places visited, experiences shared, dreams become realities.

One sensed, rounding Cape York, a decisive change in direction. Having cruised north for almost 1,000 miles inside Australia's Great Barrier Reef, repassing Lizard Island, that scene of our ignominious arrival, we turned the corner at Cape York. After a brief stop at Thursday Island where Bligh had put in on a Thursday during his famous open-water boat journey, we pointed TAKU's bow due west again. We slid into the Sea of Arafura and across the Gulf of Carpentaria, the large bight in the top of Australia. For the seven-day passage to Darwin we were blessed with a full moon, which rose each evening dead astern and during the course of each night progressed from directly astern to overhead and then as the early morning hours wore on dropped off slightly to our port bow before settling below the horizon in the last hour or two before dawn. Blessed with warm, steady Force 4 to 5 winds from our port quarter that came up off the deserts of Australia, TAKU reached smoothly down the silver corridor provided by the moon. Night watch was a joy; the course was steady and the moonlight made it almost bright enough to read outside. With strains of Beethoven's Ninth pulsing in the Walkman earphones as TAKU sailed smoothly onward on a perfect night, what more could I ask for?

The change in direction was basically imaginary, as we had been moving westward since leaving the Caribbean. The problem was that on rounding Cape York we appeared, on a standard map of the world, to be at last pointed back toward home, back toward the east coast of the United States. We had passed a psychological point of no return. Where before the world was stretched out beckoning to the west and each mile took TAKU farther and farther away from home and closer and closer toward adventure, now it seemed that each mile sailed was bringing us closer and closer toward home. Adventure, if there was such a concept, was in events left behind, around the corner of Cape York.

Voyages do that to you. Passages, too. Surprisingly, in retrospect, part of the passage or voyage that stands out on the front side is the conception and planning and anticipation that transpire. Curiously, in all my years of wanting to sail around the world and to visit different places, I had never contemplated the voyage ever ending. I could see the trip beginning, and I could imagine (often incorrectly as it turned out) scenes of it happening, but I never thought about the adventure having an end. I can picture climbers on the top of Mt. Everest. Months of meticulous planning and preparation lead to that big moment. We have all seen the picture of the conquerors, bundled against the cold, holding a flag say, of the *National Geographic Society*, which beats wildly in the wind. Such are our dreams formed. We never see or imagine the ensuing pictures, the ones that occur when someone finally says, "I guess it's time to start down." Think about it.

The expectation of the event is as important, and as much a part of the experience, as the event itself. Depending on the particular passage to be made, the expectation may run into hours, days, months, or even years. And then, suddenly, you are out there and it is happening. The marks on the chart that define your position and show your progress may indicate your physical location, but they fail to accurately indicate your psychological one. You know that there are "x" amount of miles between point "a" and point "b" and you can tell, if you have been keeping up with your navigation, when you reach the halfway point between the two. You can gauge when the distance to go is indeed less than the distance you have come. Seeing that on a chart can quicken your expectations.

Looking at the chart each day as we raced across the top of Australia, I found myself becoming irascible. I had known the world was round, of course; no surprises there. But knowing something and confronting it and living with it are different things entirely. While Celia got more and more excited about our quick progress to Darwin and beyond, I sensed the looming East Coast of home over the horizon. I became preoccupied with the disproportionate realities of where we had been compared to where we had to go. Unknowingly, I had begun to apply a psychological measure to the trip, and my psychological clock indicated that I, at least, was far further along than I knew. Nowhere in the four years of voyaging had I spent any noticeable consideration of after-the-voyage-is-over—what then? Re-entry, as yachties call it, was something others did.

Arrival in Darwin had only served to heighten my mental distress.

Surrounded by loads of cruising friends, some of whom we hadn't seen for many months, Darwin became a constant round of get-togethers and catch-ups. Since Darwin was one of the few places in Australia where one could actually see the sun set over the ocean, each evening found scores of people gathered on the shore or on decks of the anchored yachts to watch the sun disappear below the rim of the sea that stretched out unbroken to the west. For most sunset was a social event, a special panorama put on each evening for the delight of anyone who cared to take advantage of it. "Cheer up," Celia would tell me. "Enjoy the fantastic sunset." Suddenly the sunset started to represent the measurement of time, an indicator of the ultimate termination of the voyage, a beacon indicating west and "home." I loathed it.

"Maybe I'm having a mid-life crisis," I would tell friends who would listen. "You've been having that for years," would come the reply. "We all have."

29

Bali

August, Darwin
Australia

Dear Mom,

G'die as they say here. Nurse to man in hospital: "Did you come here to die?" Man to nurse: "No, I came yesterdie." Get it? The missing books finally showed up. As did the foul-weather gear, along with a whole bunch of mail. It'll be the last for a good while. The customs collector at the post office wanted to charge me duty on the American flag you sent me. I realize the small sizes may have been out of stock but three by four feet *is* a bit of overkill. When I told him you wanted my body shipped home in it after the pirates killed me in the Red Sea, he laughed and let it go. Thanks for the article "Lost in the Outback." We never got there. And we didn't see any kangaroos. The Ambon Race we hoped to enter to Indonesia was cancelled so we're off to Bali on our own, then Christmas Island and then Cocos Keeling and on to Sri Lanka by sometime in November. There aren't as many places to stop as there were in the Pacific. More as it happens.

Love from Down Under,

I had bumbled my way through Darwin and through our five windless days out of Australia followed by a perfect six-day spinnaker run into Bali, Indonesia. The plan was to spend two months in Bali enjoying magnificent beaches, delicious yet inexpensive food, and a unique culture. Expectation had put me in a better frame of mind. Eight weeks of R&R would get things ready for the Indian Ocean crossing. Timing the crossing of the Equator was important. We needed to get clear of the southern hemisphere before the cyclone season started in November, while at the same time we should not arrive in the northern hemisphere until the end of its cyclone season in October. It was also important to make as much northing as possible before the Indian Ocean northwest monsoon set in. On top of that, arriving too early at the Red Sea meant encountering headwinds for the whole of its 1,100–mile length, as well as meeting the last of winter at its northern end and in the Mediterranean. Arriving too late to the Red Sea meant good following winds, but a late arrival in the Mediterranean, which would preclude getting all the way across it in the summer and cut out the better part of a cruising season. Timing was everything.

Ideally we needed to cross the Equator sometime in mid- to late-October. With a combination of passage times and a planned month or two in Sri Lanka and/or India, we would reach the Red Sea by February. Allowing for a leisurely cruise with stops in the Sudan and Egypt and then in Israel, we could expect to be in the Med by May in time for a summer of cruising in Turkey and Greece. The more I thought about the coming months, the more interested and excited I became. We weren't really headed home, I told myself; we were still cruising. I managed to put a full stop on my confused mental state. Unfortunately, the Indonesian officials soon took care of my new cheerful outlook.

I had written to the Indonesian embassy in Washington, D.C., many months before, advising them of our intention to visit Indonesia by yacht. In due course, a formal, but friendly, reply had come, which had said, in effect:

Glad you want to cruise Indonesia . . . it's a great country . . . we look forward to having you . . . we do have some security issues so while you are there please stay away from the following seven or eight islands, which are off limits to yachts . . . there are still some 700 or 800 other islands you can visit . . . do stop in to one of our consulates and get a visa if appropriate . . . this letter is valid for one year . . . thanks for writing and have a wonderful time. Signed, the folks at the Indonesian embassy in Washington, D.C.

Armed with this letter, we had visited the Indonesian consul in Darwin and had been told that visas weren't required; the letter was all that we would need. Obviously these folks had never met Edwin

Hutepeda (his name still looms large in green ink in my passport). Will Rogers never met him either.

Edwin was the immigration official who did the final clearance on TAKU on her arrival at Benoa, Bali. I say final because clearance required traipsing to seven different offices with seven different departments to obtain individual chops on the clearance request. The last of these offices held Edwin. Any run-around can get to you, but I was prepared to be patient, with the prospect of weeks of luxuriating in Bali as the carrot that kept me moving. Edwin, in his office in Denpassar, was the quintessential official. In a starched khaki uniform with lots of braid and trimmings, he sported large aviator sunglasses. He read over the stamped clearance request and then set it aside.

He took the letter from the Indonesian embassy in Washington (good for one year), and as I watched, he ripped it into little pieces. He let them sprinkle out of his hands onto the desk. "They have no right to give you this permission. Only customs and immigration can give you permission." He stamped our passports with a ten-day visa.

"Ten days?" I argued. "You can get off a plane here from anywhere in the world and get a two-month permission to visit."

"But you did not come on a plane. Yachts carry guns for undesirable people. You should not have had that permission. Ten days."

No amount of arguing worked. Another yachtie who had the same treatment got cranky, and the result was a reduction of the ten days to 24 hours, and then he was ordered to leave the country. All of us were subject to what we felt was unreasonable treatment. We went to see the U.S. chargé who was stationed in Denpassar. She arranged a meeting with the minister of tourism, who regretfully explained, "Our propaganda to have people come visit has outrun our procedures for them when they are here. The problem is an internal political matter that only time will resolve." Edwin's word in Bali was the law.

I asked our embassy rep about our passports, which were scheduled to run out while we were in the Indian Ocean and which I had planned to renew during our two-month stay in Indonesia. "We'll send them to Jakarta. Processing may take a while," she added with a smile. "As long as your passports are off being renewed, Edwin will have to let you stay, but I can't make any promises."

Passport renewal took 21 days. Every day I would go to see Edwin in Denpassar on his request. "No passports, yet?" he would ask.

"Not yet. You know how slow government offices and bureaucracy can be." I would smile at Edwin and he would smile at me from behind his aviator glasses.

"You will let me know when they come."

"Of course."

I had other things on my mind. The SatNav had quit on the way to Bali, and I was counting on it for the trip across the Indian Ocean and on up the Red Sea. This small electronic device had become a dependable part of the crew. I had managed to fix the problem with a large rubber band and a clothespin. The rubber band would tension the clothespin, which, if it was positioned properly, would press on the keyboard in such a way as to allow it to function. The slightest change of pressure or position, and the SatNav would stop functioning. Once the screen was up and programmed, the SatNav would continue running okay, but if it stopped working for any reason, a rubber band, a clothespin, and imprecations were the only way to restart the program again.

I was desperate to get the problem fixed. In my souvenirs from the voyage I have kept a stack of telexes from Bali. From the looks of them my time was well occupied. Finally we made ready to depart. Short of a catastrophe we would get the new part in Cocos. I had worked with my clothespin and had gotten the SatNav up and running. I had also gotten out the sextant and the tables and decided that if we had made it all the way to New Zealand without a SatNav we should be able to make it all the way back home. The issue was less the need for a SatNav than the notion of having this expensive piece of equipment that was worthless when it wasn't working. We had watched boats in the Solomons, in Papua New Guinea, and in Australia wait for their Walker SatNavs (the first to break the $2,000 price barrier) to come back from repair in England. We had heard about the Walker problems as early as New Zealand, and I had decided to buy a more expensive and therefore (spot the mistake) more reliable Danish product.

Confident that things were under control, I decided to relax and enjoy the last weekend in Bali. Bali, in memory, remains smells and sounds as well as sights. Charcoal braziers in front of outdoor food stalls gave forth the pungent aromas of grilling chicken, pork or turtle *satays* (sort of miniature shish kebabs) which were served with a delicious peanut sauce. The staple dish of the country, *nasi goreng*, a sort of mixed noodle and vegetable dish, was offered almost everywhere as well. Fruit lassis, thick blended yogurt, fruit juice, and fruit pulp concoctions, smoother and tastier than any milkshake from home were the drinks of choice wherever we went. One certainly wouldn't starve in Bali. The sounds of *gamalen* music filled the air. Mountains and terraced rice paddies punctuated the landscape. The ornate temples of the local villages all blended into a patchwork landscape of delights. Everywhere there were brightly colored kites, flown all day by young boys to scare predatory birds away from the rice paddies.

Of course there were tourists—planeloads of them from Australia and from America and Europe, who had flown in to enjoy this magic island and its inexpensive pleasures, not the least of which were the magnificent white sandy beaches that ran for miles along the coastline. On the southwest side lay Kuta Beach, a warren of honky-tonk souvenir shops and fast-food, Balinese-style, joints. But Kuta, open to the thousands of miles of fetch of the uninterrupted Indian Ocean, had magnificent surf with a gently shoaling sandy beach where the waves boomed in all day long. It had become our favorite place to go and relax.

An hour of baking in the warm sun followed by an hour body surfing in the warm Indian Ocean was enough to take my mind off almost everything. It wasn't heaven, but it was close. And to top everything freelance masseuses roamed the beach and plied their trade. Some thirty Balinese women gave massages; each wore the distinctive Kuta masseuse "coolie" hat with a number painted on it. Indicating that the masseuse was officially licensed to ply her trade on the beach, the license was a way of limiting the number of women working and a means of impeding those who might solicit for less socially acceptable activities.

I could never arrive at the beach without being accosted by two or three masseuses asking for my business. "You want massage?" would be the question. If I responded, "Later," as I usually did, one would point to the number on her hat and say, "Remember me, Number Six" (or whatever her number was). Generally I didn't have to remember as Number Six would keep a practiced eye on me, holding me in ocular escrow, until I finally hired her for a massage. But I didn't mind, for at a dollar for a half-hour the massages were thorough, terrific, and one of the last tourist bargains in the world.

Fresh from my last foray to the telex office I arrived at the beach and was immediately glommed on to by Number 27, and I went through my "later" routine. I put down my beach belongings and went for a swim. The surf was the best I had seen since we had arrived in Bali, and after an hour or so of riding the waves I stretched out on my towel and felt the sun slowly drying the saltwater droplets on my back. With my mind emptying out, I half drowsed in the midday heat. I heard a voice in my ear inquire, "Massage now?"

"Okay," I replied without opening my eyes. I settled into the warm sand and tried to relax completely. I felt the lotion on my back and began to enjoy the sensual pleasure of strong hands working it into my skin. It was just what I needed to relieve the stress of the past two weeks, the daily worrying about the SatNav and the continuing hassle with Edwin. Suddenly there was a loud clamor in Balinese just above my head. Squinting up into the sun, I caught a glimpse of a very angry Number 27 berating the masseuse (who turned out to be Number 15) working on my back. A giant argument ensued around and about me.

Business was obviously not too good, and I had made the *faux pas* of allowing Number 15 to work on me when, as far as Number 27 was concerned, I had a contract with her. After some more heated discussion, an accord of sorts was reached. Number 27 knelt on one side of me and Number 15 on the other. Concluding that they had obviously decided to split the work and the fee, I anticipated the double pleasure of a four-handed massage.

How wrong I was. Number 15 grabbed an arm and began working the muscles vigorously. Not to be outdone, Number 27 grabbed the other arm and worked twice as fast. So it went over my whole body. If one kneaded, the other pummeled. While one rubbed quickly, the other almost took my skin off with the slow friction of her practiced hands. My legs were all but yanked off. The two women twisted my ankles unmercifully. Instead of a leisurely half-hour massage, I was "finished" in about seven minutes, when each, like a rodeo rider in a roping contest, threw one of my legs to the ground and jumped clear to indicate that her work was done.

I managed, barely, to put the money into the waiting palm of Number 15, who immediately distributed half to Number 27. Numbed and aching, I watched as they gathered up their lotions and disappeared down the beach, laughing, arm in arm. I felt like I had been in a Denpassar rush-hour traffic accident and had been ridden over by all of the bicycles and motorbikes that ply its busy streets. I got stiffly to my feet and made my way slowly toward the sea.

The SatNav part never came. We pointed TAKU's bow out of Benoa Harbor and setting sail, reached out across the long Indian Ocean swell. There was always Sri Lanka; I could get the SatNav part there if it didn't come to Cocos. We settled in to our routine for the passage to Christmas Island and then on to Cocos.

"I feel like I've spent three weeks being pulled in every direction," I told Celia.

"You have," she laughed in reply. "Massage?" She laughed again.

I settled back to enjoy the peace of being at sea again. The boat was sailing well under working jib (a new genoa was on order for shipment to Sri Lanka), genoa staysail, main, mizzen staysail, and mizzen. We were making over six knots and the Aries vane was steering beautifully. Above, fair weather tradewind puffers dotted the sky. Down below our SatNav's screen glowed green. With a clothespin held firmly in place by a rubber band, the SatNav tracked our position without fail as we skimmed along the azure sea.

One man with a horse competes with VAGABUNDO's plight for attention. D. Degnon

TAKU enjoys a tranquil anchorage at Eynihal, Turkey, in the eastern Mediterranean. D. Degnon

Waiting for the okay to proceed through
Greece's Corinth Canal. D. Degnon

TAKU undergoes a major overhaul, including new topsides paint, at
Manoel Island Shipyard, Valetta, Malta. D. Degnon

At the quay on Palma de Majorca, Spain, I pass three taxi loads of groceries aboard to Peter to stow below. C. Lowe

Taking advantage of Manoel Island's "superior" facilities to wash the breakfast dishes. C. Lowe

Peter and Celia take time out for some dinghy sailing in Alicante, Spain.
D. Degnon

A day at the dock in Las Palmas, Gran Canaria, Canary Islands, prior to the Atlantic crossing. D. Degnon

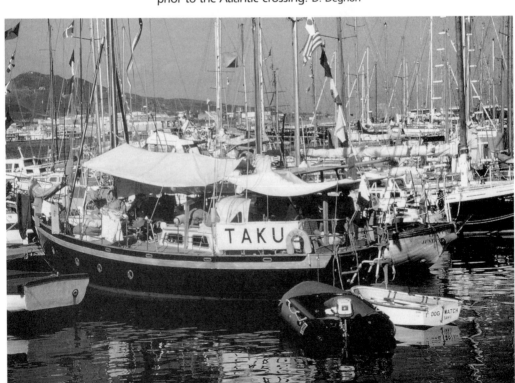

Tip finishes up a splice while crossing the Pond. D. Degnon

Motorsailing and looking for wind during the first eight days of the Atlantic passage. H. Zimmerman

Maneuvering with care alongside the ALESSANDRO VOLTA to get some fuel in mid-Atlantic. H. Zimmerman

A spirited sail through the Grenadines, B.W.I., after a six-and-a-half-year loop around the globe. P. Boocock

Rededication of the Statue of Liberty and TAKU's welcome home. D. Degnon

Dressing ship on the Fourth of July in New York City with courtesy flags
from the 45 countries TAKU visited. C. Lowe

TAKU, all sails drawing well, on a perfect New England summer day. C. B. Degnon

Sails full and by, TAKU slides briskly up the familiar waters
of Buzzards Bay, Massachusetts. C. B. Degnon

30

Transitions

February, Galle
Sri Lanka

Dear Mom,

Well, here we are about to leave Sri Lanka for Aden and then the Red Sea. It was nice seeing you at Christmas and being back in the States for the first time in five years. I admit four weeks is not a long time, but it was necessary to get back here and prepare to move on. The SatNav that I had sent to California from New Jersey for repair and that UPS lost, finally arrived here via Singapore. It's working okay. I had to go up to Colombo by train (three hours), hire an agent, and spend a day getting it out of customs. That was okay because I had done the same thing the week before when I went up to get the new sails from Hong Kong. They fit perfectly and look great, and it's good to have a replacement for the genoa and a new yankee before heading north. Also, they are getting to know me at the airport. This was the third week in a row I've been there. (They are also getting to know me on the train.) Three weeks ago all my luggage finally turned up. I can remember specifically questioning the ticket agent in Atlantic City when I checked it all through to Colombo. I told her I didn't think the airport code she had written looked right. She refused to let me see the book, but looked again and assured me that she knew what she was doing. She knew what she was doing: my bags have been in Dubai for a month, but they are finally here. Of course, the airline won't reimburse me for the train and taxi, etc. I guess I should be glad I got all the stuff. The trouble in Sri Lanka continues between the Tamils and the Singhalese, but it is all in the north near Trincomalee. I'm glad we didn't put in there. I like Sri Lanka a lot, but there is a great deal of poverty, which is depressing. Having to wait for all this stuff has meant that we won't be able to go to India or Oman but must make tracks for Aden and the Red Sea. It will be nice to get back sailing again. I figure about three weeks at sea to Aden, a few days there, and then on up the Red Sea, which will get us to the Med by May if all goes well. It seldom does, but one can hope.

Love,

"It was the best of times, it was the worst of times," wrote Charles Dickens in A *Tale of Two Cities*; he might just as well have been describing TAKU's passage from Cocos Keeling Island in the Indian Ocean, north across the Equator to Sri Lanka. This particular trip was not one that I, or anyone else, was looking forward to at all. For one, it meant saying farewell to the languid tropical waters of the southern hemisphere where TAKU had indeed languished for over three years since sliding south at the Galápagos Islands and entering the South Pacific. We had spent a quick week at an open anchorage at Christmas Island. Another five days had brought us to Cocos Keeling, where, with some 24 other world cruising boats we had prepared ourselves to move on. The pack was split as to destination between the Red Sea and the Cape of Good Hope. I preferred the former, for I had no desire to rush back to the Caribbean and then be home.

For many, Cocos was the last chance to enjoy the camaraderie of tropical cruising that many of us had shared across the Pacific. ISHMAEL, with whom we had last spent time at the Suwarrow pig roast, was there, bound for Durban and Capetown. SHEARWATER, first met in Tahiti three years before and with whom we had shared many anchorages and adventures, was there. It too, was headed for the Med. Wally and Barb aboard the New Zealand yacht SEASMOKE were there. We had met them in Cairns and had sailed up the Great Barrier Reef together, as well as spent time with them in Darwin and Bali. And TYLIANNA was there from Australia, with Frank and Anna Gonsalves and their four children aboard. We had first shared an anchorage with them in the Solomons a year or more before. GAMBIT, with our buddy-boaters Buzz and Maureen, still kept us company. And a raft of others who were casual or new acquaintances filled the surrounding anchorage.

We all delayed as long as we could. Most of the South Africa-bound boats took off, as they had less to worry about in terms of weather. We, who were headed north, had to contend with the change of seasons when we crossed the line. Finally a group of us left within a few days of each other. SEASMOKE and TYLIANNA took off. For them, the Indian Ocean would be their first big ocean crossing. Then GAMBIT, TAKU, and SHEARWATER all departed.

We all expected the 1,800–mile passage to take about two weeks. Our strategy was to run west at 10 degrees south, make a bit of a dog leg, and then work our way up to cross the Equator back into the northern hemisphere at about 80 degrees east. This tactic would put us directly below Sri Lanka with about 360 miles to go from the Equator. From all I had read, such a course had proven to be a successful strategy in the past. It actually worked beautifully for TYLIANNA, who completed the trip in just over two weeks. SEASMOKE, along with the rest of us, hit some weather. But as they were a bit ahead they squeezed by and completed the passage to Sri Lanka in 18 days.

But things turned out differently from what I expected. TAKU found herself sandwiched between two lows, one on either side of the Equator. One, actually the one to our south, became Cyclone Oscar, the first tropical depression in the area for the season, which moved south to plague the boats crossing from Cocos Keeling to Mauritius on their way to South Africa. So our pace was slowed. We got set quite far to the east and had to beat west to Galle, the port of entry at the southwest corner of Sri Lanka. GAMBIT, a more close-winded boat, managed to avoid most of the set and most of the beat and arrived in Galle three days ahead of us, as did SHEARWATER, who had left 24 hours later.

No matter, we were back in the northern hemisphere, familiar waters to us in a way. The boats from Australia and New Zealand now had to contend with feeling "upside down," the way it had felt for TAKU while she was below the line. They also had to deal with new patterns in the heavens, while for us familiar constellations began to make their nightly reappearance. All of us underwent a period of readjustment and realignment; our references had changed again.

The passage to Aden was smooth enough even though the Indian

Ocean seemed to go on forever. Bounded by Asia on the north, Australia on the east, Antarctica on the south, and Africa on the west, the Indian Ocean certainly looks, on the charts, as though it takes up a large portion of the earth's water surface. The Pacific appears to reach on forever as well, but with all of the interesting islands and anchorages and people it didn't seem that way as we crossed. Islands dot the Indian Ocean, too. Running late, we were skipping the Maldives that stretch out west of Sri Lanka; we were also skipping the Laccadives, which lie about 100 to 200 miles off the coast of India.

The Laccadive Islands, meaning the hundred thousand islands, consist of a group of coral atolls with several detached shoals and banks. They are separated from the Maldives by two major openings: the Eight Degree Channel, and 60 miles or so farther north, the Nine Degree Channel. Navigation in the Maldives and the Laccadives is dicey, and the Indian Government has prohibitions against yachts visiting the latter. Having seen a fair share of coral atolls in the South Pacific, the decision to give them a miss wasn't difficult. Once clear of Minicoy Island, which was lighted and which separated the two channels, we expected clear sailing almost all of the way to Aden and the Red Sea. The only remaining major obstacle was Socotra.

Socotra, lying at about 12 degrees, 30 minutes north and 54 degrees east, marks the transition from the Indian Ocean into the Gulf of Aden. It was widely rumored that the Russians had located a nuclear submarine base there and that visitors were discouraged in a big way. The Sailing Directions did enough to discourage one from going anywhere near Socotra, even without the pre-détente Russians. Socotra, historically reputed to be a base for Indian Ocean pirates who preyed on shipping along the African and the Asian shores, was described in classic Sailing Direction understatement as "seldom visited because it is exposed to both monsoons. It also has no harbors in which vessels can at all times anchor with safety, and the character of the natives has in the past been dangerous." Clearly, there wasn't much to recommend it!

We had all decided to give Socotra as wide a berth as possible, and TAKU did exactly that. There were perils enough waiting in the Red Sea without actively seeking them out on our own. We were coming into Arab and African countries, and one sensed a gauntlet to be run through them to the safer, at least in our minds, areas of the westernized Mediterranean. The previous year a yacht had been shot at and rammed by an Ethiopian gunboat. Yachts that had stopped in Saudi Arabia had been treated very badly. The word on the grapevine suggested provisioning in Aden or Djibouti and then staying in the middle of the Red Sea at least as far as Port Sudan in Sudan, about halfway up on the African coast. Such a strategy would keep you clear of Ethiopia and off the hazardous coast of North Yemen and southern Saudi Arabia.

From Port Sudan north, a barrier reef extended most of the way up the Sudanese/Egyptian coasts within which small yacht navigation was possible. There were numerous anchorages available; one could daysail the trip as far north as the Gulf of Suez without fearing the shipping traffic or getting caught in a northerly dust storm, which made navigation in the center of the Red Sea extremely hazardous at best. That was our plan. GAMBIT was about two weeks ahead of us, and Buzz and Maureen agreed to meet us in Port Sudan; then we could cruise up the Red Sea together. Having another boat along would provide a margin of safety against pirates or intruders, if there were any, and provide assistance in the event of gear failure or illness. Although there were lots of anchorages, there were few, if any, ports to put in for assistance once one got north of Port Sudan.

Aden was full of Russian ships, military and civilian, who called there for supplies, repairs, and recreation. I hoisted the three- by four-foot national ensign that my mother had sent, and we anchored in the shadow of a Russian light cruiser whose liberty boats set TAKU rocking violently every time they passed, which was on a constant basis. "I've had it with them," I told Celia, as I was thrown to one side from where I was working on the engine.

"Don't do anything foolish; they're bigger than we are," she cautioned. I was not to be deterred. I stormed on deck and waited for the next liberty boat to pass. I didn't wait long.

As the first wave that the launch put out hit us and TAKU began a long slow roll, I screamed at the launch at the top of my lungs. "Hey you! Slow down!" I yelled, making arm motions that I hoped would indicate the same idea.

The launch was jammed with officers headed ashore. One, seeing TAKU take another violent roll and me hanging onto the mizzen shrouds, pointed our problem out to the coxswain, who, looking back and seeing us roll, got into what appeared to be a small argument with the officer. "It's an American boat, and besides if I slow down every time it will take you that much longer to get ashore." I imagined the conversation. "And besides that's the yacht with the escaped Soviet citizen that was in the Panama Canal that we were shown pictures of in our indoctrination lectures."

TAKU was still rocking, and the officer made some gestures and did some shouting at the boat coxswain. The liberty boat slowed down. I waved my thanks. I was interested to see how long the peace would last. In a while the same launch returned from shore. As it neared TAKU it slowed down and crept past. I could see the coxswain was still annoyed, as it appeared he was complaining to whoever would listen. As he got beyond TAKU, he again increased his throttle, but he was so busy looking back to see if his wake disturbed us that he did not see the anchor buoy that belonged to VAGABUNDO anchored outboard of us.

Before he knew what had happened, he had sucked the anchor buoy into his prop and his launch ground to a halt. There he rested, pinned to the anchor buoy and unable to go anywhere. He had a boatload full of military personnel waiting to be returned to their ship. After some minutes of trying to get loose or trying to find someone to blame, the poor coxswain, who was obviously not having a good day, stripped to his underpants; in the midst of the jeers of his boatload of sailors he slipped over the side and, diving under the launch, tried without any luck to get the rope loose. Hanging onto the side of the launch in the oil laden waters of Aden, he looked very woebegone.

In the interest of international relations I grabbed a mask and snorkel and a diving knife from TAKU's cockpit locker and took them across to the man by dinghy. After a moment's hesitation, he accepted them, and after a few quick dives he resurfaced, having cleared the problem. He showed me that he had made sure to refasten the trip line to its buoy and that he had cut the line right near the buoy to do as little damage as possible. He climbed back in his launch and leaned over to return the mask, snorkel, and knife to me. He shook my hand and in heavily accented English said, "Thank you." Still wearing his wet underpants, he climbed back into his uniform and got his launch under way. One could tell from the amused expressions on the faces of the sailors in the launch that the poor driver had not heard the last of the incident.

He turned and waved again, and I motored the dinghy back to TAKU. From then on every launch gave the two yachts a very wide berth as they passed; all of them slowed down and crept by until they were well clear. Watching the cruiser I even saw that the fulltime lookout, who had been keeping us under continual surveillance by binoculars, now busily polished brass on the wing of the bridge. Clearly the harbor was big enough for both of us; peaceful coexistence had been achieved. Who knew what was next?

Provisions and a full load of fuel were aboard that would see us as far as Port Sudan, some 500 miles north from the entrance to the Red Sea. The southern entrance at the Straits of Bab el Mandeb waited, a mere overnight sail away. With everything ready, we hauled anchor and steamed by the Russian ships, waving good-bye as we went. I felt sure they thought we were from the CIA sent to spy on them. The concept of someone sailing off around the world in a small yacht was not something likely to be part of their everyday lexicon. VAGABUNDO, who was also headed for Port Sudan, followed us out of the harbor and into the Gulf of Aden. As we sailed along the coast of Yemen we could see mountains in the distance.

The general characteristic of the western part of the Arabian coast between R'as el Hadd (*r'as* meaning cape, point, promontory, hill, or peak) at the entrance of the Gulf of Oman and R'as Bab el Mandeb (*bab* meaning strait, channel, pass, or passage) at the entrance to the Red Sea is that of a low and narrow coastal plain backed by a rocky and precipitous range of mountains. The mountains rise in height between 4,000 and 8,000 feet. From October to May, during the northeast monsoon, the prevailing winds assume a northeast to east direction and, following the curve of the Gulf of Aden, blow in a northwesterly direction through Bab el Mandeb into the Red Sea.

Bab el Mandeb, where we were headed, is divided by Barim (Perim Island) into two straits. Large Strait, between the African shore on the west and Barim, is about nine miles wide. Small Strait, between the latter island and the Arabian shore, is about one and a half mile wide and shallow, having depths between five and 16 fathoms. The currents can run very strong, and if the current is against the wind the seas can be very rough. Add all the ship traffic that pours in and out of the Red Sea, and you find an area that must be treated with caution and prudence.

With some 70 miles to go from Aden we had elected to leave in the afternoon so that we would reach the entrance to the straits in the early morning and have full daylight hours to find our way into the Red Sea and to set a course for Port Sudan. Bab el Mandeb was not a place for a yacht to fool around at night. Prepared for a night at sea, we scudded along the coast for the first day of what I hoped would be about a five-day trip up to Port Sudan. Buzz and Maureen were waiting. Most of the other boats we knew, including SHEARWATER, TYLIANNA, SEASMOKE and a few others were all relaxing in Port Sudan as well. We would be there in a few short days and back on schedule, or would we?

31

A Gift of Friendship

Sahid tightens the pressure of his arm around my shoulder as the truck swerves to avoid a ship of the desert—a large camel that meets us head on in the rutted track as we come over yet another rise. Abdul, the driver, mutters in Arabic to Sahid and shifts the gears of our four-wheel-drive vehicle, sending us lurching ahead again. Wedged between the two, I am a human demilitarized zone. Sahid and Abdul are both officers in the North Yemen Navy and, like me, are temporarily on land. Like many Arab men, each has a mustache, and like most North Yemenis I have met, they are armed. Each has a .45 in a holster. I am holding Abdul's Uzi machine gun butt-down on the floor between my legs.

Each time we lurch, Sahid squeezes to keep me from falling into Abdul. I, in turn, squeeze the barrel of the machine gun to keep it from pointing into my face. I am not a gun person, and I have an image of this piece of war air-conditioning everything should it go off accidentally. I try to act unconcerned, as though I am a person who routinely drives through the desert with a machine gun between his knees and not a cruising sailor who less than 48 hours before had sailed northward past the very piece of coast we are approaching in the truck.

Blowing sand obscures the horizon and sky in every direction; dunes and desert surround us. Occasionally we pick up a camel track like the one we are now on and Abdul guns us ahead on the harder sand. He is unconcerned as to where we are and jammers on in English about having visited California and having trained with the U.S. Navy. Sahid, in the hand that is not holding me, has a large fistful of green leaves. From time to time he sticks a few more in his mouth and chews them. He has a large cud in one of his cheeks. Abdul has told me that the leaves are called *gat* and most all Yemeni men chew them regularly, as they are a mild narcotic. "The opium of the people," he jokes. He has also told me that Sahid speaks Arabic and Russian and has been to Russia to train with the Russian Navy. *"Dasveedanya,"* I say to Sahid, as I try to remember some of the Russian phrases Armen taught me. Sahid grunts, laughs, squeezes my shoulder again and mumbles something in Arabic to Abdul.

A loud thump on the roof of the cab over Abdul's head causes him to spin the truck to the left and reminds us of the fourth member of our group. Standing in the bed of the truck and holding on with one hand is our guide. He is in full desert robes and has pulled the headdress across his mouth to keep out the sand and dust. His chest is crisscrossed with bandoliers of ammunition, and in his free hand he carries his own weapon. Hearing several quick thumps, we all scan around, and from behind another sand dune comes a small gray Land Rover on a parallel course. Its gyrations are similar to our own. I, for one, am glad to see that it is still with us.

Inside it are Celia and Philip and Julie from the Sydney, Australia, yacht ISOLDE, plus the little tugboat captain from Al Hudaydah, a youthful armed guard, Ali, and the silent driver who is, as Abdul has confided to me in an unguarded moment, a major in the Yemeni secret police and the man in overall charge of this whole "incident." Although Abdul doesn't come right out and say it, he is in awe of the major, a man both to be wary of and reckoned with. Abdul's revelations have somewhat sobered my thoughts of adventure, of the welcome change from the past months of sailing TAKU across the Indian Ocean, of the absolute lark quality of the day. The machine gun in my hand is real. Sahid is Sahid and not Howard Keel about to break into song about life in the desert. To the North Yemenis an American yacht aground on one of their miles of coastline is serious; they perceive a territorial invasion. Thoughts of territorial waters, illegal entry, and espionage run through my head. Sahid, as if reading my mind, gives my shoulder another squeeze; suddenly it feels both friendly and menacing. I concentrate on keeping the machine gun pointed elsewhere for the rest of the trip.

We are on our way south from Al Hudaydah (Hodaida), North Yemen's main port on the Red Sea, to locate Gale and Ann and their ketch, VAGABUNDO, grounded somewhere between Al Mukha to the south and Al Hudaydah itself. The whole situation has an air of unreality about it. Only four days earlier we had stood out of Aden and two days before, running wing-and-wing before a brisk 20-knot wind, we turned to starboard, flopped the main across, and cinched it down tight with the vang for our passage through the notorious straits of Bab el Mandeb. Our morning position put us just south of Bab el Mandeb, and as the sun rose behind us we saw Africa off to the west ahead, dark red on the horizon.

We had been extra alert since leaving Aden because of the Red Sea's extensive concentration of shipping. As we had neared Bab el Mandeb we had been seeing merchant ships passing in both directions in a continuous stream. Gale had called on the radio and congratulated TAKU for having successfully crossed the Indian Ocean, and he had admonished me to be equally diligent as we went up the Red Sea. His morning position had put him some five miles behind, and we had agreed on future radio schedules and on a dinner in Port Sudan in a few nights.

Now, some two and a half days later, we are in our sixth hour of traveling across North Yemen. We are behind the sand curtain, away from the comfort of the sea and TAKU, en route to a lonely stretch of coastline where VAGABUNDO has come to rest.

Two days before, 24 hours after passing into the Red Sea, we received a message that VAGABUNDO had grounded the previous night. Reefed down and running with a small staysail in over 35 knots of wind, we had headed for Zubayr Island some 10 miles to starboard and 30 miles off Al Hudaydah. Safely anchored, we were soon joined by ISOLDE, who trailed us by a few hours. We had monitored the radio and awaited the news of the refloating of VAGABUNDO. The news didn't come.

Less than 24 hours later, TAKU and ISOLDE were broad-reaching for Al Hudaydah to render what assistance we could. Peter and Jennifer aboard NUNAGA, an S&S 45-footer out of Marion, Massachusetts, were also off of North Yemen, and they interrupted their voyage to tuck precariously behind Zuqar, about 35 miles due west of the spot where VAGABUNDO was aground. They were acting as the communications link among the stranded vessel, the yachts ahead of us in Port Sudan, and us on our way to Al Hudaydah. Peter was able to get a message through to a U.S. Navy vessel in the Indian Ocean, which passed it on to the State Department for information and action.

Buzz and Maureen in Port Sudan set up a round-the-clock radio monitoring by the boats that were there. They, and we, recognized the risk we were taking going into North Yemen. Still, Buzz offered to sail all the way back from Port Sudan (some 400 miles into the wind for him) if he could be of any help. "Someone has to go in and help," Buzz radioed. We and ISOLDE, being the closest, were already closing with the North Yemen coast when he made this pronouncement.

As always with cruising, things have a way of changing rapidly in directions that you least expect. No matter how complete or comprehensive the planning, the unexpected always turns out to be far different from what one could possibly imagine. Whenever needs develop, the yachtie network pulls together to help. This case was no exception. Buzz, unnecessarily, thanks us for going and adds, "You know you are representing all of us."

The better part of the long day crossing to Al Hudaydah had been spent in conference on the radio with Buzz and Philip about the port itself. The harbor has a complicated entrance and a lot of shoals in the approach. TAKU, not planning a stop in North Yemen, had only a small-scale chart, which gave me little detail. Philip's chart was not much better. We read the Sailing Directions again and again. During the day Buzz obtained from somewhere in Port Sudan a copy of the Al Hudaydah harbor chart and went over it in detail at length with us on the radio. I worked out what I hoped would be a satisfactory chart by sketching from Buzz's description. I also realized from TAKU's DR that we would be arriving just at dark; it is a major shipping port, and I assumed, correctly as it turned out, that the hazards would be well marked.

As we closed with Al Hudaydah, Peter relayed that VAGABUNDO's situation was stable; they were behind a point which kept the seas down. He also related that they were surrounded by local Arabs who had come out of the desert, were all shouting and gesticulating, and for the moment were seemingly friendly. The language barrier had kept most communication on the beach to a minimum. At dark we followed ISOLDE into the inner harbor and anchored for the night just outside the channel.

The next morning, the day of our jeep ride, we were directed alongside the dock. We tied up, and ISOLDE rafted outboard of us. We were immediately boarded by eight armed men. One spoke excellent English and seemed relieved to hear that we had come only to help our friends who were stranded. There was much conversation in Arabic, and some messages were exchanged on portable radios that the men were carrying. We were told that it was a long way to the beach. The English-speaking man, the director of the port, suggested that it would be very difficult to get there and asked how many of the four of us intended to go. I told him that we were all going, and that we would go regardless of cost.

This pleased him, and I realized that I had passed some kind of test. He told me that our boats would be very safe, that he would post an armed guard to watch them (the guard, comprised of three soldiers with guns, was already present on the dock), and that we would leave immediately. I pointed to our yellow quarantine flag and told him that we had not cleared with customs or immigration. "You may do that when you return," he told me. "Right now you should see to your friend."

Soon the four of us were sitting sideways in the back of a govern-ment Land Rover, knees bumping, and the major, Ali, and the tugboat captain, who was acting as the port director's representative, were all shoulder-to-shoulder in the front. We traveled south for several hours through a bleak and barren landscape broken only by an occasional mil-itary checkpoint. Our vehicle was waved through with a salute at each one, and the major never slowed down or acknowledged the recogni-tion. We stopped in a small village, and the major barked some orders and we were soon, all seven of us, in a small cafe eating a magnificent meal; its excellence was only heightened by the poverty of its sur-roundings.

Finally we were driven into a fortresslike building that looked sev-eral centuries old. None of us knew what was happening; all our com-munication was done with sign language. From the courtyard of the building we were led up winding staircases to the top floor. On each landing stood rather fierce-looking Yemenis with rifles or machine guns. For a moment I got the sinking feeling of being taken to prison. Before I could discuss this possibility with the others, we were stopped outside of a door, and after being directed to take off our shoes, we were led into a richly furnished room.

At one end a large Arab dressed in flowing white robes reclined on an enormous pile of pillows. He was connected by a long velvet-covered hose to a six-foot-high water pipe that gurgled and smoked in the mid-dle of the room. He also had a giant TV set that he had apparently been watching. The two men whom I came to know as Abdul and Sahid were also in the room. Abdul, acting as interpreter, invited us to sit down, and we each selected a pile of pillows and waited to see what was going to happen. From the rigors of the sea we had been somehow transported to a Fellini film that was the Arab version of Catch-22.

Our host completed a speech, which Abdul translated. It seemed our host was the chief sheik of the area where VAGABUNDO had gone ashore. He regretted that his people had not been of more assistance and hoped that things would soon be taken care of. He was at our service, and the two officers would go with us, as would one of his bodyguards. Abdul turned to me. I improvised a speech about hospitality, thanks for the concern, really glad to be here, sorry for the inconvenience, and the appreciation for any assistance. None of our cruising guides had dealt with sheik etiquette. My remarks seemed to have the proper salubrious effect when translated by Abdul; we were quickly dismissed and sent on our way. I changed vehicles, which was how I have ended up riding between Abdul and Sahid for the final three hours across the desert to the coast.

Both vehicles turn into an isolated grove of trees, a sort of oasis, where there is a compound of houses. Abdul exchanges words with a small man; I later find out he is the local sheik, and we are now under his protection. This man gives some orders, and our two-vehicle caravan multiplies to four as we near the coast. We reach a stretch of magnificent beach bordering the Red Sea and turn southward. Back at the sea, I am suddenly more relaxed. I realize what an important element it is in my life and how in tune to it my senses are. On any other day we might be a group going to a picnic, but the machine gun in my grip reminds me that we are not. As we round a bend in the coast I can see VAGABUN-DO a mile or so ahead lying canted shoreward. The tide is low and she is almost completely dry.

Our reunion with Ann and Gale is joyful; they are as glad to see us as we are to see them. The scene on the beach is chaotic. Crowds of local Yemenis testify to the uniqueness of the event. Almost all must have walked a great distance; the area is sparsely populated from what I have seen. The atmosphere is that of a carnival. One man has arrived by horse and periodically gallops across the beach to the sand dunes and back, to the delight of the crowd. The only thing missing are the vendors selling souvenirs. We all examine VAGABUNDO's situation. She sits hard aground but is not damaged and looks as though she can be refloated with assistance.

I am suddenly surrounded by a crowd of excited men who are all talking at once and gesturing wildly. One addresses me, and I say "*Shukran*," one of the few words in Arabic I have learned. The crowd gets more excited, and this man, acting as spokesman, delivers a big speech. I realize that he is telling me their plan for refloating the grounded yacht. He points at his men, up the beach, at the boat, and out to sea. He pauses for me to speak. I give it a go and try to be as enthusiastic as I can.

"I don't understand a word you've said," I begin. "I'm an English major," I add with lots of enthusiasm. "Furthermore, I don't even know where I am! But whatever you say sounds good to me. Let's go for it! What do you say?" I slap him on the shoulder, and I feel as though I have just given a football game half-time pep talk.

They don't understand a word, but they apparently like the tone of my voice and suddenly they are all pounding me on the back and nodding their heads up and down and we are somehow all together. I sense that they have a plan to refloat VAGABUNDO but that the military is holding them back. I go and speak to Abdul, who hunkers in the Land Rover locked in conference with the major, Sahid, Ali, and the tugboat captain. Abdul tells me that the navy is sending a boat and a team of men the next day to refloat the boat at no cost to anyone. They have just confirmed this on the radio. He also tells me that as it is too late to go back to Al Hudaydah, we are to spend the night with the local sheik at his compound.

I explain to Abdul that I will spend the night at the beach with Gale and Ann, and he calls on the radio. Someone on the other end responds immediately, and Abdul merely looks at me and says, "It is not permitted." The sun has set, and it is beginning to get dark. With promises to be back in the morning, we are driven off through the unmarked sand dunes and back to the local sheik's compound.

We are treated as honored guests and feasted with a newly slaughtered baby goat cooked in a pit. The sheik's four wives buzz around like bees as they serve the dinner and clear away the plates. High wooden couches are carried into the courtyard, and we are made to understand that these, normally the beds of the sheik and his wives, are to be ours for the night. They are made up out under the sparkling desert sky and the number-two wife, the most organized of the four, makes motions for us to go to bed immediately. Abdul and Sahid have headed back across the desert, and the major and Ali have disappeared.

We are excited about the prospect of getting Gale and Ann back to sea the next day and glad that they only have one more night to spend aboard their stranded vessel. We exchange whispered comments and speculations about the day and about the people we have met. The compound gradually quiets down, and suddenly wife number two is there getting us up and motioning us to be quiet and to follow. She leads us out of the walled area and over to a waiting vehicle. Her mood is happy and animated, and we sense no cause for fear or alarm. We are loaded into the sheik's Land Rover, and from his sign language we learn that he doesn't want the major to know that we are gone. The four of us are wedged into the back of the Land Rover with two of the sheik's wives and several of his older sons. Three older men ride outside, hanging precariously to the door frames.

Soon it is apparent that we are on our way back to VAGABUNDO. We roar along the beach in the moonlight; the sheik driving in and out of the waves to try to splash the three hanging on the outside. Everyone is laughing merrily. The sheik is taking food to Gale and Ann. No matter that it is 11 o'clock at night. He has been waiting for our "guards" to go to sleep. VAGABUNDO looks eerie in the moonlight with the silver waves sliding and retreating around her hull. We pull up and the sheik blows his horn until a sleepy Gale and Ann appear. We then all pile below, and the crowd of us attempt to find perches in the tilting hull. Though we speak no Arabic, and our friends from the desert speak no English, we all seem to have a lot to say to one another. Finally, at about one in the morning, we are all loaded back in the vehicle and returned to the compound. We are snuck back to our beds and left to dream the night away under the desert skies.

The next morning I get Ali to give me his gun and turban, and we take some pictures before we go to the beach to await the navy. We wait a long time, but the navy never comes. Finally the major calls on the radio, and we are given to understand that the navy isn't coming. We are made to get back in the Land Rover, and with promises to Gale and Ann to do what we can, we make the long drive back to Al Hudaydah.

We spend nine more fruitless days attempting to get VAGABUNDO refloated. We negotiate a commercial contract for Gale with the port officials, only to learn that the port officials have no intention of sending commercial assistance. Peter and Jennifer arrive on NUNAGA to add moral and negotiating support. I manage to get to town and find a small advertisement for the Hilton hotel in San'aa, the capital of North Yemen. I go to the telephone exchange and call the number and by some miracle I get through. The desk clerk speaks English and, when asked, he gives me the phone number of the U.S. embassy. Peter and I manage to call the U.S. embassy in San'aa, only to be told that the boat on the beach is British, and besides, it isn't on the beach any longer because the Yemeni Navy has refloated it.

In the strongest language possible, I tell the embassy that the boat is American, that it has been on the beach approaching a week, that I have just come from there and that it has not, contrary to what anyone has been told, been refloated. I tell them that there are two other U.S. boats and an Australian boat under guard in Al Hudaydah. The embassy says it will "look into it." I comment to Peter that if they don't look into it I'll call my mother and that'll get them looking into it damn fast.

After our call to the embassy we get confined to our boats at irregular and unpredictable times. Sometimes we are given the run of the port area, but we are never permitted to go to town. Celia runs an informal medical clinic for some Ethiopian boat people who are confined to a dhow that has been seized and brought to port. Ignoring the protests and threats of the guards, they come and ask for basic first-aid attention. We, ignoring the threats of the guards, give it to them. An officious little uniformed major arrives and screams at us to stay on our boats as we are now under arrest.

The first aid has precipitated a crisis, and we are told by the port director to desist; apparently we are making the military officials very nervous. He promises to get medical care for the refugees, for that is what they are. We are at a stalemate, and Gale and Ann are still living in the hull of their boat at the beach. Buzz, in Port Sudan, is sending telexes to the American consulate in Khartoum, Sudan, and yachts in Egypt and Cyprus are doing what they can to get assistance rolling. Buzz tells me by radio that there is a large French yacht in Port Sudan ready to come down and help, and it will bring all of the yachties. When I suggest that they may all get arrested and deported, he puts the plan on hold.

The decks of our boats deepen with sand and loose grain blown from nearby loaders. We are hot, frustrated, and at a loss as to how to proceed; evenings are spent rehashing each day. Hampered by bureaucracy, we devise new schemes. Peter and Philip work out a plan with the tug captain, who has been on the scene, and he agrees to go down with his engineer, hire local labor, and get VAGABUNDO afloat. He wants only $10,000 to do this. Peter and Philip, through an interpreter, get him to agree to $7,000. We approach the port director with this scheme; he concurs, provided we go along to help. We spend a whole morning gathering all the equipment we think we might need. Out of NUNAGA, ISOLDE, and TAKU come anchors, lines, blocks, an inflatable dinghy, tools, come-a-longs, tents, and food. We are prepared to go for the duration. We wait, but the tug captain is not permitted to bring vehicles into the port area, and all of us, at the last minute, are denied permission to travel outside the port area by "security."

The days are going by, and we grow angry and frustrated. We become snappish with one another. Two officials from the U.S. embassy finally appear. They have been in Al Hudaydah but have been unable, until this moment, to get permission to come into the port area. The male member of the duo is the military attaché, and he uses his time to look around and gather intelligence data, telling us that they are not normally allowed in the port. He also tells us there wouldn't be any problem if "damn fools like the lot of us would just stay home." We are clearly not destined to be fast friends. He promises he will go rescue the "little lady" trapped on the boat. A Texan, he is full of himself and unwilling to call the embassy to get the ambassador to request help from the Yemeni government.

We seem trapped in a situation in which we make no progress, can see no ending, and cannot quit. We know that any day the northerlies will have worked their way down to North Yemen, making VAGABUNDO's beach a lee shore and the task of refloating her much more difficult.

Finally, at the end of the ninth day, we manage to have a meeting in the port with Gale, the representatives from the embassy, and the port director. We review what has happened, and the embassy officials say they will go down the next day and get Ann off the boat and to a hotel. The Texan has told us privately that the embassy couldn't care less about the boat and that once they get Gale and Ann to a hotel and then on a plane out of North Yemen what happens to VAGABUNDO is of little interest to them. For some reason, "security" flatly denies the embassy permission to travel down the coast to get Ann.

Peter gets on the phone and calls the port director to ask him to intervene. Shortly thereafter, a phone call comes to the embassy party saying permission is granted for them to travel the next day. The following morning I speak to Ann on the radio and explain our concerns that once she and Gale get off the boat, they may not get back and the boat may not get refloated. We tell her that the Texan wants them off the boat and things wrapped up. Ann says, "I understand." The embassy party returns without her.

Meanwhile, we have been dealing with a ships' chandler named Sahid, who seems to have the run of the port and the country. He tells us that he will organize a successful attempt to get VAGABUNDO refloated. He names a figure that seems reasonable and offers the proviso that he wants to be paid only if he succeeds. We send him into Al Hudaydah to the hotel to work out a contract with Gale and the embassy officials. Suddenly, we are told the next day that we must leave the port. We are permitted to buy fuel, take on water, and purchase supplies from Sahid the chandler, who brings them to the boats. We are no longer permitted beyond the bollards where our lines are tied.

We are being forced to leave. An officer arrives with our passports; they show no evidence of our ever having been in North Yemen. Sahid the chandler seems very thick with the officials and anxious to have us gone. When I ask to take his picture before we leave, he tells me that if I take out a camera in the port area, I will probably be shot. I accept his judgment. He tells me not to worry about the boat on the beach; he promises he will take care of it even though he has never seen it.

NUNAGA, the outboard boat, casts off, and we promise to see Peter and Jennifer in a few days in Port Sudan. ISOLDE leaves; she, too, is headed for Sudan. TAKU is the last boat at the dock. A crowd of guards and one or two officials watch. I give out my supply of magazines, some months old, to the guards. To the little major who has shown up I give *More Items from Our Catalog,* a satirical spoof of the L.L. Bean catalog, which offers, among other treats, babies in pink, yellow, black, or camouflage. I hope he will pass it on to the "secret police" so they can get a view of what decadent American life is really like. I remind Sahid of his promise to get the boat off. He smiles, his eyes hidden behind dark glasses, and says, "Yes, yes. Don't worry."

As we are about to cast off, there is a commotion on the dock, and the old Ethiopian man whom we helped pushes through the guards and beckons to Celia. He and his boat and family and crew, all refugees from the strife in Ethiopia, are still confined and under port arrest. For several days we have been floating parcels of food and clothing to them in a bucket attached to a line when our guards have been occupied elsewhere. The guards make a half-hearted attempt to push him away, but he stands fast. He indicates to them that he wishes to cast off our lines; they being guards and he being a seaman, they defer.

He reaches down and shakes Celia's hand; taking her hand, he puts something in it and closes her fingers around it. Celia takes the helm as I push us off and clear us from the dock. I gather the lines one by one, each removed from its bollard by the old man.

As we maneuver away from the dock, the old man gives me a small, slight wave. It is a seaman's "fair winds" wave, a wave of tribute and communion, the kind we give fellow cruisers when they leave port and put to sea. After raising the main, I go back to the cockpit and con TAKU out of the harbor. We turn the stern and our backs to the land and once more look seaward. We are headed back to a world that we think we understand.

"What did he give you?" I ask Celia.

"A gift," she replies, opening up her hand to reveal five small shells, "a gift of friendship."

32

Details

Rec'd from VAGABUNDO

Dear Dom,

Let me describe what happened after you left Al Hudaydah. I returned to VAGABUNDO and Ann with the people from the U.S. embassy. The colonel was my interpreter and in fact stayed with us to refloat the boat.

VAGABUNDO was on sand. There was a trough about six feet deep next to the boat. The sheik who controlled that area assembled between 90 and 100 people to push; some pulled, some lifted, to slide the boat into the water. Fortunately, we were in a large bay and the water was calm, which was a real asset. In addition to the people, the sheik also had four small fishing boats standing by with lines attached. VAGABUNDO was hauled back into deep water where we anchored while we went back to thank our friends.

After our experience, I promised Ann that we would ship the boat to the Mediterranean. We finally got space on a northbound Danish freighter. It planned to discharge her cargo in Marseilles, France. Orders were changed enroute. We were put back into the water in Sète, France, near the Spanish border. From Sète we sailed down the coast of Spain to Gibraltar. That part of our voyage took over a year. We sailed from Gibraltar to the Canaries and then on to the U.S. Virgin Islands. We then sailed direct to Florida where VAGABUNDO is now up for sale.

Regards,

Months passed before we found out what had happened. Philip, sitting in his cockpit one day in Port Suez, looked up and thought he saw

VAGABUNDO going by on the deck of a freighter bound for the Mediterranean. As it later turned out, he had. The eventual receipt of Gale's letter cleared up the mystery. But the year was now moving into April, and TAKU had over half the Red Sea still to sail. Catching up with Buzz and the gang in Port Sudan, we worked our way north in consort, moving when the wind allowed and staying holed up in various little watery indentations in the desert when the wind howled down from the north on the nose and made sailing difficult. We were in no hurry, hoping to arrive in the Med by late spring. We contented ourselves with looking at the unvarying desert scenery and adding new words to our nautical lexicon of Arabia.

Pushing north day by day we catalogued *bu'rat* (bay), *cor* (swamp, wadi), *djeziret* (islands), *jabal* (hill, mountain), *khawr* (wadi, cove, inlet, bay, lagoon), *marsa* (anchorage, cove, inlet, bay, bight), *qita'* (rocks in water), and *sha'b* (reef). I read that the Red Sea loses over eight feet of depth in the summer months because of evaporation. Though the scenery was unvarying, the dry desert backing on the moist sea provided a fascinating contrast as we moved along. On two occasions we saw a lone camel rider on the bluffs riding along miles from anywhere. And then, finally, we were in Egypt, at least according to geographers, although it looked the same as the Yemeni and then the Sudanese coast we had been sailing along.

After setting the anchor and backing stern-to the government quay between GAMBIT and a New Zealand boat called REHUATA with Bob and Ann and their two children aboard, it was time for a breather. We had met REHUATA in New Zealand, and suddenly here they were again. Another American yacht, TOAD HALL, arrived at the same time. I had met Peter Bollman in the Galápagos and saw him briefly again in Suva; now here we were bumping into one another in Egypt.

As new arrivals, we were directed to the local customs office in town to receive our clearances, have our passports stamped, and complete all the formalities of entry. The customs official, in full regalia, greeted us politely and asked for copies of our crew lists.

"Where is your official stamp?" asked the official, as he peered across the desk at us. After what was now turning into years of dealing with officialdom and their requests, I was prepared. I reached into my bag and pulled out a rubber stamp I'd had made in Fiji, which had the boat name and home port on it. Taking out the stamp pad that I also carried, I stamped the copies of TAKU's crew list for the official. If he was surprised he didn't show it, but rather turned to Peter and said, "You?"

Peter gave me a glance of annoyance, for he had obviously not run into the rubber stamp routine before. He looked the official in the eye and said, "I don't have one."

"But you must," smiled the official. "Otherwise I cannot process you."

"That's ridiculous," replied Peter. "I've never needed an official stamp before."

"But this is Egypt," shrugged the official. "If you want to get cleared you must stamp your crew lists." He busied himself filling out forms and then stamped my passports and handed me my clearance. Then he turned again to Peter. "Here is the name of a man in Hurghada who will make you such a stamp. He is the brother of my wife." The official scribbled a name and address on a piece of paper and slid it across the desk to Peter. He waved us away. Peter was fuming.

"I was mentally prepared for *baksheesh*, but this is outright larceny," Peter told me as we made our way downtown and started looking for the address on the piece of paper. Soon we passed through the market area where vegetables, fruit, eggs, bread, and all sorts of exotic, unrecognizable spices were for sale. The interaction between the vendors and the buyers, all in their traditional *djellabas*, gave a vibrancy to the air. After the confinement in North Yemen and the weeks working our way north from Port Sudan, the festive energy of the market was infusing me with a new energy.

Suddenly Peter stopped, and I watched as a large grin spread across his face. He disappeared behind a mound of melons into one of the market stalls. I followed him and watched as he held out his hand with some coins in it and pointed to a basket on the counter. The old stall keeper nodded, and when Peter held up one finger the vendor took an object and wrapped it in newspaper. He picked some coins from Peter's palm and passed him the package.

"C'mon," said Peter, turning to me and now obviously happy. "I didn't spend all those months in third grade for nothing." I trailed him back towards the customs office.

"But your stamp?" I asked.

"Got it right here," Peter replied with a mysterious smile.

The official was surprised to see us back so quickly, and I could see him preparing himself for an argument with a stubborn American. He was even more surprised when Peter asked for his crew list back. Peter unwrapped his parcel from the market and took out a potato. "Here is my ship's stamp," he proclaimed. He took a Swiss army knife from his pocket and deftly cut the potato in half. Taking half in the palm of his hand, he dug at it with the knife blade.

"But that," said the incredulous official, "that is a potato."

"Nonsense," said Peter, "it just looks like a potato." Turning to me, he asked if he could please borrow my stamp pad.

"That is not an official stamp," sputtered the official, "that is a potato." He was obviously over his depth with Peter, who was busy inking his newly made stamp on my proffered pad. "A stamp must have the vessel name on it," the official went on, obviously trying to forestall Peter.

"Exactly," replied Peter, pressing his inverted potato on the bottom of his crew lists and smiling broadly at the official. "There," he said as he finished the last copy. He handed me back the stamp pad. The official looked carefully at Peter's newly stamped crew lists and nodded. Suddenly I saw Peter start and grimace, and I watched his face darken. I could see the trouble: Although Peter had carved TOAD HALL in the potato half, it had imprinted backward.

"LLAH DAOT" read the newly imprinted words on the bottom of Peter's crew lists. "It *looks* like third grade," I whispered to Peter. I contemplated the trip to find the official's wife's brother and his rubber stamp factory. We stood there waiting. The official took Peter's newly stamped lists and put them in a folder. He filled out a clearance and gave it to Peter, and then he stamped Peter's passport. "Welcome to Egypt," he boomed. "I must tell the brother of my wife to beware of potato sellers." He laughed and directed us from his office.

"I don't get it," I said to Peter. "I was sure he wasn't going to let you get away with that."

"Neither do I," replied Peter. "We never carved words in third grade, only pictures. I forgot that it would print backward."

The words "print backward" jogged a thought. "Of course," I said to Peter. "In Arabic the writing reads from right to left. It probably looked fine to him." We both laughed.

"I wonder what would have happened if we had done words in third grade?" Peter mused aloud.

"We might have gotten to meet his wife's brother," I replied as we strode down the dusty street under the spring warm Egyptian sun.

33

Out of Egypt

"American sailing yacht, you must stop! Yacht TAKU, you must not go any farther; you must come to the dock!"

"Do you think they'll shoot?" I ask Celia.

"Let's not find out," she replies. Reluctantly I swing TAKU's bow around, and we reverse course, moving slowly into the current that has been propelling us along northward through the Suez Canal. We have been stopped at a major checkpoint, a large building with a dock built on the side of the canal every 20 miles or so to control and monitor traffic. Contrary to canal regulations, we are traveling on our own; we left our pilot behind a few hours ago.

Not that travelling through the canal is difficult. Approximately 80 miles long, the Suez Canal linking the Mediterranean to the north with the Gulf of Suez and the Red Sea to the south, has no locks and is basically a large ditch cut through the land to connect the two bodies of water. At the northern end is Port Said on the Mediterranean, and at the southern terminus lies Port Suez, where we have started. Traffic is closely monitored and permitted to move in only one direction at a time in convoy because the canal is narrow.

A convoy generally is comprised of about 25 ships. There are two southbound ones and one northbound per day. The majority of the ship traffic takes place during daylight hours, and no convoys are permitted to begin at night. At the southern end the ships start into the canal at daybreak and slide along at a rate of one every five minutes. Simultaneously, a southbound convoy enters from Port Said.

There is a large lake approximately halfway where the convoys pass. The southbound convoy is timed to reach the lake first, and it anchors there; as soon as the last of the northbound ships passes, it weighs anchor and proceeds on south to the Red Sea and ports beyond. At the northern end of the canal there are two channels, each about five miles long, leading into the Mediterranean, so as soon as the northbound convoy enters the exit channel, a faster, southbound convoy starts through the other to go nonstop to Port Suez, where the pilots are dropped, and then onward. Thus, every day, year round, in some 24 hours approximately 75 ships make the transit.

Vessels arriving at Port Suez are scheduled through by the canal commission after the proper paperwork is completed and the fees are arranged for by a shipping agent who, knowing by radio the arrival time, has the formalities finished and out of the way to minimize delays. For yachts, the procedure is different but no less complicated.

Having no agent, we had no way to call ahead and make arrangements. We had heard that there were agents available at Port Suez, for a fee, to take care of the considerable paperwork and to arrange for the transit of a yacht. They vied to attract the yacht market. Years before (how could it be years?), before TAKU had even departed the Caribbean to head west, I had heard stories of the Suez Canal agents. "Watch out for the Prince of the Red Sea; he's a crook," we were advised by one yacht. "Use Moses, the taxi driver; he's difficult to find but the cheapest by far," came other advice. I had filed this information in my mind and had made a note on the appropriate chart: "Avoid the Prince of the Red Sea. Moses is the man!"

"Moses is the man!" Who better to lead us through the intricacies of the Red Sea red tape and out of Egypt? Reading the notes, I remembered the conversations and reminded Celia. "I don't know why people get so excited about things. Remember being told about the Prince and the whole bit?"

"I'm sure it can't be as they all told us," Celia answered. "Except for your go-round with the ship's chandler in Hurghada, the Red Sea trip has been wonderful."

I had to admit I had gotten a bit excited in Hurghada soon after we arrived in this most interesting and friendly country. "Will Rogers never met the Hurghada's ship's chandler," I rejoined, trying to avoid the topic.

"Will Rogers never met a lot of people, according to you," replied Celia, not letting me off the hook.

"I was only acting; I told you that," I went on. "I wasn't serious."

"Well, you convinced me and most everyone else," Celia said.

In Hurghada and anxious to get ashore and off to Luxor with Buzz and Maureen, we had made all the necessary arrangements to leave the boat. REHUATA said they would keep an eye on things so that we would not have to worry about changes in weather or people going aboard while we were away. The only thing holding us up was the ship's chandler. He had a monopoly on all goods and services delivered to yachts and shipping in the port of Hurghada. My order for fuel and water was promised within 24 hours. We waited three days, until the trip to Luxor was about to start. Each time I saw the chandler he told me the supplies were on the way to the boat. He had taken all of our jerry cans and all of the water containers we'd been able to scrounge up, and he'd never brought them back.

The irony of the situation was that immediately outside the port area was a filling station where diesel fuel was available at about 12 cents a gallon. This was where the chandler bought the fuel, using jugs supplied by his customers. The price to the boat was approximately one dollar a gallon, a nifty profit for a 10-minute delivery. On top of that, the chandler asked for payment in U.S. dollars only, gave a lousy rate of exchange, and then asked for a delivery fee. "Foreigners" were not permitted to haul fuel into the port area, so we were virtual prisoners of the system and dependent on the chandler's whims.

He came by every day looking for business, and I finally hit on a scheme to get our fuel—or at least get our jugs back. I got him to come on board; we were stern-to off the quay and got on and off TAKU by using the dinghy as the water was too shallow alongside to allow us close to the dock. Once he was on board, I demanded that he produce our fuel. I had discovered that the Egyptians routinely screamed at one another and that in Egypt the sticky wheel did, indeed, get the most grease. The chandler made another excuse: "Perhaps tomorrow; today it is too hot. You will get it. Don't worry."

The chandler asked to be returned to shore. Then I pulled my surprise. I had decided that a "when in Egypt" approach might work. "I am holding you here till we get our fuel," I said.

The chandler laughed until he realized that I was serious. He called to the army guards on the dock to ask for help. One ran off to find someone who spoke English and returned in a few minutes with the port director, who spoke rapidly in Egyptian with the chandler. I started to scream. "This man promises us each day that he will bring our fuel. He never does. He will stay here until we get it. If we do not get it, I will throw him in the water, and he can swim to shore." I was shouting like a camel driver. Some anguished remarks from the ship's chandler seemed to suggest that perhaps he could not swim.

"Captain," pleaded the port director in his most reasonable voice, "I am sure he will bring whatever you want; just bring him ashore."

"He never brings anything," I shouted. "I keep him here."

A crowd of onlookers gathered. Soon the port director was shouting at the chandler, who shouted in return. It was a full-fledged yelling match. I was sure they were exchanging information about ancestry and reputations. The port director had the last word to me—in English. "If you bring him ashore, he will go now and bring your fuel and water. I, myself, shall stay here until it comes. I apologize for your inconvenience."

I decided to give it a try. I returned the chandler to shore, thanked the port director profusely, told him I was sure he had other work to do and not to wait, and he in turn told me to call at his office if the fuel did not come immediately. Within the hour we got everything we ordered. Celia, for the rest of the day, eyed me warily and told me that I needed the trip to Luxor far more than she thought. I assured her I was only acting, but she remained unconvinced.

I was in great spirits upon returning from three days in Luxor and ready to proceed north once again toward the Med. On arrival in Port Suez, I was disappointed to learn that Moses the taxi driver was gone. The Prince of the Red Sea, however, was still very much on the scene. While TAKU was on the approach to Suez, a large motor launch, carrying a distinguished-looking Egyptian man dressed in European clothes and toting an attaché case, drew abeam.

Before we could do anything, the launch was maneuvered skillfully alongside and the man stepped across to our deck, even though we were still doing five knots. He dismissed his launch, which took up station astern, and introduced himself as Mohammed, the nephew of the Prince of the Red Sea. He expressed the Prince's regrets that he could not meet us himself and allowed that the Prince would be most happy to represent us in our arrangements with the Canal Commission in organizing our transit as he has done for "thousands of his yachting friends from all over the world for years."

Remembering our chart with the warning to avoid the Prince, I asked about the details such as price and was given a quote of $125, which I already understood to be a fair price. I was told that I need do nothing, that the Prince himself would see us once we got anchored, and that his office would serve us in any way it could. Before I could say "pyramid," the launch had recovered Mohammed and sped off. We had little time to contemplate this experience because we were immediately approached by another launch full of screaming doubles of the ship's chandler.

This second launch proceeded in a haphazard manner and almost rammed us while the men on board yelled at the driver, screamed at each other, and exhorted us to hire the man at the bow, Ibrahim, as our agent. The more we waved them off, the more tenacious they became. "We will do your arrangements for 200 dollars," one shouted, while another screamed, "He is a good man; you can trust him." The others kept encouraging the driver to smash the launch alongside so that Ibrahim could join us.

They were a comical bunch, but they were serious. Fearing for TAKU's topsides, I cut the engine on one of their approaches, and they flew by. As we came to a stop, they slowed and approached more cautiously, still shouting all the while. I waved the card Mohammed had left us and shouted, "The Prince of the Red Sea represents us. If you have business with us, see our agent."

Apparently it was the right technique, as the launch veered off, and after a moment of silence all on board started their shouting again as they went off in search of other prey. And thus we decided—careful debate, reflection, discussion and thought having been replaced by impulse—to hire the Prince. The decision turned out not to be a bad one, and the Prince, bearing a gift box of pastries, appeared on board once we had anchored.

Dressed all in white European clothes, including white leather belt and shoes, he looked like he belonged in a shuffleboard game in Florida, but he was indeed a shipping agent and had, now that we had seen the competition, an obvious monopoly on the yacht trade. With Mohammed hovering behind him holding his briefcase, the Prince filled out some forms, asked when we wanted to transit, explained how the system worked, told us the location of his office and, collecting our money, disappeared. He was slick, competent, pleasant, and much easier to do business with than the basic Egyptian screamer. I was happy with the choice.

A later meeting with Mohammed confirmed the time of our transit. For the crews of TAKU and GAMBIT (and for a fee), the Prince had even arranged a car and driver for a day trip to Cairo; thus we were able to view the pyramids and visit the museums during the time we had to wait before we could commence our transit. He obviously had taken over Moses' taxi business as well.

After a day in Cairo surrounded by millions of people it was nice to be back aboard TAKU. Both boats had been told that the pilots would come aboard at 0430 the following day so that we could get underway and be in the canal by first light. With visions of Cairo's teeming crowds and thoughts of the wine-dark uncrowded seas of the Mediterranean in our heads, we all turned in for an early night. Our pilots came not at 0430, but at 0200. We discovered that, unlike the Panama Canal, the Suez pilots go only as far as the halfway point; by getting us going early, they could get home well before evening. We also learned that yachts did not travel by convoy, but rather went independently and were required to keep well to the side when ships of passing convoys were encountered.

By early morning the big ships of the northbound convoy had overtaken us and begun to pass, one every few minutes. As they approached we pulled way to the side and regained the center after each had gone by. The procedure was straightforward enough except for our pilot's continually insisting that we go "faster, faster" as he wanted to get home. He also reminded us constantly that we "must" give him a present at the end of the day. We had decided, on the advice of other cruisers, to give him a five-dollar bill but to put it in a sealed envelope to be opened once he had left TAKU. Otherwise, we were warned, the pilot would scream and demand more and try to embarrass us into giving in. This gift, or *baksheesh,* is part of the Egyptian style—as is the screaming.

We anchored next to GAMBIT at about 1600 and gave our pilot the envelope as the launch came alongside to retrieve him. This turned out to be too soon. He ripped open the envelope and extracted the bill, waving it in the air. "This is an insult," he shouted for the benefit of the approaching launch. "I have never had such a small tip in all my years as a pilot." This is the *baksheesh* way: dramatic, loud and colorful, but entertaining.

Wise to the ways of trade by now and aware that five dollars is a very good tip, we were not intimidated. Rather we sat and watched the show. Celia, at one of the pauses, said, "I am sorry we have insulted you with such a small tip. Since you obviously don't need it and don't want it, give it back, as we can use it." In a moment the bill was gone, swallowed up by one of the pockets of the pilot's brown wool greatcoat, which he had worn all day to ward off the cold. Just as quickly, the man disappeared with the launch. As he left he yelled that we must be ready at 0300 the next morning to finish the transit.

As always, early morning, especially with numbers like 0200 and 0300, comes sooner than you expect. We reluctantly dragged ourselves out of warm bunks at 0215 and dressed against the chill early-morning air. Our pilot didn't come at 0300 as we expected, and so we sat, getting more and more annoyed, until finally at 0415 we saw the pilot launch speeding in our direction. The launch stopped first at GAMBIT, and we could just discern, in the dark, the shape of her pilot clambering aboard, wrapped in a heavy overcoat. With a rush and swoosh of water, the pilot launch bumped alongside TAKU. But there was no pilot wrapped in a greatcoat to jump on board.

We were momentarily puzzled until the driver of the launch shouted above the din and racket of his engines, "You give us *baksheesh,* and we will go and get your pilot."

"We are not giving you anything," I shouted back. "We have been waiting for hours for a pilot, and we have paid our agent for all of the arrangements!"

I must not have sounded very convincing, for he repeated his demand.

I saw that GAMBIT had raised her anchor and was proceeding toward the canal, and in a moment of inspiration I moved to the bow and started raising our anchor. "We are picking up our anchor now, as we are late for our transit, and we are leaving. You'd better go get our pilot." I turned decisively away from the pilot boat and continued raising the hook. In a moment I heard the launch gun her engine and felt the roll from the wash as she roared away to shore.

"Now what?" asked Celia.

"Now we merely follow GAMBIT; they'll be right back with the pilot."

"I'm glad you didn't cave in," Celia told me, "but what if they don't come back?"

"They'll come back, and if they don't we'll just follow Buzz and Maureen. How can we get lost? It's a straight ditch all the way to the Med. Besides, do you think they'll let a vessel proceed through the canal without a pilot against the southbound convoy? Think of the problems if there was a collision; the whole canal would be closed."

As we motored slowly along we could pick out GAMBIT's stern light and outline ahead of us just turning north out of the lake where we had anchored and into the canal itself. Off in the distance I saw the lights of the pilot boat approaching. As we hadn't gone far, I took TAKU out of gear to await the pilot. But instead of coming to us, the launch roared off down the canal. We waited a few minutes and then got slowly underway again. The sky was getting lighter as we turned into the canal, where we were quickly confronted with the first ship of the southbound convoy.

Keeping well to the side, we proceeded northward, passing vessel after vessel in the southbound convoy. We could not see GAMBIT, which had disappeared far ahead of us. We were concerned, but at the same time we started to laugh. "We may be the first vessel to transit without a pilot," Celia said.

Now several hours later we are still proceeding without a pilot when we are ordered to pull into the checkpoint. I have a very uneasy feeling inside that the Egyptians are not too happy. "I hope we don't get arrested," I voice my concerns aloud. Without answering, Celia jumps to the pontoon with our bow line and with a deft twist secures it; without waiting for the stern line, she charges up the ramp to confront the official who is charging down.

"Where is our pilot?" she screams. "We might have been killed or gotten lost or run down! How dare you make us proceed without a pilot. We paid our fees. I want to speak to our agent. Why should we have to pay the launch to bring him to the boat? Where is our pilot?" Celia is still screaming and stomping her feet and waving her arms. The poor official looks befuddled and tries to calm her. "You don't . . . he's coming . . . he's coming . . . he'll be right here . . . please . . . just a few minutes."

"Don't just a few minutes me," shouts Celia. "He was supposed to come at three A.M. and he didn't and the pilot boat wanted *baksheesh*.

Baksheesh, do you hear, to bring him." Celia sounds like one of the taxi drivers in Luxor. The official is pleading with her to wait just five minutes.

"She's lost it! She's really flipped," I think to myself.

"Five minutes, please," asks the official placatingly as he turns and retreats up the dock.

"Celia . . .?" my voice is tentative. Something tells me you have to speak very calmly to disturbed persons.

She wheels on me and shouts "What?" and at the same time she gives me a wink and her face dissolves in laughter. "I saw that man coming toward us and decided that we would be here all day getting yelled at or worse. Then I remembered your performance with the ship's chandler and decided to beat him to it. Did you see his face? I don't think we'll get into trouble now."

Over Celia's shoulder I see the official prodding a pilot in a greatcoat to hurry. The official stays way up the ramp, not wishing to incur Celia's wrath again. The pilot says in English: "I am Ahmed, your pilot. We are sorry for the situation. But you should have waited for a pilot . . ." Before he can continue Celia goes after him.

"We did wait. The pilot boat never came back. They wanted *baksheesh!*" This she shouts, and seeing Ahmed wince, I know we will hear no more from him today. He holds up a hand.

"I have brought you some warm bread; perhaps you have not eaten."

"Thank you," I reply, breaking off a piece and trying it. "The bread is delicious." Celia tries some as well for we both know the Arab custom of providing food and also that a guest who accepts food is honor bound to do no harm.

"Would you take some coffee, Ahmed?" I ask.

"I'll make it while you get us under way," says Celia, disappearing below.

I start the engine and, pushing the bow out from the pontoon, get us under way. "I will steer if you like," says Ahmed. "I will steer you all the way to the end of the canal." He takes over the wheel, and we are off.

"I'll check on the coffee." I duck below. "You deserve an Academy Award," I tell Celia.

"Well, you weren't too bad yourself with the ship's chandler. Too bad our pilot isn't named Moses."

"Why?" I ask.

"Well, who ever heard of being led out of Egypt by Ahmed? Somehow it doesn't have the right ring to it!" We both laugh. We gather up the coffee, the bread that Ahmed has brought, and ourselves and go on deck to watch the canal slip by and to allow Ahmed, the pilot, to lead us out, at last, from Egypt.

34

Correspondence

June, Larnaca,
Cyprus

Dear Mom,

Things have been happening fast for a change. TAKU is safe in a slip in the Larnaca marina, as are the dozen or so boats that came up the Red Sea this year. We had a nice three weeks in Israel, where we tied up with GAMBIT at a tiny marina in Haifa. Made a couple of trips to Tel Aviv and an overnight one to Jerusalem. Also went and visited a kibbutz, which was interesting. Celia has gone to Rhodes, Greece, to take a job for a month or two as mate on a 70-foot British charter boat. I've pulled our poor old Volvo out and sent it off in a truck with a Cypriot named Minolus, who reportedly does great mechanical work and who thinks he can save the engine. I am busy doing repairs and trying to write, which, in a marina, is difficult. Every time I sit down to type, I hear a knock on the deck, and it is one of many friends just stopping by to borrow something or to say hello. I find that I have to work late at night to get anything done. The marina is so huge and the docks so long that it's easy to waste half an hour just getting to the showers and back. Almost all of the boats including TAKU have bought bicycles (little ones with 24-inch wheels) to facilitate getting around. Bob from the New Zealand yacht REHUATA calls us "the hole-in-the-wall gang" because we look like a bunch of desperadoes when we ride out in a group. The young man you said called from Framingham, Massachusetts, has gotten in touch with me. He's actually in his mid-fifties. His name is Jack Corcoran, but everyone calls him Buckets because he's a retired deputy fire chief. He will be coming on board as crew; I expect him to arrive in the next day or two. As soon as the engine is back, we'll be heading up through Turkey to Greece where Celia will rejoin. Her parents are coming in August for ten days, and my friend Jack McHenry from school is coming for a week in August as well. Several of us had planned to winter in Larnaca, but we've all changed our minds now that we've seen it. Not much to do here. Looks like Spain may make more sense. That would position us to return to Yugoslavia next summer before crossing the Atlantic. Buzz and Maureen are talking about wintering in Turkey, but I think sunny Spain sounds more inviting. I finally got the club boom fixed; it snapped in two when the bowsprit broke in Australia. Bruce Martin aboard the Kiwi yacht RUAH is a wonderful carpenter and scarfed a new end on to the broken boom. I went to pay him, but he refused. He told me that he was glad to be able to do something for me. I said that I didn't do anything for other people as I didn't have those kinds of skills. "You're our writer," he told me. "You write about what we all are doing and that's for all of us and we appreciate it." It's nice to know that others think of me as a writer, but Bruce's thought that I am "the group's writer" is a big role to fill. I hope I am up to it.

Love,

August, Rhodes, Greece

Dear Mañanas,

Here we are back in Rhodes. All roads seem to lead to Rhodes! (Ha! ha!) I think this is the fourth time now. As I wrote you from Cyprus, Buckets came aboard. Then I got a mysterious telex from a French couple who were arriving the next day for a two-week charter on TAKU. Thing was I never heard of them; actually, one turned out to be the brother of an old colleague. A friend I had casually invited to come sailing in Turkey couldn't come, so he passed the invitation on to this couple who thought that he had told me. He hadn't. Anyway, Pierre and Hélène came aboard, and Buckets and I cruised with them for two weeks up the coast of Turkey as far as Marmaris, and then we shot over to Rhodes, where

they left, and Celia returned after her stint on the big 70-foot
ketch. The trouble with the Med is that it is crowded; there are
probably 400 boats in Rhodes, moored three deep around the
inner harbor. There are also so many harbors in the Med that you
rarely see anyone you know, unlike the South Pacific where you
saw the same boats "down the line" as we used to say. I miss the
camaraderie. Celia's parents came, and we went on a ten-day
cruise back down the coast of Turkey and back to Rhodes. Then we
repeated the same tour with my friend Jack. Actually, Turkey is
extraordinarily beautiful. Lush forests, and mountains off in the
distance, and wonderful protected anchorages everywhere. Much
of it was part of the ancient Greek and Roman empires so there are
abandoned ruined cities and temples everywhere. Most are not
visited by western tourists as they are too inaccessible by land.
Having a boat is a real advantage. The people have been extremely friendly, and the food is delicious and cheap. Trouble is, old man
winter is peering from behind this paradisiacal scene, and it's time
to get moving. We're headed up to Bodrum, Turkey (formerly
Halicarnassus), and then across through some of the Greek isles
and on up to Athens. Then through the Corinth Canal and into the
Ionians, down around the boot of Italy, through the Straits of
Messina, across the top of Sicily and on to Palma de Majorca by
early December. That's a lot of miles to cover, but winter is coming. When are you guys off for Japan?

More as it happens,

December,
Atlantic City,
New Jersey

Dear Buzz and Maureen,

How things have a way of turning around! I hope you guys are well
settled in your snug little berth in Turkey. It's neat that you got an
apartment to stay in and don't have to freeze on the boat. After we
left you in Greece we made it through the Corinth Canal ($200 for
a mile-and-a-half ditch with no locks) and on up to the Ionians. I
think Corfu has to be one of my favorite places in the whole world.

It is about 25 miles long and rich in flowers and plants and trees as well as lovely old towns (some medieval) and wonderful vistas everywhere. Bundling up in a sweater, going ashore at dusk, walking up the cobblestones to the plaza, and sitting in a cafe as it grew dark was neat. There were chestnut sellers on many of the corners with little charcoal braziers going, and I really fell in love with the place. Would you believe I had to pull the engine again as my friend Minolus and his helper installed an oil seal backwards and we got oil trickling along the shaft into the bilge every time the engine ran? That held us up a week, and we were already behind schedule. We shoved off December first with almost a thousand miles to go to get to Majorca. Remember, I said we should all be snugged down by December first. I was right. We hit terrible weather and had to turn back and wait a day; then we had to motor with no wind all the way to the Straits of Messina and got through there and over to Palermo, and it was like someone threw a switch and winter started. We had 40 knots on the nose, and the Italian weather forecast called for *mare molto mosso,* which translates as very rough seas. We started for Palma, but made little headway, and after a day headed back to Palermo. I called home to tell them what had happened and found out that my mom was in intensive care in the hospital with a bad prognosis. TAKU was stuck between a rock and a hard place as they say. I couldn't leave, as we had to get somewhere for the fast-approaching winter. Palermo had no slips, so we shoved off and scooted back around Sicily, back through the Straits of Messina and down to Malta, where in 24 hours we hauled the boat and winterized it and packed and left Buckets there to finish up. Got on a plane to London in hopes of getting tickets there to go back to the States. Wow! Got to London and called home and would you believe, my mother answered the phone. Yes, she was in intensive care. No, she wouldn't stay there. Yes, the doctor said she could go home. When was I coming? Aaaagh! We spent a few days in London enjoying civilization and the Christmas season and got cheap seats on Air India to New York. By the time I got to New Jersey my mother was back in intensive care as the doctors had let her out too soon. The prognosis is again poor. She, a fifty-year smoker, has emphysema. They don't think she will get out of the hospital this time. Celia has gone home to Connecticut and plans to take some courses. I am with my aunt at my mother's, going to the hospital twice a day, and trying to learn all about the personal home computer. Not sure how all of this will play out but will stay in touch. Have a great Xmas!

Snug Harbors,

May, Atlantic City

Dear Mañanas,

Thanks for your letters and good wishes. The funeral confusions have finally settled down and all of the loose ends are beginning to be tied up. The doctors were amazed that my mother lasted for five months. Somehow after she had her eightieth birthday party last month she just got weaker and weaker. The hospice people were great, but it has been a long winter. On a brighter note, Peter is coming back to Malta to help sail the boat across the Med and the Atlantic. Celia finished her course work and is coming back, as is Buckets, who has been hanging out in Boston for the winter. I wish I was back in the Pacific; I envy you guys.

More as it happens,

June, Malta

Dear Buzz and Maureen,

TAKU seems to have survived. The yard here is painting the hull before launching. The price was about a fourth of the estimates I got while I was in the States. Peter, Celia, and Buckets are all busy doing boat work while I finish up some letters. I agree that Tunisia will be more interesting than the European coast of the Med. It's wonderful that we will be able to rendezvous here in Malta and cruise together again. We look forward to your arrival in a few weeks. Hope the rebuilt engine purrs like a kitten!

Fair winds,

35

Port to Port

As always, things turn out differently than expected. GAMBIT and TAKU cruised the Tunisian coast together. Being back in company with old friends was fun and with another yacht to share experiences on foreign shores life was more relaxed. We ate in exotic little cafes, took train trips to Tunis, and shopped in the *suks* for local merchandise. We explored the ruins of Carthage and sat in cavernous rug-seller emporiums drinking tea and looking at pile after pile of oriental rugs. But the end of July neared, and we needed to be in Gibraltar by September to get ready to cross the Atlantic in the fall.

There would barely be time enough to see a little of Spain before heading to Morocco and out to Madeira and the Canaries. We were a day out of Bizerte on the north coast of Tunisia bound for Spain's Balearic Islands. These islands, Ibiza, Majorca, and Minorca, lying in the crossroads of the Western Mediterranean, had welcomed sailors for thousands of years. But there was no wind. "Now I see why Odysseus took nine years to find his way home. Without an engine we might drift out here for weeks at a time." I had learned that in the Med there was either too much wind or no wind at all.

I called GAMBIT on the radio to make a morning position check as we had lost sight of her at dusk. She was always able to make about a knot better than TAKU when under power, and I expected her to be a good 15 miles ahead of us. "We've had a bit of trouble," Maureen told me when we made contact. "Our Volvo that Buzz completely rebuilt in Turkey threw a rod through the side of the engine, leaving a big hole in the engine and damaging the starter. We're dead in the water."

"Where are you?" I asked. Maureen read me their coordinates from their SatNav. I checked them on the chart and found that we were about four miles away. "We're on our way," I told them. "See you in about an hour." And within the hour we had sighted GAMBIT's familiar yellow hull resting stock still in the unrippled blue Med. We soon drew alongside.

'We'll just have to sit and wait for some wind," Buzz told me. "Then we'll sail into Minorca and see about getting some engine repairs done. You guys go ahead; we'll be okay."

"Look, suppose the wind doesn't come up for a few days or it comes up too strongly?" I was remembering the *mare molto mosso* of the previous winter. " I have a better idea. We'll take you guys under tow and head toward the Balearics, and if the wind comes up we'll let you go and sail in company with you till you get in safely. If the wind doesn't come up, we'll tow you into port, and you can get your repairs underway and not get stuck in the Med for another whole season."

Buzz agreed, and mumbling nasty words about the Volvo company, he rigged a bridle and we were soon under way at five knots for the island of Minorca some 175 miles away. The flat calm continued, and GAMBIT bobbed along behind TAKU like a child's pull toy on a string. Maureen had called us on the radio to tell us not to make supper as their freezer, which ran off the engine, was full to the brim with meats that were all thawing out at once. At supper time we slowed and pulled GAM-BIT alongside while Maureen passed us stuffed porkchops and all of the trimmings.

"I don't have to navigate or stand watch," she told us, "so the least I can do is cook. Steak and eggs for breakfast!"

By morning we were a bit under 100 miles out. There was still no wind. Buzz and I conferred on the radio. "I have been reading the various books we have on Spain," he told me. "As much as we really want to go to Minorca, getting to the mainland is harder from there. Looking at the engine, I think we're going to scrap it and get a new one and that will be a lot easier to do in Palma de Majorca. How do you feel about giving Minorca a miss and going straight on to Palma? It isn't that much farther. Or if you guys really want to go to Minorca we'll go there and then figure out how to get over to Palma. Are you there, Dom?"

"Yeah, Buzz, I was just giving Peter the new course for Majorca. We're not dropping you guys now. According to the SatNav it's about 90 miles, and I figure that at this rate if it stays calm we'll get in around midnight. Dinner ashore tomorrow night. Besides I always wanted to see how to put in a new engine. Don't forget we have a Volvo, too."

By ten that night we can see the loom of the lights at Palma, and by one in the morning we have maneuvered GAMBIT to an anchorage in the outer harbor and TAKU is safely anchored as well. There is still no wind. After breakfast we once again take GAMBIT in tow; soon we are both anchored side by side in the approved Med style, perpendicular to the quay in two open slots in the heart of Palma.

Palma remains a blur. We ran into many old friends who were passing through. Buzz found an outfit in town that sold a Dutch-built engine called a Vetus that would fit GAMBIT, and the new engine was soon at the quay in a crate waiting to be installed. Buzz, an engineer by trade, quickly got to work, and in a few days we were able to warp GAMBIT alongside the dock, and by rigging a sling with the boom and some extra tackle, we could lower the new engine into place.

In the meantime, we on TAKU busied ourselves with boatwork, provisioning, sightseeing, and going to the movies, as Palma's cinemas had first run features in English with Spanish subtitles. Plans to cruise Spain were revised each day as it was now mid-August.

Buzz was making good progress, but the task was a one-man job. He had to install a new exhaust system, new shift levers and cables, new gauges, and a new shaft and prop that had to be put in with scuba gear. It all took time. Buckets found himself a cheap apartment in Palma and announced that he had decided he would move ashore for a while and give up the sailing life. In a day he was gone. And then, during our third week in Palma, we all went one day to GAMBIT and stood by while Buzz proudly started the new engine. We were finally ready to head for "Gib." The summer was over, and no one had seen it go by.

The farther west we sailed the more detached I felt from the sense of cruising; it was as though the world had shrunk. Years before I would have been overjoyed to be cruising Spain's Costa Brava and Costa del Sol, but instead we sailed from port to port barely noticing any change as TAKU moved toward Gibraltar and the Atlantic. Where heretofore the world seemed to stretch endlessly off to the west with years and years and miles and miles to go to get all the way around, the distance and time remaining was now finite, measurable, and believable. Gone was the carefree feeling of being off in another universe, cut loose from life at home.

The occasional Australian and New Zealand boat with whom TAKU shared harbors still had that sense of excitement and adventure. For them, their familiar worlds lay far away across the Atlantic, the Caribbean, the Panama Canal, and the vast Pacific. Everything they saw was new and wonderfully foreign to them. East Coast Americans have this affinity or connection with Europe; it's as though it is right next door. Europe seems familiar territory. We know it, despite the fact that the languages and cultures are different. And I still had this sensation of needing to move on, that there was somewhere I had to be. Time and distance were shrinking proportionately. No more of the kicked-back, take-it-as-it-comes life.

My cousin Tip arranged for a month's leave from his job with the government to join us. Crossing the Atlantic was something that he had always wanted to do and for which his earlier passage from the States to the Virgin Islands had merely whetted his appetite. He planned to come aboard in the Canaries in mid-November, and I had promised to have him across the Atlantic and in Barbados so that he could fly home in time for Christmas. I could always sail back to the Med. Why, just a few weeks sail across the Atlantic and I'd be there, and then I could really relax and spend the time necessary to see everything. This change in attitude, when I allowed myself to get in touch with it, surprised me. Cruising, I had learned, was much more people than places. I missed the sense of close sharing that had gone on in the Pacific and in the Red Sea.

October, Gibraltar

Dear Mañanas,

Hi from the rock! There really is one. The last day sailing down the coast of Spain we could see it like a beacon looming larger and larger in front of the bow. The weather has been magnificent, and now that we are here, I can relax a bit. The prevailing westerlies start any time now, and I was hoping we'd make port before we had to beat. There are about 25 cruising boats squeezed into the tiny marina here. Some new friends and lots of old one. A merry old bunch to say the least. Gib is neat: old winding streets that used to be cart tracks, little cafes, interesting shops and chandleries and every kind of boat part that you would ever need. We're off in a day or two for Morocco. I sound so casual when I write that, but it is just across the way. Then out the Strait to Madeira, about a five-day passage, and after a few days there, we'll drop down the 250 miles or so to the Canaries and make our departure from there. Write c/o AmEx Barbados.

Happy Halloween,

October, Madeira

Dear Mañanas,

Well, we made it to Madeira. I have found a second place that I have really fallen in love with. The first was Corfu; the second Madeira. We are tied up to the breakwater in Funchal with almost all the same boats that were in Gib plus a few more. Madeira is quite steep with lovely winding roads and lush vegetation. It is Portuguese and you can almost sense a going back in time. I feel like I might have stepped off a British ship-of-the-line that has put in here for last-minute provisioning before heading to India or elsewhere. There is such a sense of timelessness about the place. That's particularly welcome given my recent sense of time rushing by. Of course, it's fall again. Autumn, I guess, is my favorite season of the year. The days get shorter, and there are those marvelous early evening times that in the summers were merely hot afternoons. I realize that I was in Corfu at about this time last year. There must be something seductive about the fall for me. Darken the day, put a slight chill in the air, put on a warm wool sweater and even socks, and wander the streets. It's how I imagine the London of Dickens' time. For some reason I always think of it as being autumn or winter in his books, not spring or summer. It's the romantic in me. Or is it? At any rate, we had a pleasant few days in Tangier and saw lots of interesting markets and people, but I am glad this is the end of the Arab countries for awhile. Constantly having people trying to get you to buy things, or go places or look at things, gets to be wearing after a bit. The passage to Madeira was an uneventful five days. Either we are getting better at it, or in fact, the passages are indeed routine and uneventful. Well, gotta go. Most of us are meeting in a little cafe we found for *empanadas,* which are wonderful skewered meat and vegetables. The local wine is nice, too. We expect to be in Grand Canary for a week or so getting ready for the last crossing. We're off for there tomorrow. The next letter will be from the Caribbean.

Fair winds,

36

The Pond

Ishmael, the questing seaman and narrator of *Moby Dick*, reflects about sailing around the world: "Round the world! There is much in that sound to inspire proud feelings, but whereto does all that circumnavigation conduct? Only through numberless perils to the very point whence we started, where those that we left behind secure were all the time before."

Twenty-two days out of Las Palmas, Gran Canaria, in the Canary Islands, we will, if our navigation proves true once again, make landfall in Barbados in the West Indies on the ensuing day. We will, as well, have crossed the Atlantic (referred to by many simply as "the pond"). And we will, in the jargon of the crews on the multitudes of slick racers we have seen, have finished "t.a." (transatlantic to the uninitiated). Lastly, being in Barbados will put TAKU some 90 miles to the east of Bequia, a small island in the Grenadines.

On arrival in Bequia we will close our outbound track (something circumnavigators speak of) and finish, at least geographically, TAKU's voyage around the world. We had last called in Bequia some six and a half years before—before turning westward toward Panama and the Pacific. Thus far our t.a. passage has been what would be classified as ordinary, if crossing an ocean in a small sailboat could ever be described that way. With four of us on board, a sense of comparative luxury exists compared to passages made across other oceans.

A note taped to the bulkhead in the galley shows the work schedule for the trip: Day 1, cook (except breakfast, which is do-it-yourself); Day 2, wash dishes; Day 3, sweep floors and clean the head; Day 4, free. This schedule has worked without a hitch. We have been more than adequately provisioned, and even at this stage of the voyage we have grapefruit and oranges from the Canaries remaining and edible. Bread has gone by, as have most of the salad ingredients (there are still a few heads of cabbage left; it keeps almost forever), but the meals coming out of the galley are as varied and unusual as the cooks preparing them. Washing dishes every fourth day has not been much of a chore, though all of us, at times, have wished for paper plates, and having someone sweeping up and cleaning the head every day has reduced this sometimes onerous task.

So, too, with watch standing. We do two hours on and six off round the clock, which gives everyone adequate off-watch sleeping time. The Aries vane has steered flawlessly, even after all of these years, and during the light–air parts of the voyage (of which there have been a few) when the vane won't track, we have employed our new autopilot, which I installed in Gibraltar to replace the 12-year-old one, which had finally gone terminal. Even the SatNav was doing its job, keeping track of our position as we moved along.

I had established the watch-standing assignments by trying to best suit the personalities of those on board. Peter, back for a second time, was a reliable and experienced watchkeeper. Tip, also back again, had not been aboard since the first offshore passage, but was an experienced sailor as well. I told Celia that I would sandwich Peter and Tip's watches on either side of our own. "That way," I said, "if there's a problem they can call, in the first hour, the person who has gone off, or in the second hour, the person due to come on."

I gave myself the 0600 to 0800 watch. I had found that I like to get up early at sea, and once it is light I can rarely sleep; I enjoy a bit of breakfast as well. Peter, I decided, would precede me on the 0400 to 0600; he is not, I had discovered over the years, a morning person, and he would much prefer to sleep until lunch than to get up for breakfast.

Thus went my reasoning. Celia got the 0200 to 0400 watch by default. Tip inherited the midnight to 0200 watch, and when he learned about it said, "You mean I'm off from six until midnight and then have to get up for only two hours, and then I can sleep for six more? Fantastic!"

So for 22 days the passage has been routine; the twenty-third day will be the same—two hours on watch keeping an eye on the course and the sails and a good lookout. During the off-time in the day, chores are done and meals are cooked. I have, as well, limited our sail changes as much as possible to the daylight hours, having no urgent schedule that would require otherwise. I am surprised at how quickly the sail changes go with four people. Doubling the size of the crew causes a geometric progression in how fast the jobs get done. No wonder the old sailing ships carried such large crews. I begin to feel that previous ocean passages have been mere dress rehearsals where all the mistakes have been made and that, finally, everything is coming together in a performance that one can be justifiably proud of.

On three occasions we have set TAKU's bumblebee-striped spinnaker and carried it as long as the wind stayed aft and remained favorable. We have set and handed the mizzen staysail as conditions warranted. I love this sail best of all. It is lightweight, extremely easy to set and douse, and provides a substantial increase in sail area and speed. With the exception of the storm sails, which I hope to never see out of their bags again, we have gone through almost the entire wardrobe of canvas. We have carried up front, with the twin downwind poles, various combinations of sails; these have included the unhanked, wire-luffed running staysails, a combination of one running staysail with poled-out yankee or #1 genoa, and in lighter airs a poled-out, red-and-white-striped 600-square-foot drifter. Suddenly I feel like we are really sailing across an ocean rather than merely making a passage from one port to another.

The wind, for the latter half of the passage, has been out of the east to eastnortheast, and as our projected course is southwest to west, we've been almost continually dead downwind (ddw we refer to it on board) for a number of days. We have gybed back and forth every day or two to hold as close to our trackline as possible and to favor the slight shifts in wind direction that have occurred. Another factor that impels us to gybe across is an attempt to find the tack with the most comfortable ride for the swells that are running. After long hours on one tack we decide to try the other "in case it might be a little more comfortable." It never is. We have had an uncomfortable cross-swell for the entire trip, and we never figure out what has caused it. With the wind now holding between 10 and 15 knots, TAKU is averaging an easy six knots and logging between 135 and 150 miles each day. "Rolling home," as the old chantey used to go.

The first third of the trip was not as pleasant. With less than five knots of wind after leaving Gran Canaria, we were forced either to sit or to motorsail. Hoping to get across before Christmas, I elected not to sit. Under sail, with the engine turning over slightly better than slow rpm, we were able to do between 90 and 100 miles a day as we tried to conserve our fuel. TAKU has a range of 700 to 800 miles under power, clearly not enough to go all the way across the Atlantic. I was concerned about the wind; if it didn't fill in we would, at some point, have to drift and wait.

On day five we sighted a merchant ship on the horizon and raised it on the VHF radio. The vessel turned out to be an Italian tanker en route from Brazil to the Mediterranean. It also turned out to have a load of fuel on board. The ship reported no wind for the preceding three days, which for us was a bad sign. The elusive trades were being more elusive than ever. The ship also reported sighting a number of sailboats headed west and not very fast. The ship's captain turned out to be an avid yachtsman, and when we asked him if he had any spare fuel he promptly altered course in our direction and within minutes was doing tight circles around TAKU to take the way off his ship.

When the tanker came to a stop, we were told by radio to come along the lee side and tie up. Although the wind was slight, the ocean swell rolled the tanker sufficiently to make tying up alongside hazardous to our hull and especially to our rig. We lay about 10 yards off and had a conversation. The crew wanted to pass us a four-inch-diameter fuel hose and to fill us up to the decks, but we explained that we only had a three-quarter-inch opening and not only couldn't handle the hose but couldn't handle a full boat of fuel. The crew of the tanker (the ALESSANDRO VOLTA) lined the rail to yell and to wave hello while Celia spoke on the VHF with the captain. He expressed disappointment that he couldn't give us a few tons of fuel, but he asked us to stand by. They would give us two 60-liter plastic wine casks full of fuel, but first they had to empty the dregs and clean the casks a bit. I pictured our injectors being clogged by a so-so vintage chianti. We wallowed alongside like a small pilotfish next to a big sleeping whale and waited.

Celia went down below and dug out a bottle of wine and put a ribbon on it to give as a present to the captain. Peter, on his own, wisely dug out our Italian courtesy flag, which, when he ran it up to the portside spreaders, elicited a round of cheers from the tanker's crew. Tip, on the other hand, ignored the gaiety of the moment and began to get agitated about how close I was maneuvering TAKU to the tanker. "Back off," he yelled at me. "They'll crush us if they hit us."

Confident in TAKU's maneuverability, I got annoyed. "Look," I shouted back, "it's my boat, and if I choose to wreck it by getting it smashed by a tanker, it's my business. Besides, if we get shipwrecked here, our rescuers are right alongside. You could probably just step aboard and not get wet! Relax!" Tip was not mollified.

The captain appeared on the waist deck of the tanker and beckoned us closer. Peter had rigged fenders, and we came slowly alongside. I watched carefully for the roll of the tanker; for all my bravado I didn't relish terminating our voyage in mid-Atlantic and going off to Italy in a tanker as supercargo. There was much laughter as we passed the bottle of wine to the captain, who was simultaneously passing a bottle of wine to us. Wine seemed to be the gift of the day.

"What else do you need?" they asked us in broken English. "Water? Food?"

"No, nothing, thank you. We just need wind!"

"Sorry," shrugged the captain, looking dismayed, and then brightening, "but the fuel will help you find wind, yes?"

"Yes!" we all replied enthusiastically, and everyone laughed again. The crew passed us the end of a line while we passed them a line at the same time. Getting that sorted out took a minute. Then, one after the other, the two 60-liter former wine casks, now drums of fuel, slid down the line to Tip and Peter who hoisted them aboard and secured them.

"Can I give you a position?" I called jokingly to the captain.

"No, no," he laughed.

"Do you need the containers back?" Peter called across.

"No, no," came the answer again.

"Can we pay for the fuel please?" we asked. This time the "no, no" was very emphatic.

"Good luck," the captain called. "I am afraid we must go." We pulled slowly away as the ALESSANDRO VOLTA set her engines in motion. We took photographs and waved our goodbyes as we set off westward once again. With much hooting of whistles and waves from the crew, the VOLTA pulled quickly away and was soon a spot on the distant horizon, leaving us alone again in possession of the ocean under a blue, cloudless sky.

We never needed the fuel. Within 24 hours the trade winds filled in, and we carried the two containers of fuel the last 2,000 miles of our voyage, lashed on deck unused. The wind held to Barbados, but it brought with it for the first few days a heavy coating of red sand all the way from the Sahara. The sky looked extremely hazy, and the sun had a ring around it for days. The rigging, the sails, and the decks seemed odd when we looked at them covered with sand while we were hundreds of miles from Africa and the desert. We saw no other vessels except for one sail on the horizon two days out of Barbados. Now, with only a day to go, I think back over the 1,900 miles we have sailed since our contact with the VOLTA.

We've set and handed sails, sighted a whale, and spent a hot day on the galley floor disassembling and rebuilding our Volvo's starter motor, which had decided to retire in mid-ocean. Tip, master mechanic that he is, traced the problem to a worn-beyond-repair solenoid. Even though Minolus had rebuilt the engine itself, the auxiliary parts were still the originals and beginning to show their age.

"Tip, can't you really fix it?" asked Peter. "You seem to be able to fix everything."

"I wish I could," Tip replied. "Are you sure you don't have a spare solenoid? You should probably carry one, you know."

"Tip, we've made it almost 40,000 miles without one. There are lots of spare everythings we should carry, but if you worry about all of them you never get away from the dock. We've got a good boat, good sails, lots of food, and a good crew. That's enough."

Tip continued to mumble about spares and showed Peter where the solenoid was broken and was going on about springs and rods and things that I didn't want to hear about.

Suddenly Peter raced up the ladder to the cockpit and I could see him rummaging in the port cockpit locker. Soon he returned carrying a very full and heavy plastic bag. He set it on the floor in front of Tip. "There," he said. "Buzz was right. You didn't want this stuff, Dad, but I stuck it in the locker just in case."

Tip opened the bag and pulled out piece after piece of Volvo-green engine parts. A spare piston emerged, followed by rods, springs, gaskets, impellers, pumps, bolts and washers, and at the bottom of the bag the damaged starter from GAMBIT's dead engine. Buzz had offered me all the miscellaneous "junk" he had stripped off the engine, and I had thought, "What do I need all these old parts for; we've just had the engine rebuilt and only have to get across the Atlantic." Peter, wisely, had stowed the bag on board.

Even I could see that GAMBIT's starter, which had been hit by the thrown rod, was damaged beyond use. But Tip rolled it over, and there, still attached and undamaged, was the solenoid, an exact match to ours. In a matter of minutes Tip and Peter had replaced our useless solenoid, and before I knew it they had TAKU's engine up and running. I had to admit that I felt better inside.

"See, Dad, if we hadn't rescued them, then they couldn't have rescued us," Peter said. "Like you say, you never know what's next." You never do.

For the past four days we have listened to the Big RA, or Radio Antilles, the voice of the Caribbean, playing selections of Caribbean Christmas music. The favorite of the year is by Barbados' own Red Plastic Bag, who sings about finding Maizie (the title of the song) driving him crazy by "making movements with Santa Claus," who apparently has come not by sleigh but by B.W.I.A. (British West Indies Airline). The song is played so often and is so catchy that we are all humming "Maizie" in spite of ourselves. The Big RA exhorts us to shop, as Christmas is only a few days away; we merely check the compass, the horizon, and the sails, and sit in the cockpit under the tropical sun and marvel at the incongruity of it all.

We have thought, each in the solitude of our watches, of the future. Watching the nightly array of falling stars, I have begun to try to find a perspective on the circumnavigation. The Southern Cross, low, but still visible on the horizon in the early morning hours, reminds me of places visited and other oceans crossed. Is there life after circumnavigation? What kind of accomplishment is circumnavigation when you finally sit down and realize that you have done it? Now that it will be completed, what will it be worth, tangibly and intangibly? For me, the lure of the sea and of adventure is still very strong. Celia is more interested in getting back to shore and some more formal higher education. Tip, taking time off from an interesting career, is experiencing an adventure of measurable dimensions. My adventure has been my career, and its dimensions have always seemed to be measureless. Now, I am not so sure. I am not, like Peter, headed back to school, with hopes of owning a car, making money, and getting into the fast-food fast lane.

For a long time (six and a half years), life has been largely determined by the weather and the ports toward which TAKU sailed. With less than 200 miles to go to that imaginary point where we will cross our outbound track and mark the geographic end of our route around the world, I am struck by Ishmael's words.

Have we passed through "numberless perils" to arrive *only* at "the very point whence we started?" Are all those that we "left behind secure" there before us? Of course they are. The realization hits me. Our arrival may just be "an arrival" in the sense of a passage completed. Perhaps Ishmael is suggesting that the value of the circumnavigation is not in the arrival as much as it is in the doing of the adventure. This thought contents me for the moment. I think of places visited, of friendships forged and kept, of 40,000-plus miles of sailing and the multitudinous things that I have learned upon the waters of the world. Am I different from when I left? Of course, but in what specific ways I cannot determine until I indeed get back—and may never indeed determine. On this day before landfall I am content to think about the myriad events that when strung together, make up a passage—this passage.

37

Familiar Shores

LOG ENTRY

New Year's Morning

Off Bequia, W.I.

0600- Sails full and by, course west-southwest, speed five knots, weather clear, winds east 15 knots, seas slight, Bequia in sight. Crossed outbound track completing circumnavigation of the world after six years, 143 days since departing Marblehead. What now?

April, St. Thomas

Dear Buzz and Maureen,

By the time this gets to you guys you will have made it across to Panama and be getting ready to transit the canal to head back up toward San Diego. It was great catching up with you in Martinique, and wonderful to be able to share a last anchorage on this side of the Atlantic. We have been working our way slowly up the islands and revisiting places. It's not the same. Thomas Wolfe was right, "You can't go home again," but home, wherever that is, is where TAKU is headed. I thought for a bit that I might want to stay in the Virgin Islands, but I think I need to sail back to the States first and really complete the trip around the world. To stop here now would leave things incomplete. Sort of like not reading the last chapter of a book you've labored through. I kind of thought people would notice TAKU; you know . . . "Hey, there's the boat that just sailed around the world." But, as usual, I was wrong. We're just part of the scenery. Good luck on your transit. I expect we're going

Puerto Rico, Bermuda, and then New Jersey and back to New
England. How easy it all sounds at this point.

Hope the tehuantepecer doesn't get you!

May, St. Georges
Bermuda

Dear Mañanas,

Arrived here on the tenth. Boy, is it cold. Took us seven days from
San Juan. We had sailed overnight from St. Thomas to San Juan,
and we no sooner dropped the hook in San Juan Harbor when I
heard "Yo! Ho!" shouted from the shore. The only person I know
who does that is Buckets, and when I went ashore in the dinghy,
there he was. He was in San Juan on a bit of a vacation with a new
lady friend, and they were at the fort that overlooks the harbor
when we sailed in. He was telling the friend that the boat down
there was like the one he had sailed on, and then he saw it was
TAKU and started yo-hoing from the fort. Of course we couldn't
hear him, so he jumped in a cab and followed us as best as possible all through the inner harbor, he on the shore and us on the
water, until we anchored. His friend had to go back to the States,
but I asked him if he wanted to sail to Bermuda, and he said he
did, and he did. Small world. It's hard to believe that we are a scant
500 or 600 miles from the States and that once there, you're there.
I wish I was headed for Japan like you guys, but that would have
added two years to the trip. Being gone nine years instead of seven
probably wouldn't have made any difference. Lots of boats here.
Every day another one or two stagger in. Many have ripped sails
and broken rigging from a wicked northeaster that they got caught
in between the U.S. and here. We plan to sit here for a week or two
until the weather really moderates; it is still too much spring and
not enough summer. Then we'll make landfall in Atlantic City in
time to go on up to NYC, the Big Apple, for the Fourth of July.
Holden Caufield said that when you start remembering things you
miss people a lot, or something like that. He was right.

Sayonara,

TAKU rolls gently in the North Atlantic swell as she slides up the coast from Atlantic City, New Jersey, toward New York City and the coming Fourth of July celebration. It is night. We are enshrouded in a cocoon of darkness that is pierced, however slightly, by the loom of our tricolor masthead light. The light does not appear to penetrate very far, and through the rainsqualls and showers that accompany us we keep the best lookout we can. The autopilot is doing a good job steering, which allows me to move about the cockpit. I scan behind us to the starboard side, and then bend to look off to port under the sails toward land, the lights of which continue to slide by. We are about two miles off. Behind us somewhere is Brigantine, named for a ship that foundered there, Seaside Heights, Beach Haven, and Ship Bottom. It's easy to imagine how the last got its name. Also astern are Barnegat Inlet and Barnegat Light.

I am reminded of Walt Whitman and his poem "Patrolling Barnegat" and the lonesome, edge-of-the world perspective he was able to evoke. Here, offshore, you can almost feel the tug of the land on one side and the insistent call of the sea on the other. TAKU rolls along, bow wave hissing, oblivious to both.

We have decided to go to New York for the glorious Fourth of July, to see the rededication of the Statue of Liberty, and to pretend that the big celebration in her honor is really a welcome home for TAKU and her crew.

The Fourth of July has been an annual benchmark on TAKU's voyage around the world. I remember celebrating the near-completion of the initial refit in Marblehead, Massachusetts, by sitting on the rocks at the edge of the harbor watching the fireworks go off. A year later, we were bundled in warm clothes and celebrating landfall in the haunting Galápagos on my first day below the Equator. I remember the chill of the Humboldt Current sweeping up from the cold Southern Ocean had been a surprise to the four of us then on board.

A year later I would be saying, "A year ago we were crossing the Equator at the Galápagos!" We would be at a cookout on the beach of a small island in the Va'vau group of the Kingdom of Tonga. Friends from several American boats had gotten together for a potluck cookout and Fourth of July celebration, including Bob and Jane on BROWN PALACE who would go on to share many anchorages with TAKU for the next two years.

The evening was perfect—the warm, tropical moonlit night that we all dream about but seldom experience. The wind lowed in the palm trees, the dinghies bobbed at the water side. As the evening got late the talk died down, and we all sat wrapped in our own thoughts until suddenly Bill announced, "We can't have an official Fourth of July without fireworks." With that he went off in his dinghy to retrieve SINTRAM's flare gun, some flares, and an outdated hand-held signal.

The first flare of the parachute flares went "pffffft" and splashed off in the night without igniting. The second one did the same. "Great fireworks, Bill," someone commented. "Watch this," he replied, firing his third and last. It went with a bang and illuminated the area in red. In the glow we were all able to see one another. The water was red, the palm trees were red, and the sand was red. All of us cheered except Tony from PANACHE, who noticed that the burning flare was settling down and about to land in his dinghy. We all stood transfixed as providence took a hand and at the last possible instant carried the flare beyond the dinghy to hiss untroubled into the lagoon.

The next few Fourth of Julys were more memorable by where TAKU was than by any specific events. They, in retrospect, give geographic punctuation to the circumnavigation, highlighting on the one hand the passage of water under TAKU's keel and on the other hand a progression that at first took me farther and farther from my homeland and finally and oddly, seems to bring me back toward home. So rather than measuring, like Prufrock, our lives out in coffee spoons, we measure them out, in part, with Fourth of Julys.

The early morning haze slowly lifts as we manage to round Sandy Hook under full sail. There are sailboats on the horizon as far as I can see, all making for New York and the festivities. I don't know how crowded it will be. "I hope, at least, we'll be able to see the statue," mused Celia.

Some six weeks less than seven years from TAKU's last visit, she sails once again under the Verrazano Narrows Bridge and into New York's upper harbor. Despite ourselves, we are excited—even more so when we find a place to anchor late on the second of July close to, and in plain view of, the Statue of Liberty. "Home and hosed, without the hose," I comment as we furl sails, put on sail covers, and dress ship with our code flags and with a large number of courtesy flags from the 45 countries we have visited in our 45,000-mile odyssey.

We revel in the festivities. The parade of ships is magnificent, and like all the other tourists who have sailed here, we take picture after picture. The anchorage is perfect for viewing the rededication of the statue, and I find myself spending almost the entire time I am in New York out on deck just watching things happen. The impressions are spectacular, and I enjoy the hooting of the thousands of horns, which seems to be the yachts' way of giving applause. Except for a few minor collisions, everything is orderly. People seem to be on their best behavior, and fortunately, the weather cooperates as well.

After the fireworks on the Fourth, many boats up anchor and head for home. We decide to get a good night's sleep and then to move on ourselves on the fifth. It's a decision shared by many. As I fall asleep I realize that I am back at last and that the voyage around the world is, indeed, over. The thought comforts and disquiets me.

Boats evaporate the following morning. We are in no hurry, as we are headed up the East River and on into Long Island Sound and must wait for the tide. An "Ahoy TAKU" brings me on deck.

Next to us is NERISSA, a classic wooden ketch with friends Chip and Martha Jordan aboard. We met first in Tahiti and had last seen each other in New Zealand. They have been back in the States for a year. We tie NERISSA off our stern and go aboard for a morning of stories and discussions of what readjustment is all about. Their readjustment consists in part of a new baby daughter and enrollment in law school.

With the day waning, we say goodbye to Chip and Martha with promises to meet in New England later in the summer. I take down our flags and hoist sail and realize that TAKU is the only boat still at anchor. Everyone else obviously has places to get to, obligations to fulfill. We take a few tacks through the now almost empty New York Harbor for fun. And it is fun. After years of sailing toward a destination, I am now sailing for the pleasure of it.

There are scads of boats headed up the East River with the tide and most pass us. One I don't know yells, "We saw you in Martinique!" I wave in response. Another, a goldplater charterboat, is one that we had first seen in Greece and then on and off since then. The man at the helm waves and mouths something to me. I nod as though I understand, but with the engines running, I haven't heard him.

"What did he say?" Celia asks me.

Suddenly I realize that he has mouthed two words: "Welcome

home!" He knows that we have just returned. We wave enthusiastically, and he smiles back, knowing that we have understood him.

That night in a quiet anchorage on Long Island Celia and I sit on the cabintop and watch the sun slowly setting off to the west. "Well, it was certainly a memorable Fourth. Nice of them to give us that big welcome," I remark.

As we sit reflecting on the evening, a small daysailer comes by with a young couple in it. They draw alongside, luffing their sail to slow their speed. "We really admire your boat," says the man. "It's a real boat. It looks like a boat that could cross oceans. It's the kind of boat we dream about getting someday."

I am tempted to ask him to make me an offer, but instead reply, "Thank you. She is a good boat."

The man nods. "Has she . . . ever crossed an ocean, I mean?" asks the man. For a moment I don't know what to say. Words fail me, and I merely reply, "Yes." As I say it, I realize that I sound a bit short.

But he is not put off and asks again. "Which one?"

For a moment I think to pick an ocean, and then I just smile and say, "I guess you could say she has crossed all of them as we've just finished a seven-year circumnavigation."

"My hat goes off to you," says the man. "It's fantastic to meet someone who has done what many of us want to do. Someday! Well, congratulations and welcome home!" He trims a little on his sheet and his boat gains way. The distance between our boats increases, and finally he is a little smudge on the horizon as the sun goes down. I realize that I am indeed home. We are back in the United States at last. Within a week TAKU will be on a mooring in the Connecticut River, and I will be working as a yacht broker, and Celia will be off to school. But for now, on this last "official day" of the circumnavigation, I am content to sit on the cabin top and to watch the stars appear. I realize that I cannot pretend to be still off somewhere around the world. People have welcomed me home. I have accepted and acknowledged those welcomes. For a few minutes I will look at the sky and imagine myself anywhere in the world I want to be. Then, recognizing the familiar shores of home waters I will also recognize that a voyage that had started so long ago had, indeed, come to its end.

38

Loose Ends

So there you have it. Just like that, like reading a long, wonderful book that you really love, and finally you turn the last page, and you see that words run out three quarters of the way down, and then there is nothing but white space. You try to read more slowly, to make it last, but finally you run out of words and close the book, the story over. I have a few loose ends to tie up here, a few more things to tell you, and then you too will have to close the book on this adventure.

I have a word or two to add on some of the characters in this story. Buckets finally sailed all the way around the world on a variety of other people's boats, and it also took him seven years. Buzz and Maureen sold GAMBIT, which Buzz had owned for more than 14 years, and are now in the garage-door-opener business in San Diego. Tim is happily working as a handyman in California and sailing now and then with friends. Bob and Jane sold BROWN PALACE and retired to Hilton Head. Dave and Marcia are still cruising aboard MAÑANA. Having made their way back across the North Pacific from Japan to Seattle, they are now en route to Mexico.

Armen went back to teaching and to being a partner in a travel agency. Cristina disappeared. Tip is back working for the Navy and has the civilian rank of an admiral in the engineering division. Celia graduated *Phi Beta Kappa* from Wesleyan and settled in California. And Peter, as crew aboard FIONA, a Westsail 42, completed a passage from Tahiti to Bermuda via Pitcairn Island, Cape Horn, Chile, and then the Falkland Islands. He went on to captain a C&C 44 from Boston to Greece and now manages a sailing school in the Bahamas.

TAKU sits five minutes away in a local boatyard, shrouded in tarps against the harsh New England winter. She's a little tired and worn, but ready to go again. I, on the other hand, sit snug in our house here in Beverly, which was built by Captain Thomas Bridges, a sailor of the Revolutionary War period. The house, more than 200 years old, overlooks the harbor that leads to the sea beyond.

"Our house" is mine and Catherine's, for I married Catherine Baker, who had been my editor at *Sail* magazine. We are the happy parents of Martha, our new baby daughter. We sail TAKU whenever possible, and a recent summer found us cruising her to Nova Scotia and back. In his "Four Quartets" T.S. Eliot wrote:

> *We shall not cease from exploration*
> *And the end of all our exploring*
> *Will be to arrive where we started*
> *And know the place for the first time*

So we come to the end. Or is it, for you, a beginning? For those of you who are wavering, you can, as Ulysses did, bind yourself and still hear the Sirens sing. But if you do hear the Sirens sing (for they are everywhere and sing when you least expect it), and you feel and fear the lure of being swept and sunk upon the shoals of a cruising life, don't despair. By all means go! Up helm! as Ahab said in *Moby Dick*:

"Turning to the steersman, who thus far had been holding the ship into the wind to diminish her headway, he cried out in his old lion voice—'Up helm!' Keep her off round the world!'"

"Up helm!" Find *your* "old lion voice." "Keep her off round the world!" Go while you can. You will discover that the shoals of a cruising life are not shoals at all, but infinite depths and spans of oceans upon which one lives the very richest life the world can offer, beyond your imagining, beyond my telling.

Fair winds!